TESTIMONIALS:

"Thank you for the privilege of reading your book. I thoroughly enjoyed your insights. You have certainly captured the subject matter in a logical and sequential fashion."

Bonnie Scheid – Author of "Recycle Your Life"

"The language in your book is easy to read."

LaMont Russell – Graphic Designer

"The book is a true testament to the things that are necessary for individuals with barriers to employment to obtain, and maintain employment."

Curtis Tatum – Vice President of Workforce Development, Goodwill Industries of Kansas, Inc.

"Roger does a good job of exploring the importance of ATTITUDE which I have always thought was almost as important as job skill."

Dean Day – Retired Benefits Manager and Business educator

"Your book contains a wealth of practical information for persons who are looking for ways to improve their lives. The attitudes and behaviors that allow a person to achieve their goals are described in ways that are clear and understandable. Many people can benefit from the ideas presented in this book, especially those wanting to improve their economic situation. I appreciate the balanced way in which the book includes the spiritual part of life along with the mental, physical and social aspects."

James Wenger, PhD
Regional Conference Minister

"An effective and practical tool for men and women preparing to be released from a prison setting to be productive and happy in society."

Chaplain Oscar Gomez –
Hutchinson Correctional Facility
State of Kansas

JOB and LIFE OPPORTUNITIE$: MOVING UP

TATE PUBLISHING
AND ENTERPRISES, LLC

Published by Tate Publishing & Enterprises, LLC
127 E. Trade Center Terrace | Mustang, Oklahoma 73064 USA
1.888.361.9473 | www.tatepublishing.com

Published in Association with Roger A. Eichelberger dba: Diversified Business Services, LLC

Tate Publishing is committed to excellence in the publishing industry. The company reflects the philosophy established by the founders, based on Psalm 68:11,
"The Lord gave the word and great was the company of those who published it."

Book design copyright © 2016 by Tate Publishing, LLC. All rights reserved.

Illustrations by Anita Swartzendruber of His Story Art, Inc.
Cover design by Shelley Plett
Author Photo Lifetouch by Olan Mills Corporation

Published in the United States of America

ISBN: 978-1-68301-333-4
1. Self-Help / Personal Growth / Success
2. Business & Economics / Careers / General
16.02.26

Table of Contents

PREFACE... xi

ACKNOWLEDGEMENTS xiii

INTRODUCTION xiv

CHAPTER 1 – ASSOCIATIONS WITH PEOPLE 1
  1 Open the Door of Opportunity 1
  2 The Yes Look 3
  3 Don't Run From Advice 4
  4 Friendships Pay Back 5
  5 Life Can Be Much More.. 5
  6 More Than the Coffee Break 6
  7 Benefits of Community Involvement 6
  8 Compete With Competition 7
  9 Networking Connections 7
10 Confidence Circle 9
11 Complimenting Others' Successes................................. 10
12 Sharing Your Gifts... 10
13 Gossip is Like Fire 10
14 Get to the Point... 10
15 Respecting Co-Workers 11
16 Respecting Your Boss/Supervisor 11
17 Dinner Manners.. 11
18 Crossword Puzzle.. 13

CHAPTER 2 – EMPLOYMENT APPLICATION 15
  1 When to Apply 15
  2 Personal Information 16
  3 Availability.. 16
  4 Work History 16
  5 Education.. 16
  6 Employment Test Tip 17

CHAPTER 3 – PREPARE FOR INTERVIEWING................. 18
  1 Arrive Early 18
  2 Think Before You Commit 18
  3 The Hand Talks.. 19
  4 A Lesson in Listening... 19
  5 Pay Attention to Small Stuff 19
  6 Choose Encouraging Words 20

7	A Smile is Contagious (Illustration)	22
8	Read About Interviewing	22
9	Willing Workers Wanted	23
10	Handling Information	24
11	Making the Right Impression	25

CHAPTER 4 – ORGANIZE SELF ON THE JOB 27

1	A Time to Keep It Personal	27
2	Work Ethics	27
3	Computer Ethics	28
4	Keep Work Desk Area Clean	29
5	Distractions Cost Time	30
6	Keep Copies of Important Information	30
7	Answer Mail Immediately	31
8	Get on Key Mailing Lists	31
9	Avoid Foul-ups	31
10	E-Mail	32
11	No "I" in Team	32
12	Importance of Following Through	32
13	Trusty Companion	33
14	Hidden Writing Skills	34
15	Working Smarter	34
16	Goes With the Territory	35
17	Time Management	37
18	Taking Notes at a Meeting	38
19	Signing In and Out	38
20	The Three Ring Rule	39
21	Think and Then Do (Efficiency)	39
22	Texting and Social Media	40

CHAPTER 5 – EMOTIONAL ISSUES AT WORK 42

1	Handling Conflict	42
2	Keep a Good Attitude	42
3	Facing New Challenges	43
4	Embracing Criticism	44
5	Differences of Opinion	44
6	Learning from Mistakes and Failures	44
7	Be Flexible	45
8	Be Proactive	46
9	Activities to Complement Job	46
10	Develop Lasting Values for Life	46

11	Bullying	47
12	Mind Over Matter (Thinking Ability)	48
13	Dealing with Stress	48

CHAPTER 6 – PREPARING FOR JOB EVALUATION 51

1	Good Attendance is Important	51
2	Body Language Talks	52
3	Make Suggestions With Questions	55
4	It's the Boss's Business	56
5	Day Planner	56
6	Avoid "I Can't"	57
7	Working Chain of Command	57
8	What is Clean Clean?	59
9	Be Adaptable	59
10	Review Your Job Description	60
11	With More Knowledge Comes More Responsibility	61
12	Go the Second Mile	62

CHAPTER 7 – OFF WORK AND AT HOME 64

1	Importance of Family	64
2	Commit to an Exercise Program	65
3	Leave Personal Business at Home	65
4	Free Time	66
5	Planning Personal Goals	66
6	Read the Newspaper Regularly	71
7	Watch Area Job Openings	71
8	Appreciates Nice Home	71
9	Eating Healthy and Stretching Grocery Dollars	72
10	Develop Prayer Life	74
11	Vacationing	75
12	Sports Talk	75
13	Getting Better Sleep	75
14	Helping Hand From Spouse and/or Close Friends	78
15	Limit Screen Time	79
16	Unemployed Young Adult	80
17	Cherish the Moment	80

CHAPTER 8 – FINANCIAL PLANNING 81

1	Develop Your Own Business Plan	81
2	Credit Cards	82
3	Increase Your Credit Score	83

4	Too Much Debt?	83
5	Figuring Net Worth	84
6	Making Life Investments	85
7	Develop an Organized Budget	87
8	Watch for Windows of Opportunity	88
9	Value Personal Contacts	89
10	Envision More for Yourself	90
11	Guarantees In Life	90
12	Investing Locally Pays Back	91
13	Successful People Like Seeing Others Do Well	91
14	Tips to Getting a Loan	92
15	Hard Times Build Character	92
16	Start Saving Sooner	93
17	Filing Information	94
18	Barter to Save Cash	94
19	Making Smarter Purchases Saves Cash	96
20	The Paycheck	99
21	Insurance	100

CHAPTER 9 – DOES MANAGEMENT CARE ?. 102

1	The Company Policy Manual	102
2	Be Loyal and Supportive	102
3	An Agreeable Personality	103
4	Working a Second Job	104
5	Entrepreneurship	104
6	"That's Our Policy!"	104
7	Show Appreciation for Gifts	104
8	What is Total Quality Management?	105
9	Respect Clientele Visits	105
10	Stay Off the Grass	106
11	Maintain Clean Work Vehicle	106
12	Your Life Ambitions	107
13	Company Exhibit	107
14	Be More Professional	107

CHAPTER 10 – ENABLING RESUMÉ 110

1	Preparing Your Resumé	110
2	Extracurricular Activities	110
3	Things Around Us Matter	111
4	Balanced Life Adds Character	112
5	Opt to Serve as a Volunteer	115

6	What's Your Hobby?	115
7	Join Professional Organizations	115
8	Attend Convention or Seminar	116
9	Enroll in Classes	116
10	Update Yourself	117
11	Computer Software	118
12	Job Fair	118

CHAPTER 11 – GOING THE SECOND MILE 120

1	Empowerment Acts as Fuel	120
2	Encourage Group Involvement	120
3	Entertaining Guests at Home	121
4	Goodness Gracious	122
5	Being Courteous	122
6	Make it Right the First Time	123

CHAPTER 12 – CONSIDER THESE CLOSELY 125

1	Joy in Seeing Others Become Successful	125
2	Don't Wait, Call Before You're Late	125
3	The Test is Getting Rest	125
4	Change With the Times	126
5	Adapt to Criticism	126
6	Permission to Post Material	127
7	Prepare for Bad Weather	128
8	Confidentiality	130
9	Your Smart Friend	130
10	Avoid Indifference	131
11	Have a Backup Plan	132

CHAPTER 13 – STRENGTHENING CHARACTER 133

1	Is a Mentor Like a GPS?	133
2	Sharpen Up Your Presence	133
3	More Than Skin Deep	134
4	Demonstrate Integrity	135
5	Sense of Humor	135
6	First Impressions are Lasting	135
7	Appreciating Your Job	136
8	A Compassionate Personality	137
9	Extra Personal Care	137
10	Use Uplifting Language	138
11	Allow Time for Deep Thoughts	138

12 Mirror Mirror on the Wall 138
13 Music—Great For Our Well-Being 139
14 More Than Listening 139
15 Practice Makes Perfect 140
16 "In God We Trust" 141
17 The Gift of Grace 142
18 Re-alignment 143
19 Reputation 143

CHAPTER 14 – FORGETTING THINGS TOO EASILY? 145
1 Invest in a Planner 145
2 Improve Planning Techniques 145
3 The Mental Edge – Mind Over Matter 145
4 "A Picture is Worth a Thousand Words" 146
5 Saying Less Can be More 147
6 The Unforgettable Character 148
7 More Tips For Remembering 149

CHAPTER 15 – WANTED: *QUALIFIED WORKERS* 151
1 Marketing Your Strengths 151
2 Customer Appreciation 151
3 Productivity 152
4 Quality Over Quantity 152
5 Calculating Risk Taker 153
6 Psyched Up 153
7 Smiling is Contagious 154
8 Non-Smoker 154
9 Social Etiquette 155
10 Team Unity 156
11 Modesty is the Policy 156
12 Hands Off 157
13 Positive Approach 157
14 Strength Comes From Patience 157

CHAPTER 16 – RISING TO THE OCCASION 159
1 When The Going Gets Tough, The Tough Get Going 159
2 Leadership 160
3 Working the Extra Hour 160
4 Scanning Saves Time 161
5 Problem Solving Strategies 161
6 Living a Simpler Lifestyle 162

7   Thanking Others 163

8   Becoming Spiritually Excited 163

9   Motivated 164

CHAPTER 17 – MORE IMPORTANT TIPS. 166

1   Favors Have Limits 166

2   Clutter-Free Mentality 166

3   Up Front Seating Bonus 166

4   Respecting Others' Personal Space 167

5   Friends For the Right Reasons 167

6   Subtle Remarks 168

7   Conducting Meetings Effectively 168

8   Speaking With Effectiveness 169

9   Street Wise 170

10 Power of Forgiveness 171

11 Raising the Bar 172

12 Enjoy Picture Photos 173

13 More About Entrepreneurship 173

14 Coming From Abroad 174

15 Freedom to Make Good Choices 174

CHAPTER 18 – LOOKING TO THE FUTURE 176

1   Life Under the Magnifying Glass 176

2   With a Circle of Believers 176

3   Breaking Bread 177

4   To New Beginnings 177

5   A Decision For Eternity 178

6   A Fresh Start 179

7   Time Capsule 180

8   Dreams Can Come True 180

9   Wishing You the Best 181

10 The New You With Commitment 181

NOTES AND RESOURCES 183

OTHER SOURCES TO READ 188

WORD INDEX 189

APPENDIX 194

1   Resumé Form 194

2 Monthly Budget Sheet... 195
3 Financial Balance Sheet (figuring net worth) 196
4 Answer Sheet (Body Language, Crossword Puzzle)..................................... 197
5 Personal Inventory of Possessions... 198
6 For Focus Group Meetings.. 201

PREFACE

This self-help book has been written to give words of encouragement for young people or adults struggling to find a satisfying job. All eighteen chapters give suggestions and tips for the unemployed, underemployed, and/or underpaid lower income persons trying to improve themselves. Many of the suggestions shared in this book have come from experiences in my own life.

You will find that some information may sound over-simplified, or at other times may sound unimportant. In either case, be patient with me. I make a similar claim as Charles Ray Van Nice wrote in the opening part of his book, *Tact and The Teacher*: "The views here set out make no claim at completeness; they rather aim at stimulating thought…"[1]

Looking back at my younger years, I feel God was already preparing me to write this book. Also—and more importantly—God allowed me to go through many hardships while He was there all the time, teaching and guiding me when things were not going in the right direction. I came from a caring, loving home with Christian parents. They emphasized a good work ethic which made me who I am today. They also encouraged me to continue my education after high school. Hesston College, a private 2-year Christian church college in Hesston, Kansas, contributed greatly to strengthening my beliefs in Jesus's teachings.

Another purpose in writing this book lies in my commitment to give back what so many people have done for our family. We were blessed to have extended family and friends help us in so many ways! Great Uncle Wilbert Graber once told me, after I asked him what I could do in return for his generosity, "Just pass it on to someone else needing the same help." What a profound statement!

While my aunt Donna Horst was still living, we decided there should be a biblical emphasis to these writings, which places the emphasis where it should be, living a more wholesome life.

King Solomon is one of my favorite writers. He wrote practical instructions (in Proverbs) for successful living. The Proverbs were inspired by God, for all of us to read and apply in our daily living. In the introductory referencing remarks before the book of Proverbs in the Living Bible, it states the "Author: Principally Solomon…," wrote the book of Proverbs in "10th century B.C. and later." In chapter 1:2, "he wrote them to teach his people how to live—how to act in every circumstance."[2]

LouAnn, my wife, and I are blessed with two children, a son and daughter, their spouses, and grandchildren, whom we love very much. Each one is very special to us. And like all families, we have had our good times and more challenging times. In a perfect world, we might have only peace and happiness all the time, but there is no perfect situation here on earth. There is good news though; we can ask God to lift up our spirits to help us through the rough periods in our life. We must put our hardships and difficult experiences behind us, reach out and find new beginnings.

As I was reminded from Dr. David Jeremiah in his Sunday morning sermon June 9,

2013, the book of Psalms in the Bible is packed with scriptures giving encouragement to those who will take a little time each day to read biblical passages.

So along with my own experiences in family life, teaching and business, there are instances throughout this book where I use practical biblical references and lessons learned by me to give depth of understanding.

Thank you for choosing to read this practical self-help book. I hope you'll find some things you may want to apply in your own life. I also realize you may be taking a big leap of faith as you read all the words of encouragement that are shared in the pages ahead. Please consider my intent of wanting to help you get empowered in a new way! On the other hand, you may have already put some or many of these ideas and practices to work in your life, and I affirm you. Congratulations!

Disclaimer:

Some important thoughts about my writing…I do not claim to have all the answers! My writing is somewhat like an autobiography. Many of the ideas and opinions have come from my life experiences; and now, I'm sharing because I have a passion to help and encourage others, like many other people have done for me. You'll find information from me and other authors, which may or may not fit your life perspective. As a reader, you can sort out what is best for your situation.

As the author, I am not a psychologist, doctor, or sociologist. I am an educator—a teacher. I've tried to create new value options for my readers to make choices for improving their income level, if they choose to do so. My reader should consult a professional for counsel if there is any doubt whatsoever before applying suggestions. Therefore the publisher, and myself as author, remind the reader that we are not donating or selling the self-help book as advice for a cure-all, but hope to offer only suggestions and ideas for improving the reader's situation. And for that reason, we disclaim all liabilities or personal hardships or problems which may occur from, or after, the publication and reading the information in this book.

ACKNOWLEDGEMENTS

Special thanks to...

- the following people who helped by reading manuscript material and giving advice before being published: Bonnie Scheid, John C. Murray, Byron Ediger, Joel Klaassen, Melinda Just (publisher's editor), Ardell Stauffer, James Wenger and my wife, LouAnn whose patience, support and depth of personal understanding provided excellent editing suggestions.

- our family members, son and daughter, who always support, inspire and allow me to ask for their advice; each one of our grandchildren, who supported us and made suggestions for improving the reading of the book; as well as our parents, grandparents and extended family for all the patience and lessons they taught us while growing up.

- Dr. Melva Kauffman, past professor, who often encouraged me in college to broaden my communication skills to write.

- David Adams, past principal who affirmed me as an accomplished teacher and leader at the Vocational Center.

- Dr. Gerald Steele, my professor, who allowed me to teach and learn from him as a graduate assistant while working on my Masters Degree.

- My Aunt Donna who encouraged me to include a biblical context.

- Chris, a fellow college professor who taught similar classes, for encouraging me to write a book about protocol expected of hourly employees on the job.

- my deceased uncle, Calvin Eichelberger, for the lessons he taught me in learning to enjoy the lighter side of life.

- Free Press for support and hanging in there with me for several years, while giving counsel and waiting patiently until I finished the book for publication.

- family, friends and other contributors who I missed giving credit for advice or material.

- Counselors and Chaplains, who said they needed a book like this, and encouraged me to finish my writing, so they could use parts of the book to help persons struggling with job and life related challenges.

INTRODUCTION

D o you want to feel better about where your life is taking you, earn more, and have time to do more things you want to do? If you answered yes, this self-help book has suggestions that might interest you. This book has especially been written for job struggling Americans.

Each one of us wants to have choices leading to pleasant outcomes for ourselves. As a suggestion, consider starting off with just a few topics to read and study. Take your time. There will be choices—your choices! These choices may be your chance of a lifetime!

The central theme focuses on helping struggling minimum wage earners who are experiencing difficulties and searching for a better quality of life. A good share of the book's emphasis is about receiving a better wage.

You are not alone!

Maybe you're earning all you want and that gives you happiness. That is OK. It's important to feel good about where your life is leading you! As you read, look for helpful ideas that will inspire you.

The news reminds us daily of the large number of underemployed or unemployed people seeking a good job. Several years back, a report from CNNMoney.com says, "But many economists and labor market experts say job growth and the economy overall would be significantly stronger if employers could find the skilled workers they really need." In the same report, Jeff Summer quotes, "Supply and demand is completely out of whack." He said he is "hearing across the board, across industries, companies indicating they can't exploit market opportunity because they can't find people with the right skills…"[1]

Could these employers back then, and possibly now, be saying they would like to hire more help if they could find workers with the right kind of skills and character traits to fill their needs in the workplace? I think so!

As I studied another article found in the Wichita Eagle in 1991, the study pointed out, "The average U.S. manufacturer rejects five out of six job applicants because they are not skilled enough."[2]

What kind of skilled workers are they looking for to hire now? Could this still be happening in today's economy? I would guess it's even more serious today. This leads to important issues in this book.

In an article titled, "Survey: Fewer skilled workers," taken from the "National Association of Manufacturers, Towers Perrin Co., survey of 400 U.S. manufacturers," I found the following as the "most common reasons for rejecting entry-level applicants:" The first and highest percentage is "doesn't adapt well," followed by "poor reading and writing skills, no work experience, poor math skills, poor verbal skills, and failed medical, drug test."[3] I'm wondering if "no work experience" may mean there had not been good work experience preparing them for the next step.

Even though the findings above are not studies done recently, perhaps my reader can still identify with one or more of these problems today. Whatever the case, my intentions are to offer many suggestions to you, my reader, as we try to find and fix these weaknesses leading to a better job and lifestyle. There are many ways you can choose to improve each day and prepare yourself for having a better standard of living. Some of my readers may have to make special adjustments or work doubly hard because of physical impairments or other handicaps.

As I thought more about the previously mentioned statistics, the report may not fit your situation. Whatever the case, you may want some changes to happen sooner rather than later to experience a better quality of life. I will explore hundreds and hundreds of tips to do better in the following chapters.

With more ambition to learn and understand the little things that may make a difference, your life can become more meaningful and productive. If you're earning a smaller income than you want, experiencing poverty conditions, if you're out of a job, working only part time, wondering how to arrange things to work in your favor, then this self-help book has helpful information for you. A few new thoughts and reminders in this book may be just the ticket you've been looking for. Even only a few paragraphs out of one chapter may include one or two choices or options which could accelerate you in the right direction.

My hope and prayer is that many of the stories and suggestions will challenge you. Again, I do not claim these suggestions have all the solutions for everyone—only thoughts for your consideration. In fact, there is so much more information out there in other resources than I could ever hope to bring to your attention. Not every tip will work for everyone. There will always be problems that creep up in life. The way we deal with challenges today may help us to be stronger and better-prepared to deal with similar problems later.

When I played varsity basketball in high school and college, I can remember arranging time for many hours of dedicated practice to play well enough to make the team. It took much dedication in practicing technique, patience, and determination to shoot a higher percentage of shots and make the moves to help win a game. It felt very good after continued practice to step up to the free throw line during a game and sink important shots when it really counted. Continued practice paid off again and again in competition. I hope this book encourages you to treat your days, weeks, and months as a special time to practice and examine where you are going and how to get there. It may take dedicated practice for you to make the difference you want for yourself.

Have you ever hiked in the Rockies or other mountains where the paths were very demanding? Maybe it was the strenuous practice of preparing for a race or a competitive event? In either case, it becomes a grueling challenge of "mind over matter." It usually pays off in the end with some exciting rewards! I hope the same will happen to you. Practice hard and prepare well so when you experience tense times on or off the job, you'll be ready for the challenge. Keep your mind focused on reasons why it is so important to train yourself to meet the demands facing you today by:

- creating a burning desire within yourself to be more than you are presently;
- applying the hidden rules of middle income people while becoming more successful;
- devoting yourself to finding resourceful reading to engage you in fulfilling your dreams;
- choosing options that allow you to reach greater heights of understanding;
- developing a vision for your life, to become all that God wants you to be;
- contemplating ways to put new ideas to work in your favor;
- focusing on continued daily study and meditation to improve your quality of life;
- practicing advice shared by others— while finding their secrets of success;
- beginning to enjoy life and experiencing new vibrant friendships;
- applying learned interpersonal relationships so badly needed in the workplace;
- and working hard to deserve those good wages and fringe benefits that come from hard work.

When I was teaching in the classroom, I always told my students at the beginning of the course that through hard work and determination, it was possible for them to receive an "A" in the course. The same can work for you as you work toward becoming an A-1 employee. But what might be the formula for your particular success story?

First—this could be your choice for change. Tell yourself you want to be the best that you can be! You're not going to let other people discount your potential by discouraging you.

Second—begin to work on your character assessment with determination. Practice improving your understanding, and learn more acceptable job expectations every day so your actions speak loudly and happen automatically.

Third—this part of the formula is big! Channel all your thoughts in a positive direction as you pleasantly interact with people. Friendships lead to more friendships and friendships pay off!

Improve your people skills; talking and responding to others is an area that some of us will continue to work at the rest of our lives—including myself! All through my lifetime, I've had to work hard at this. Repeatedly, I pinch myself and step back and say, I could have done better at this or that.

Zig Ziglar in his book *Top Performance* says "85 percent of the reason you get a job, keep that job, and move ahead in that job has to do with your people skills and people knowledge."[4]

I will come back to this issue many times.

Have you ever felt pressed to do something and didn't do it because you thought you couldn't? I've had that feeling even in the case of writing this book. It was time to write rather than only think about it. The time was now for me to act on my premonition. Rather than just watch and hear people talk about what they should be doing, I wanted to step out of the box and provide tools in this book, which have potential to help you!

We all know the playing field (work in this case) changes very rapidly. Let's assume you want to be the kind of person who can "change to the beat of the drummer." What do you want immediately out of this time in your life? The key to all this change is probably being able to change quickly…to being interactive internally and externally. Try committing to "be adaptable," as my son would say. This means practicing to be receptive and understanding of others' expectations spontaneously. This will take much effort on your part. It doesn't happen by only reading tips in this book. It must be rehearsed over and over again to best improve mannerisms. It may take months to make these changes, but it can happen. Practice improving your character, understanding, and acceptable job protocol every day so your actions happen automatically. As you read suggestions in the chapters ahead, choose the ones which will benefit you most. Like I've said before, many will apply, some will not. If you want to, give the ideas a priority rating. Mark up this book if you have purchased it. Remember, it has been written for you, so you are in the driver's seat. As the author, I hope you will experience more joy because you have been practicing and applying new tips and techniques faithfully.

Across the country in the workplace, in the classroom, during a conference, at evaluation time, on coffee break, sweeping the floor, in a jail cell, someone is saying, "I'm trying to get it right! Why can't I have a good job? Why was I laid off? Why can't I earn the pay I deserve?" It just doesn't seem right for so many people, like you perhaps, to be left out of meeting your potential.

Remember, you are not alone!

I hope you will appreciate the words of encouragement in this self-help book, and even the implied thoughts many times. My book can make a difference in the way you see people and the way people see you. We all can develop the potential to be responsible for leaving a good first impression with people we meet. Today's economy, maybe like never before, requires that employees have depth of character, organizational abilities, and technical skills. It's about accepting a broader understanding of job protocol (diplomacy expectations) and appropriate workplace skills.

As I said before, I'm sure you are probably already practicing numerous tips that are shared in this book. Go ahead and pick out additional tips that may work for you. Use this self-help book as your workbook toward starting a new you—like making a New Year's resolution. You may have to re-read parts over and over until it feels right. If it still doesn't feel right for you, go on to the next topic.

Increasing your job potential starts with you! When I was a high school senior, we considered the motto, "Try and Try Again" as our graduating theme. It is the same today. You have what it takes! Now all I have to do is convince you of that.

Develop the whole person—mentally, socially, physically, and spiritually—as you become more knowledgeable. I believe you will be convinced you have made a good investment as you read and contemplate putting many of these ideas and tips into practice. Please allow many of these choices for change to become part of your new personality. I pray that my words of encouragement in this book have a positive effect upon you and the lives of your family members for generations to come!

CHAPTER 1

ASSOCIATIONS WITH PEOPLE

*Those who have a magnetism about them are uplifting
to be around and draw others to them!*

OPEN THE DOOR OF OPPORTUNITY

Opportunities come or go on the job and in life from the decisions we make. How is it going for you today? What would make your day? As you answer those questions, this could be the first step to walking through a door of a new opportunity. What's it going to look like when you open the door?

Let's say I'm taking a road trip. I'll begin with a whole lot of planning first. What amount of money will be set aside for this trip? How many miles will be traveled and which highways will be selected by my GPS? Where will I stay? In the end, I want to have had a good experience!

Decisions are necessary to have a good experience and receive the best end result for the money. When a person plans well several days in advance, an overnight stay will probably be more enjoyable. In my case, I made several contacts with key people before decisions were made in finalizing the trip. Then, it was like opening the door. Now I could look forward to an enjoyable trip knowing there was a plan in place.

The same preparation can be so valuable at our jobs every hour, every day. Hopefully, the thoughts, reminders and suggestions in the following chapters will open doors to give you more options as you make decisions.

You may have already made conscious efforts to consider changes for your own actions— relating to others and earning their respect. This has potential for adding value to your life. Chapter 1 emphasizes the importance of building strong associations with other people. Becoming responsible for the things you do and say can build character; this helps to build strong associations with people. If you are not yet on this path, the time could be right as a beginning to follow your dreams.

The following is a suggested list of performance objectives and examples to get you involved—some for today, tomorrow, or for the future if you choose to do so. As you will discover, the list is in no way complete. The purpose of this list is to give you encouragement as you read the book and plan ahead. Circle the boxes that fit you at this time:

- ■ Encourages others by sharing cheerful thoughts
- ■ Describes success in daily life from a positive perspective
- ■ Identifies with people who live their life in a way you admire

- Selects motivating reading material
- Takes a stand on distinguishing good behavior from the unacceptable
- Extends help to helpless and disadvantaged people
- As an employee, consistently works productively for your employer
- Forgives others for their weaknesses and mistakes
- Demonstrates a life of integrity within the community
- Plans a realistic, personal monthly financial budget
- Solves problems patiently and with determination
- Models family as an important treasure in life
- Reads about other people's goals and achievements
- Observes how others react and relate to others
- Associate well with those who are salaried
- Rewards self and others for accomplishments often
- Chooses to study the Bible often
- Takes advice from individuals who are making good choices
- Conscientiously creates a healthy environment
- Supports management and the boss faithfully
- Feels thankful for tasks and projects in your job which give you joy
- Gives of self and money without expecting something in return
- Works on computer with good time-management practices
- Tries hard to relate well to others—being genuinely courteous to others
- Modifies plans to improve situation daily
- Considers praying each day to God
- Prepares to be more efficient on a daily basis
- Summarizes and evaluates accomplishments for improvement
- Appraises net worth each year
- Combines efforts when possible
- Chooses living standards within financial means
- Generates positive influence with people
- Takes time to laugh with others, not at them
- Respects and honors parent(s)/family always
- Rearranges schedule with flexibility to accommodate others
- Outlines new life goals on paper each year
- Compiles daily agenda in monthly planner
- Records written notes in effective manner
- Considers learning about biblical Christian conduct
- Solves problems using good problem-solving practices

- Displays good common sense behavior
- Volunteers time for special events in community
- Completes and follows through with projects to the end
- Shares personal belongings with others in need
- Considers being committed to a set of personal beliefs aligned with God

In conclusion, consider developing your own performance objectives as you read or after you finish reading this book.

YOUR NOTES:

THE YES LOOK

If you are employed, are you enthusiastic about your present employment? I enjoy seeing employees who are genuinely motivated about their job! Do your actions and stature show respect for your employer?

When employees are motivated for their job, they stand straight with a "yes look" of good posture. The employer may prefer the person on the left to hire and train for promotions. This person tries to:

- hold their head and body in good posture.
- make eye contact with the person when speaking
- focus his/her expression on the positive.
- show a respectful manner even in troubling times.

If you do not feel as interesting and enthusiastic as you would like to be, step up with an "I can" attitude.

your body speaks louder than your words

3

Consider action now! Take a deep breath and stand up straight. If you have handicaps, practice being all that you can be. Begin to focus on job areas that you can appreciate. Feel your energy coming back. You may be surprised what can happen in life when you give 100 percent. This choice has helped me. It could help you!

DON'T RUN FROM ADVICE

Primary to acquiring advice is learning to "obey your father and mother."[1] In Proverbs 1:8 we're also told, "Listen to your father and mother."[2]

Don't run from advice, for that will, undoubtedly, bring on more insecurity and unhappiness sooner or later. If you do not like to take advice, you may not be able to handle change. When a person allows another person to give advice, it can build up a bond of friendship and respect.

People who are constantly running away from a problem may not feel good about solving challenges. Rather, I hope you're a person that thrives on getting as much information from as many sources as possible, and is not afraid of helpful criticism. When reading Jonah, Chapters 1 and 2 in the Bible, Jonah was trying to run away from the call of God. This story has been told over and over, and passed on from generation to generation. It has been passed down through the ages by scholarly people all the way back from the 8th Century BC.

The Living Bible tells us in the prelude of the reference edition that "Jonah was a prophet born in Israel and called by God to preach repentance to Assyria, the nation that was shortly going to destroy Israel in 722 BC. On receiving the call, Jonah's nationalistic spirit would not allow him to offer salvation to the pagans, so he attempted to flee from God by ship."

As I understand the story in chapter 1 of the book of Jonah, the Lord had called Jonah to go to this big city of Nineveh (the capital of Assyria) to tell them how wicked they were. Instead, Jonah prepared to go another way, not listening to God. He went to Joppa where he found a ship going to Tarshish. While Jonah was traveling the high seas, God caused a great storm to toss the ship around until it was nearly destroyed. The sailors were frightened and everyone was crying out to their gods and throwing cargo over the sides to lighten the ship. All during this time, Jonah was sleeping soundly in the lower cargo of the ship. The captain was surprised to find Jonah there sleeping rather than helping the others. "What do you mean," the captain roared, "sleeping at a time like this? Get up and cry to your god, and see if he will have mercy on us and save us!" After that "the crew decided to draw straws to see which of them had offended the gods…and Jonah drew the short one." After that the crew asked Jonah all kinds of personal questions. "Then he told them he was running away from the Lord." Everyone was frightened! They knew Jonah couldn't get away from God and asked him what they should do to calm the storm. The storm was at its worst. Then Jonah said, "Throw me out into the sea and it will become calm again. For I know this terrible storm has come because of me." They didn't want to throw Jonah overboard but nothing worked to help the situation, and it was bad! So bad "they picked up Jonah and threw him overboard…and the storm stopped!" Everyone "stood there in awe," shocked at what they witnessed. Immediately they sacrificed to the Lord and "vowed to serve him."

At that time, the Lord caused a great fish to swallow Jonah. Now "Jonah was inside the

4

fish for three days and three nights." Can you imagine the anguish Jonah went through as he was tossed around in the fish belly darkness, seaweed and half digested fish food?

At the end of chapter 2, the story ends with Jonah pleading with God to forgive him and to give him another chance to obey his command. Jonah promises to turn all his thoughts to him once more. God heard Jonah "and the Lord ordered the fish to spit up Jonah on the beach, and it did."[3]

Every time I read this biblical passage, I'm taken back with its magnitude. Jonah learned there is nothing more important than listening to a trusted friend.

FRIENDSHIPS PAY BACK

What are ways to work together with others on the job and in your personal life? Probably first and foremost, apply generous good will with people in general! Make treating people as you want to be treated one of your primary goals in life. This can become automatic with sincere practice rather than having to think about it each time you meet someone. Allow this to become part of your personality with family, co-workers, friends, and reaching out to people who are struggling. Most often, financial gains come first through people, not things.

Build on your history by saving business leads that you may want to pursue at a later time. One way to do this would be to save business cards. I usually write the date, a brief note on the card and file alphabetically in a card holder. By having a quick reference to review in the future, the note may be beneficial to you.

Consider finding ways to remember people's names through the practice of association. When you meet someone later, you can smile, and with a little luck, say their name. This is a very important investment of your time and energy. More will be said later about ways to remember people's names.

LIFE CAN BE MUCH MORE

We need to be the most we can be so our face glows with enthusiasm and initiative. Your personality could radiate with the love of Jesus' teachings. You can choose to be inspired by the Bible's Ten Commandments in Exodus 20 and the Sermon on the Mount in Matthew 5. Read and think about those texts. If your heart is in step with the teachings of Jesus, you have potential to become more than you are now. Life can be much more!

It can become a thing of believing and desiring the fruits of the Spirit. As written in Galatians 5:22 and 23, "But when the Holy Spirit controls our lives He 'the Lord" will produce this kind of fruit in us: love, joy, peace, patience, kindness, goodness, faithfulness, gentleness, and self-control."[4]

If trials and tribulations try to trip you up, and evil forces may well try to do so, continue praying to the Lord. Allow the Holy Spirit (the presence of God within us) to shape your happiness every day.

MORE THAN THE COFFEE BREAK

I wore out a 1/2" electric drill on a summer afternoon. As I look back in retrospect, it broke down because I didn't give the drill a break. I had drilled 50-plus 1/2" holes through 8" concrete. I'm sure that if I would have allowed the drill to cool down for a few minutes, the drill would probably have been OK. That's how the body works. If you've been working really hard, you also need a break from the stress of the day.

The dedicated worker functions better if the body is given a short break after working very hard for a couple of hours straight. The body will normally be more efficient and effective with others after approximately a 10 minute morning or afternoon break. Give yourself a rest time away from repetitive work. If the job is taxing and you are in charge of the work load, let the body recuperate by giving it a change of venue and a change of body motion.

Just about all employers encourage a break if there has been heavy productive work or activity for a couple of hours. Try to use good discretion about when and how long the break should be!

Your brain won't burn up or malfunction like a drill if it's worked too hard.

BENEFITS OF COMMUNITY INVOLVEMENT

How do you get more involved with the community? Reaching out to others around us builds friendships. For starters, shopping at home is appreciated very much by both local business merchants and other people who are community-minded. This involvement goes a long way toward building bridges in your local community. How far out is community? One of my friends, who owns a store locally, asked me why I buy products out of town periodically. I shared with him that shopping out of town in the wider community of associates where I have worked seems important to me occasionally.

One way to be surrounded with a caring community is to take time to find a civic group to attend. As time goes on, you may want to join a community group. If you're interested, say yes and try it. Get involved in small group discussions. You can benefit from volunteering to do projects with others. When you respond to others' needs, reaching out and helping them, it can make your own problems seem trivial and unimportant. If asked to do something like this, you can show a caring attitude about them. Sharing stories with others can be a growing, enriching time together. Being part of the community in this way has been a real source of support, strength and encouragement for me and my family through the years.

There are advantages to being neighborly. Take something to your neighbor or watch for a chance to do a random act of kindness for them. Blowing the snow off their sidewalk, helping the neighborhood safety watch, waving to them, throwing the paper onto their porch if they're on vacation, inviting them over, and getting to know them on a first name basis are all part of being neighborly. Show a genuine interest in them. Neighbors are important! Neighbors can watch each others' premises when gone. Neighbors can become friends, visiting on the porch together and sharing stories. By the way, laughter is good medicine for the soul as you laugh and share together. As you become helpful to others, you may discover:

> **Great things can happen to those who give and keep on giving without expecting something in return. This may take time, but the rewards are great!**

COMPETE WITH COMPETITION

Competition can strengthen a person or organization. Rivalry can be good or not so good. It's a matter of how rivalry is treated. Past experiences have given me a real spirit of competition. Persons who are or have been coaches usually have a drive to compete that is hard to explain. Also, persons who have studied and prepared to work in sales might say that "if there is a will, there is a way" to get the job done right. Athletic competition can strengthen the mind and body through practiced skill training. Competition in sales can do the same if the group pulls together with a collective goal. Teamwork is at the heart of successful competition. Teams are easily defeated if one or two members are going in another direction, act with selfishness or envy, or someone is a slacker. Each needs to unselfishly pull their fair share of the weight.

There was a time when I observed a new steak house being built directly across the street from another. At an opportune time, I posed a question to the manager. Why do you seem so excited about another steak house starting up on the other side of the street from you? Won't you attract less business if they are so close to you? His theory was that by having more competition in one area, all the businesses can benefit. More choices create options for customers to continue coming back into the area. It gives more visibility for market share; the result—more profits. Competition can strengthen the desired results if people and organizations all pull together and organize cooperatively with one another.

NETWORKING CONNECTIONS

Why or what is networking? My definition of this is: "surrounding yourself with people who you may want to work with in the future." Develop a circle of friends and community business people. Attend job fairs. Introduce yourself to employees at companies of your choice. Learn to make friends with people who you feel are trustworthy and genuinely interested in being helpful. As you increase friendships, look for opportunities to help others, also.

What is the connection between networking and finding a good job? Allow friends and their friends to help watch for that special job. Do not underestimate what friends can do for you! I encourage you to surround yourself with people who want to help you in some way or another. Advice from a friend you know (word of mouth) is very, very high on the list of ways to find a good job. A small percentage of good jobs are advertised publicly. The following quote by Bowman addresses this fact: "It is estimated that up to eighty-five percent of the available jobs are never publicly announced."[5]

The following gives two more examples of networking. Let's say you're a computer technician and planning a trip to Kansas City on Saturday to attend a Royals baseball game. While you're there on other business, allow some extra time. If you're interested in computers, pick out a computer store where you may want to order a product or have on your list as a resource. Allow ample time to browse or purchase an item. Visit with the business clerk or owner. Get a catalog. There's a chance someday you may need to order an item from their store. Maybe they'll even special order something for you. Sometimes it's not what you know but who you know that will help at a later time.

Also, while in Kansas City to attend the Royals game, you stopped to fuel the car. While fueling the car, you start a conversation with a man from the area standing next to your fuel pumps. You're simply being friendly. During the conversation, you find out his business needs help with AutoCAD software and he asked about your interest in checking with them further. He encourages you to come look him up and visit their plant sometime soon. You were able to come back to Kansas City the following week to help him solve a technical problem. He and others at his company were very pleased you were able to help him solve the technical problem. This was a great way to add to your network. Now you probably have another specialty AutoCAD software person to call upon for technical help at a later time.

Here were just two examples of the hundreds of ways you can build upon the strength of your network. Surround yourself with people who want to help you in some way or another... to make your life easier…and to make your job easier.

Do you have a close friendship network with any of the categories below? These are the persons you learn to trust and know as friends. They may be the people able to help you at some point in the future. Build on strengthening acquaintances similar to the people on the following list. Remember, this list is only a beginning for your network.

- Hair stylist, dentist, doctor, pharmacist, lawyer
- Restaurant business owner, retailer, news reporter
- Accountant, computer guru, teacher, professor
- Policeman, city employee, pastor and staff
- Established licensed plumber, carpenter
- Banker at one of the local banks, reputable insurance agent, accountant
- Local service station owner, auto mechanic

Think About It- Connect with More Good People!

Any one of the above may want to know you as much as you need to know them. Your network would not be complete without family members, church members, and neighbors. Many of these persons may someday become your closest friends and soon become part of your confidence circle, which is discussed in the next section. People in your confidence circle can be trusted to a higher degree to hear your struggles and successes, persons you can confide in, and to get confidential advice. Remember, good jobs are found through friendships.

Group support is powerful. Find friends who can have a good effect upon you.

CONFIDENCE CIRCLE

My definition of a confidence circle is: a closer network of friends; a group of persons who are friends that talk with each other often. Each person would help you no matter what the circumstance. Building a confidence circle may come from building upon a closer network of friends. This group of friends can be counted on to help solve problems and celebrate your successes. A confidence circle is like the spokes on a bicycle wheel. For the wheel to work right, it needs a hub and many good spokes. You are that hub. As the hub, you are surrounded with spokespersons who are ready to give support and enjoy good times together.

Consider strengthening this part of your life. This is a serious process of developing very close friends. One of the keys here is having persons who respect you. They would not share your private stories with others. Each friend is very protective of one another's close friendship.

This is not new. It is primary to building a strong foundation for a family, business relationships, and/or a person who wants to advance in the job world. Most often, when two or more persons are gathered together and working at something together, the outcome is stronger.

Challenges could go through more scrutiny with a group of close friends. Better ideas and creativity can come from having more minds resolving the same problem or mission.

COMPLIMENTING OTHERS' SUCCESSES

Can you be happy to see others having success? In Romans 1:28-32, the author talks about the penalty for persons that become full of every kind of wickedness such as greed, hate, envy, and bitterness.[6]

Read more about this in the book of Romans.

To enjoy seeing others get ahead is a pretty tough challenge to handle sometimes, right? But peace of mind can come over a person who has this attitude. If our hearts are in the right frame of mind and want to relate well to others, kindness will come out, giving both you and them a win-win situation. From now on, I challenge you to say only uplifting words as you compliment and enjoy others' successes.

SHARING YOUR GIFTS

People who hope to increase their pay base might want to consider giving of their time and sharing their gifts. This may already be one of your priorities. After a long day on the job, spending time with your family or friends is valuable. And, then to share your time with others who need help. Yes, we need to take good care of ourselves, too. However, life does not stop with me, I, and myself. The employee looking beyond self could have more potential by giving time to others. This starts simply with awareness and consideration of our priorities. Sometimes our own challenges seem to keep us from helping others until we get our own life in order. Good employees are not selfish. Good employees can hopefully rise to the next level of excellence—this involves helping others look good. Giving of your time, resources, and money can help you from becoming self-centered.

Another level of giving involves giving to an organization or someone who is struggling. There is something unexplainable that happens when you extend yourself or volunteer by giving a portion of your time and/or income!

GOSSIP IS LIKE FIRE

If you are working to become more effective on the job, avoid cheap talk that will reflect negatively on the company or another person. My mother-in-law once said, "If someone gossips about another person, they'll probably gossip about you also." No one gains from cheap talk. Practice building people up rather than tearing them down. Apply the golden rule, "Do for others what you want them to do for you."[7]

Make the other person look good and be known as having a helpful attitude.

GET TO THE POINT

Have you ever had someone ask why you are "beating around the bush?" If you sense during a conversation the other person is in a hurry, try to "get to the point" and take less of his or her time. Usually, people in a work setting don't have time to hear you talk around the issue. Get to the point quickly in your communication. Time is money for people who have a busy schedule. On the other hand if you sense the other person is in a big hurry and you still want to do a better job of getting your point across, you could say something like this: "Let me think about it more and I'll try to give you a better answer at lunch tomorrow."

RESPECTING CO-WORKERS

Dr. Marlene Caroselli begins her booklet by quoting, "It has been estimated that 95 percent of our workplace success depends on an understanding of other people."[8] Some ways to understand others, as mentioned earlier, are being a good listener and showing interest in them. If you want respect from others, treat them with respect.

What should you do when someone mistreats you again and again? You may want to confront the person by asking why it's happening. Next, ask another person you know and trust who can help you with the situation.

The benefits of respecting all staff personnel at work can be rewarding. Why not become a valued co-worker?

RESPECTING YOUR BOSS/SUPERVISOR

When difficulties come between you and your boss or supervisor, I'd advise you to call him or her and set up an appointment. Give your supervisor a chance to ask additional questions. In this way, we are giving them the respect they deserve. And, try to avoid allowing others to sway your thoughts in a negative direction toward your boss.

It's a good idea to respect management at all times. This will most likely help them to notice that you are grateful for your job and willing to work productively.

If you have tendencies to go around your boss, you may want to pray and respond by acting on this problem and know how to change. Jesus tells us that "If two of you agree here on earth concerning anything you ask for, my Father in heaven will do it for you." [9]

Let your supervisor go to upper management for getting questions answered. It's worth making it a priority to listen well to your boss. Working for a business is a privilege. Try to find an outcome that will make both you and your supervisor a winner!

DINNER MANNERS

Whole books are written about meal time manners, wow! What a difficult thing. Eating manners could have a higher priority among people in general. Companies are often looking at employees who are healthy and well-mannered for the long term as they train and promote them through the ranks. You will be an investment for them if they hire you.

While having a meal with others, your table manners may be another way of representing the organization, company, or family. Impressions are made from people watching your table manners. They may relate it to future work habits on the job as well. Other subtle things are learned about an individual while eating, such as respect for others and the art of conversation. There needs to be a politeness about eating patterns at all times even though there's no one around. As you are considered for a new position, and you do not know when this will happen, think about how you would fare with some of the pointers below.

Remember, the following are some American traditions for the most part. Take a minute or two to read through the suggestions. Check those you want to give more attention to.

- Follow the lead of the host or hostess to be seated
- Don't interrupt the host or a guest who is talking at the same table
- Respect the waiter or waitress; be patient
- Avoid touching the spoon on the glass while stirring or leaning back on chair
- Chew small bites of food slowly, quietly, and with mouth closed
- Pick up finger foods such as raw carrots, celery, and a half piece of bread
- Focus on conversation that makes dining pleasant
- Use the utensils in the order of proper etiquette
- Say, "Please pass the ____ to me, thank you." Don't reach for food dishes.
- Wait to begin eating until the last person at the table is served
- Share conversation with those closest to you when dining at a long table
- Roll spaghetti correctly onto your fork
- Wait to talk until after chewing food with your mouth closed; take your time while eating
- Avoid controlling the conversation at the table; share pleasant appetizing thoughts
- Show an interest in others' conversation—be a respectful listener, too
- Include those who have not yet joined in the dinner conversation
- Turn away from the table and cover your mouth if you must cough
- Excuse yourself if you must leave the table
- Be complimentary about the taste of the food
- Keep the dinner jokes light and clean
- Tip the waiter or waitress 15 to 20 percent; this may be their only pay
- And, show appreciation for the invitation by sending a thank you note.

TABLE MANNERS CROSSWORD PUZZLE:

ACROSS

1 Please do not _____ your mouth full.

5 Be polite & specific, rather than saying pass _____.

7 Take your _____ while eating.

9 Eat _____. Enjoy your food and dinner guest(s).

11 Place the _____ on your lap before eating.

12 Eat from a dish, not the _____.

13 Please pass the dish _____ potatoes.

15 Tip the _____ 15-20%.

16 Treat family with respect such as a _____.

17 Be careful so food doesn't fall off the _____.

20 Green finger food.

22 Don't _____ your seeds or waste on the table.

23 Last two letters of a mid-western state.

26 Something people put on bread.

27 Don't reach across the table for the _____.

30 I think _____ makes the water taste better.

32 Practice saying yes rather than _____.

34 Tell your _____ how good the food tastes.

35 Don't take _____ while dining out for dinner.

37 Compliment the _____ of the food.

39 Don't talk about _____ at the dinner table

13

40 A poor practice to _____ through your food.

DOWN

2 Kind of wood to make a salad spoon in East Indies.

3 Set the place settings with the _____ left of the plate.

4 Another name for the fork, knife and spoon.

6 Say _____ before you start eating.

8 Don't make _____ for foolishness.

9 Please don't be a _____-off at the dinner table.

10 The opposite of the waiter.

14 Don't _____ it, eat your veggies.

18 You shouldn't laugh _____ someone.

19 Offer to pay the _____ if you did the inviting.

20 Type of food popular in Louisiana.

21 Type of meat, called _____ chops.

24 Follow the lead of the host or _____.

25 Keep _____ clean and light at dinner time.

28 Include others in the _____ conversation.

29 Chew with your _____ closed.

31 Begin to _____ after the host takes the first bite.

33 Sauerkraut has a distinctive _____.

36 Eat an _____ of corn with holders.

CHAPTER ONE SUMMARY

Ending the first chapter on dinner manners should not be surprising. Our mannerisms, when we're visiting with people, tell others what we're all about. We want to communicate, so that people will feel comfortable associating with us. This is basic and very important to becoming a good employee and even more, becoming successful.

CHAPTER 2

EMPLOYMENT APPLICATION

WHEN TO APPLY

Keep in mind, there are many approaches to finding and making application for a job. There is still, in my opinion, no better way than to meet and visit with someone one on one. If I were an employer, I'd still want to see someone face to face early on in the application phase. I guess it's like the saying, "different strokes for different folks."

Some businesses encourage you to make application on-line. I chose Google and typed in the following, "online employment application," and found employers in our area who were hiring.

After reading this self-help book and reviewing options, you're probably almost ready to make preparations for a good-paying, full-time job.

It's generally a good idea to drive up at the place of employment by yourself. There may be exceptions, such as having a handicap, or other reasons. If you can, pick up the application first and then take it home so you can fill it out completely. Whether you're picking up the application, taking it in, or going for the interview, first impressions are so important, as I remind my reader in Chapter 13. If you plan to fill in the application at the place of business, why not take a rough draft to help you with important information to complete the application.

I'm recommending you take a resumé along at the same time as you give them the completed application. Paper clip the resumé to the filled out application. One example of a resumé form, in the Appendix, can be copied and used for this purpose after removing APPENDIX title with white-out. Chapter 10 addresses the resumé. As you fill out the application, such as, who employed you in the past, you can simply print in the phrase, (see my resumé).

Monday morning and Friday afternoon are probably the least effective times to call in to make arrangements for a job application. I'm recommending you contact the employer on a Tuesday, Wednesday, or Thursday between 10:00 and 11:00 a.m. or between 2:00 and 3:00 p.m.

Another very important issue—do you know someone who has been encouraging you to make application at a particular place? If you do, ask them for advice about making application. Also, ask them if you can use their name as a referral. Second, if this place of work still appeals to you, give them a call to see if they're accepting applications. If they are, and you still believe this employer would be a plus to work for, give them a call and ask them what time would be best to pick up an application.

Remember, first impressions are lasting and timing is primary. Thank them politely for the information.

PERSONAL INFORMATION

The first thing you usually see on an application is "please print clearly." Printing clearly can be either eye catching or hard to read. Practice making your words and letters appealing. That is basic to getting someone's attention or losing them.

Being completely truthful while filling in the answers on the application is very important. Sometimes the employer may already know your family or even your history, so don't assume they do not know you.

Avoid leaving empty blanks. If you have no answer for that space, draw a line in it, to mean you haven't skipped over it accidentally. Do not leave gaps in your application; that may create doubt in your reader's mind. Read the questions thoroughly, so a yes does not mean no and no doesn't mean yes. Try hard to be affirmative with yes answers.

All employers want a telephone number where they can reach you. Consider giving them a number so you can be reached easily. The employer wants to know if you are easy to reach or only when it is convenient for you.

AVAILABILITY

If you are interested in the open position, show enthusiasm and genuine interest on your face as the potential employer asks about your availability. You have gone in to make application to work at that particular business. You are telling them you want to work for them.

In the space where it asks "When can you begin?" fill in the word, immediately or negotiable. Give the total hours available per week—instead of 30-40, place an asterisk in the blank and drop down to the open space with another asterisk to share you are available as many hours as the supervisor asks you to work. This also might indicate you would consider a salaried job. This indicates to the employer that your job comes near to being first in your priorities. By handling it something like that, if you can, you are telling the hiring employer that you are flexible. Employers like to hire people who are flexible and adaptable.

This is no time to tell the employer you cannot meet their demands.

WORK HISTORY

Fill in your most current working job first, then your job before that, and so on. Do not use old phone numbers or guess what the telephone number was, thinking the past employer has the same phone number or even the same address as before. In fact, you could call your past supervisor(s) and ask them for their telephone number along with the extension number where they can be reached. Share with them you are needing this for making application for the new job at _____ . If there are barriers to rebuild, do it and move on. If you did have a good experience in the last job, share with them briefly how much you had appreciated it. Ask them if you can use them for a referral and remember to thank them for their efforts.

EDUCATION

Schools attended—be complete in answering this question so the employer forms an opinion about you doing things completely and correctly. This may be the place for you to fill in the space with an answer (see resume).

EMPLOYMENT TEST TIP

Keep a perspective for most jobs; you are filling out an application for an employer who is wanting to hire someone to help them make a better profit.

CHAPTER TWO SUMMARY

This is your chance to share who the real you is in professional ways.

CHAPTER 3
PREPARE FOR INTERVIEWING

ARRIVE EARLY

Prepare to go early for the interview. Arriving early has advantages. If your trip is a short distance of about 10 miles, you should add extra minutes for any unexpected interruptions. More time is added to find a parking place, check on the right entrances, brushing yourself off or read a sign before you actually arrive at the destination. Sometimes the person who arrives early may receive helpful benefits such as:

- learning information that will help you later if offered the job
- hearing news about something important that happened to someone
- meeting new people who are waiting for the same purpose
- having time to clear your mind and focus on why you are there
- gaining hints from others about interviewing
- looking confident after taking some deep breaths
- receiving unexpected encouragement from others
- experiencing the feeling of being in the flow of things
- being invited into the interview ahead of someone who is late
- demonstrating that you are responsible with time management
- opportunity to dialogue with the interviewer's assistant

The assistant may be asked by the interviewer later, "What was your first impression of the individual?" Arriving early has the potential to strengthen your interview process.

THINK BEFORE YOU COMMIT

Try not to take on too many outside responsibilities, especially while you are concentrating on preparing for a job change or interview. Arrange more free time in the evenings for things that come along regarding the job change. Evaluate your commitments to see if they align with your job-change goals.

When you accept new commitments, it may be even more important to be able to follow through immediately. Develop a plan to be effective, and meet deadlines.

When you say yes, you want to be ready to do a good job. Do you feel compelled to say yes to everyone who asks you to do something? Sometimes it is difficult to know when to say no.

As you plan ahead, you will want to do even better at prioritizing your time. Eliminate lower priorities which can help increase your effectiveness. During this period of time in your life, pray to Jesus as he asks us to pray in Matthew 7: 7-8. It's very important to have free time for meditation while evaluating routines. Find ways to build upon your strengths. Pray that you can be at your best for thinking things through!

THE HAND TALKS

Have you ever had someone give you an evaluation of your handshake? If you haven't, you might want to try it. Your next employer may check out your handshake, along with other factors, in determining your potential. He or she may want you to represent the business with a firm handshake. One time after shaking a person's hand, I felt like apologizing for shaking it too hard. In some business circumstances, the handshake is a way to begin a meeting. As I've learned, in other settings handshakes are not needed, which helps to avoid spreading germs.

Practice does wonders for us. The handshake should be firm with some movement in the forearm up and down from the original position. How long do you shake hands? Perhaps one to two seconds is all the time needed. Get some advice from other business people. Sometimes the hand shake is longer for giving affirmation to a friend.

In an interview situation, watch the other person for a clue and be quick to offer your hand if their hand is offered to you. Otherwise, do your greeting verbally. If a person offers you a handshake at the beginning, you may want to take the lead as you end the conversation to show how much you appreciated the meeting.

A LESSON IN LISTENING

By not listening to a co-worker, it could signal that you don't think they are important. In an interview or meeting, stay focused on **watching and listening** to the other person speaking. Give this person your full attention. Try not to take too much of their time by talking about insignificant information. Answer their questions and avoid getting sidetracked on something else. The interviewer's time is valuable. Be sure to look at his or her eyes during the discussion. Allow the interviewer to lead in the discussion.

During a scheduled interview or formal meeting, try to evaluate if you're talking too much. By showing genuine interest in the person speaking to you, they may feel more open about giving you their undivided attention and perhaps even a job offer. When talking with this individual again at a later time, repeating their name is important! Remembering to say their name shows to them your earlier conversation was important to you.

PAY ATTENTION TO SMALL STUFF

Misspelled words and grammar on the application will not help you get a job. Start looking up words in the dictionary immediately if you do not feel confident to spell well. Soon, you'll probably know how to spell much better.

When a track runner tries to improve upon the last race, diligent practice may result in a faster finish. As some say, "you get back what you put into it."

I heard once that when Gene Stephenson was coach of the Wichita State University baseball team and was being interviewed on television; he mentioned giving credit for some of his winnings to the small details that may be overlooked by an opponent. Paying attention to the small details is a good idea, especially if you're arranging for investments of time and/or money. It's even more important if you're doing this for someone else, for instance your employer.

Improving upon small, personal ways of saving might be a way to improve your financial gains. If you're not doing it already, some day you may want to include this as part of improving your personal goals. Many employers look for prospective employees who are wise financially and stable in the use of their money.

Following is another illustration of how a small savings developed into big savings. Employees who work in manufacturing, such as drafters, often develop many prints each week. Sometimes drafters make several prints per day. Within one blueprint, there may be hundreds of arrows on dimension lines to show size. What if one day the head drafter says to the department drafters, "From now on, we'll not fill in the arrowheads; and in doing so, we'll make a substantial savings in the course of the year."

For example, one of the drafters wants to know how much it will save if none of the arrow heads are filled in. The answer to this question is—in one day, approximately two seconds are saved for each arrow not filled in to make a solid arrow. What if approximately 100 arrows are made per day by one person. Each day, there is a savings of 200 seconds or three minutes and 20 seconds. During a 40-hour week, there is an approximate savings of 16.7 minutes. The savings in a four-week month are approximately 66.8 minutes. And, in one year or 11 working months, there could be a savings of approximately 734.8 minutes or 12 hours, roughly speaking. If the company charges $32.00 per hour for your time, then $32 times 12 hours was being lost by filling in the arrowheads. That was a probable loss of $384.00 before and is now a gain of $384.00. My math also shows me that if you add up the spread of the loss vs. the gain, the result is a savings of $768.00. If you multiply this number by 10 for 10 drafters in the department, it totals $7,680.00.

If more savings can be made with other small processes, it adds up to bigger profits for the company. This is a classic example of how small changes can add up to big savings at work or at home. If the company makes more profits, who knows, some may come back to you in getting a raise or promotion.

In conclusion, if you bring something of significance to someone's attention, be cautious about an appropriate time when they are not so busy, and can listen to your idea with time to talk. And yes, much more will be said later about many other details.

CHOOSE ENCOURAGING WORDS

Positive feedback is appreciated. As this happens, both individuals can be encouraged and built up. For the one hearing positive feedback, it's like being given gold. Affirmation of this kind is needed. Practice it daily and develop it to the point that it's part of your personality. For the person giving positive remarks, a respectful rapport will develop between co-workers.

Communication of this kind is valuable. Employees using positive reinforcement can be more effective than otherwise. This results in a higher rate of productiveness in the work environment when practiced conscientiously.

Saying yes in an assertive tone of voice and expression deserves an exclamation point! Your yes tone can be "of sound mind," sincere, honest, upbeat, and heart-felt. Supervisors like to hear from this person. Your effectiveness may increase when sharing positive reinforcement with others. However, "You cannot just be a 'yes' person and survive," said a friend of mine. At times one has to say "no," as already discussed a couple pages back under the topic "Think Before You Commit."

People not only like to hear affirmation, but also the use of their name. This takes the conversation to a higher level. We can help to make a big difference in the lives of others around us. If you have not yet adopted this habit, you might want to try it. You may enjoy the response you get by genuinely encouraging someone as you call them by their name!

A story heard by my wife at a workshop by Dr. John Valusek years ago sponsored by Hesston Corporation, now AGCO, was called, "Get your dipper out of my bucket."

This is the gist of the story: As the day began, a man named Bill started his day with breakfast. He was energized, ready for action with another full schedule at work. As he arrived at his desk, a co-worker commented that he looked tired and asked if he stayed up late. That conversation made him feel a little tired, since he must be looking tired. He attended a meeting, and while conversing with a co-worker, she mentioned the color of his shirt made him look pale. Now, he was feeling even less energetic. After listening to another negative comment, he felt like saying, "Get your dipper out of my bucket." His bucket was drained of confidence. He had not been encouraged by others. The lesson to learn from this story—as an employee, he would have greatly benefited from more affirmative comments at work. We can have the potential to join in creating an atmosphere of positive feedback most of the time.

Have you ever felt like people were only taking away your energy level and not giving positive remarks to energize you? Giving others encouraging words is one way to help them feel confident. Even a smile signifies you acknowledge them and gives the other person encouragement. Employers are looking to hire persons who energize fellow team members.

The words and phrases following encourage and energize others rather than exhausting them. As the opportunity arises, consider saying these and other similar phrases to encourage people you work with daily:

- What a good score!
- Way to go!
- I'd call that a good job!
- Terrific job!
- That was a noble thing to do!
- Sensational!
- Now you're on the right track!
- Excellent!
- Thank you!
- How did you do it so well?
- Quite an improvement!
- That's a good way to handle it!
- I appreciate working with you!
- I can count on you!
- That's much better!
- What a good idea!
- Thanks for the advice!
- We accomplished a lot today!

- Figured that out quickly, didn't you?
- I'm fortunate to work with you!
- Got it down, don't you?
- Very interesting suggestion!
- Satisfactory work!
- Exactly what we wanted!
- Good going!
- That's admirable!
- That's probably the best answer!
- Job well done!
- My, what a creative idea!
- This is worth a reward!
- Very convincing!
- Hurray for you!
- Okay, that looks good!
- Quite favorable!
- Great work!
- Keep hanging in there.
- Awesome!
- Couldn't do that good myself!
- Positively yes!
- Very well done!
- That will give life to our project.
- Congratulations for choosing encouraging words!

- God willing, you can do it again!
- Mighty deserving for you!
- You've hit a milestone!
- Good judgment!
- You've given the project your best!
- That's thoughtful of you to do!
- Good work! Brilliant!
- You know what's important!
- That will produce good results!
- That will give life to our project!
- Marvelous!

A smile is contagious!

READ ABOUT INTERVIEWING

It would be well worth your time and energy to read more about interviewing. One book I read was entitled *The Job Hunter's Final Exam*, by Thomas M. Camden, published by Surrey Books. Camden had some very good true and false questions followed with supporting rationale in the chapter called "Interviewing." Again, I would suggest you find and read more sources about interviewing.[1]

Let's do some pretending. You see a Job Ad on-line or in the paper that invites people to come interview. You may feel the Ad matches your qualifications. Before you call for an inquiry from reading the Ad, take a power nap for 10 minutes so you're at your best. If you are tired, set the alarm. Considering the job interview, make sure you have some clean, full length, pressed clothing for the season. Your clothes do not have to be the latest style but I'm recommending you look dressed up. Clothes must be wrinkle-free, free of lint, and go together. You can't afford to sound sleepy on the phone, so take some stretches and flush your face with water. Now, before you call, there are more things we want to think about before you jump in the car and go. Think of several different times you could go to interview, in case they ask you on the telephone.

Next, do you have some reliable transportation to the place listed in the Ad? Is the car clean and quiet? What do you want to say to them when they answer their phone? They may ask you what your ambition is in life. Make it short and reasonable. If it's an answering service, do what they ask and politely give them a courteous form of thank you. "This is your chance," regardless how you might feel. Socially, and this is big, you would want to show them you are polite and can hold a mature conversation with them. For starters you might say, "I'm calling about your Ad," (and tell them where you learned about the job). "I'm interested in coming to apply with you." Wait for them to inquire about you. You are going to think about this long and hard, right? Make your conversation short and reasonable. By the way, before they speak, have a pencil and paper ready to take some notes about names, phone numbers, and location of their business. Let's say they make an appointment for you to come apply, now what? Ask them for directions. Again be sure to thank them. Now, you've learned the job opening is only five miles away, what a break. Prior to going, prep your hair and put on your best happy face with just a little bit of cologne or deodorant. Check yourself in the mirror. Each time you interview, think positive thoughts, such as, "they may need someone just like me."

Prepare to take some cash, oh about five $1.00 bills and a $10.00 bill for a soda or coffee if the occasion comes up. Whether you're hired or not, try to be poised, excited, hopeful, and glad for this opportunity. Avoid being disappointed if it takes more tries before someone offers you a job. This can be expected, no matter who we are. Consider each interview as a learning experience. Prepare again for the next interview from the things you learned at the last one. Companies want to know if you have a "stick-to-itiveness." Many places are looking for people they can train for the long haul, since it costs them big bucks to hire and train. For that reason and more, interviewers are looking for people who have potential, are socially adjusted, and have personalities to meet their customers.

WILLING WORKERS WANTED

Opportunities may become available to you that may very well help strengthen your job situation. Sometimes we can ask ourselves—what could I be doing to help myself be the willing worker I really want to be? A couple of examples are, being willing to take classes or an internship to help with communication skills as an employee. Be willing to take advantage of a class that helps prepare you for something new on the job. What would happen if we gave ourselves an exam, marked off the areas to improve, and focused on areas of weakness to become a more willing worker?

When I was a teacher, asking for some feedback and requirements from employers was important for me. I wanted to teach and strengthen those weaknesses for students. As a teacher, I continued to encourage my students often to consider ways that could help them qualify for a good job sooner, rather than later. You can do the same.

Ask not what you can do for yourself but what you can do for them, referring to the employer.

Willing workers may get the breaks! Unwilling workers may not get the raises! Are you willing to:

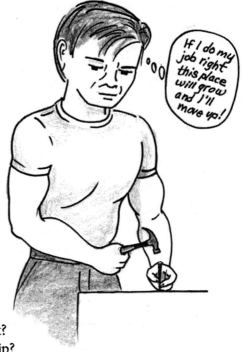

- take orders?
- practice restraint?
- handle the blame?
- listen, listen, listen?
- try again and again?
- be patient with others?
- thank others sincerely?
- learn by doing it calmly?
- forgive other's ignorance?
- go slowly and efficiently?
- build quiet personal character?
- accept another's point of view?
- allow others to air their feelings?
- have patience in troubled times?
- do work without being rewarded?
- work hard beyond the call of duty?
- have quiet moments without talking?
- bear disappointments without complaint?
- give glory to the boss for his/her leadeship?

I hope your answer was a resounding yes to each question above.

HANDLING INFORMATION

Don't tell everything you know. It's been said that you want to come out of an interview feeling you didn't say everything you wanted to say. I wonder if sales and working with people are similar. Employers want persons who get to the point and do not waste their time. Prioritize and only give what you're asked to give until you know the other as a friend or close acquaintance. Telling someone too much may also indicate you have a problem or have trouble handling information. Telling an acquaintance too much information is not good.

If information shared with you as a trusted employee or friend is confidential, the wise thing to do is continue to keep it confidential.

I was visiting with a person recently about what I was doing after he asked the question, "What are you doing now?" I caught myself wanting to tell too much about what I was doing even though he said he wanted to know. The real truth is the other person may have only asked out of trying to show interest in me. The other person may not have had the time for a long conversation. The acceptable thing to do is say something they would enjoy hearing and be brief! You might want to talk about the lighter things that don't involve your opinions. I try to work at this challenge myself.

This same person shared with me about a meeting he recently attended. At the meeting, an individual stood up to share how a local group was doing a project incorrectly. Do most people want to hear how something is being done incorrectly? Probably not, so…as you communicate with others, politely share what you feel is necessary and above all, leave them feeling good about the conversation.

MAKING THE RIGHT IMPRESSION

Check out the nature of the business before interviewing. Preparation before the interview is big. Visit with someone who works for the company in the area of your interest. What are the expectations you must meet to make the right impression?

Practice your lines, perhaps in front of a mirror. How does the up-coming job interview compare with past jobs? Sometimes the interviewer is trying to match you up with a job that is compatible for your success. Representing yourself correctly means also going to the interview by yourself. Think of something pleasant as you meet the interviewer. Prepare notes several days in advance and try memorizing your lines. However, as stated before, you do not have to share everything!

As I shared with my 20-year-old grandson, clean cut hair styling, coupled with flushing the parts of your face that are shaven, with an after shave such as Mennen Skin Bracer, gives the smiling face an energized look of confidence. My wife suggests for the women, a clean, cared-for hair style with touches of make-up can be energizing.

For both men and women, avoid far-out dress unless you're dressing for a specific job. "Dress for success." Wear medium-dark clean seasonal clothing and one step up better than the job you want. A hat or cap may not be acceptable for most interviews unless you are interviewing where it is very cold. Strong scented fragrances or too much distracting apparel are not good. Wearing clean, comfortable, hard-toed construction shoes to an interview for a construction job or a maintenance job may be okay, but not for most jobs.

If you are interviewing, pay very close attention to the person you are interviewing with rather than thinking of the next thing you want to say. Review the first topic of this chapter, "Arrive Early." Put your best smile on as you prepare to greet the interviewer. Maintain eye contact and show good posture as you allow the interviewer to be seated first. Normally, you would not use first names in an interview. Do not use vulgar slang language, one-word answers, chew gum, or fold your arms. More will be said in Chapter six, with the topic, "Body Language Talks."

CHAPTER THREE SUMMARY

Now remember…only answer interviewer questions with short courteous answers and to remember the interviewer's name.

Another important item for you before your interview is to write a cover letter. Find examples of a cover letter, then insert specifics that describe you and your situation. Set aside valuable time to prepare an errorless letter for introducing yourself. Begin by sharing why you want to arrange for an interview. This two or three paragraph letter should give the right impression about your strengths, experiences, willingness to work, and goals in a new job! Share your telephone number and when you can be available to visit for the interview.

CHAPTER 4

ORGANIZE SELF ON THE JOB

Consider your time on the job as a privilege—your responsibility for the sake of both yourself and your employer.

A TIME TO KEEP IT PERSONAL

Do you use company time or the company phones for personal business? If you've done it a few times, consider not doing it and make a conscious effort to avoid the practice. Do personal business off company time. You will then have more time on the job to do the work for which you are being paid.

Conducting personal business during work hours costs companies a loss of profits. If you are responsible, re-evaluate and start saying: "I care. I have respect for my employer. I'll be very careful not to do personal business on the job." Here are examples of doing personal business on company time to avoid:

- Quitting early or lateness for personal business
- Reading a book unrelated to the working job
- Wasting time, visiting about non-job things
- Sending personal text or e-mail to a friend
- Calling in sick to do personal business
- Making a grocery list for shopping
- Taking longer breaks than allowed
- Arranging for a personal party
- Running personal errands

WORK ETHICS

"There are studies that show companies with strong ethics policies put twice as much net income on the bottom line," said Larry Axline, Managing Director of Management Action Planning, Boulder, Colorado.[1]

That was true then and is probably still true today. It probably holds true also for work ethics. It's simply the way we think about our work. In many cases work is associated with factories, offices, schools, hospitals, mines, construction and manufacturing. How about work camps, working laborers, work detail, iron worker, workshop, for instance?

What is your association to work? Speaking realistically, having a good work ethic is about liking to work hard. Very few people like to hear someone say, "You should work harder." Just try thinking about it differently. Why not try working smarter on the job. Talk about work in another way. Maybe it's about using some of the following words instead of the word work: end product, duty, business, activity, benefit, quota, practice, account, project, task, obligation, or productivity. This may help improve the way you perceive your own assigned work ethics on the job and the employers profit line.

Employees who have good work ethics try to put their best foot forward on a daily basis. When giving your best, you can bank on having a better chance toward future wage increases.

What are more examples of explaining what a good work ethic is all about?

- Wanting the employer to be very successful
- Putting your all into a job rather than doing as little as possible
- Appreciating hearing compliments made about your employer
- Never talking negative about your employer
- Telling others about the good product which the company produces
- Providing excellent services to the company customers
- Encouraging good teamwork and striving to be honest
- Employees are hard-working people, accomplishing much in a day

COMPUTER ETHICS

Consider the business computer ethics below for yourself at home and in the workplace so you and the company grow:

- Record all purchased software; use only certified software
- Stay with assigned equipment and software
- Do not take credit for using another person's work; respect copyright laws; resist plagiarism; and be respectful of others' information
- Keep computer and work station clean, free of dust and clutter
- Be considerate of loud computer sounds or loud music around others
- Do not play games on company time or cheat on calculations and measurements
- Avoid eating and drinking next to the computer
- Stay focused on tasks and assignments in chronological order
- Avoid any activity that might create a conflict between departmental personnel
- Respect equipment, software, and supplies as company property
- Do not enter into an unlawful contract of work-related activity
- Conduct affairs with highest ethical standards and report any suspicion of foul play, violations, or misconduct; and pornography
- Do not take little bribes with the intent of influencing business decisions
- Do not access company material or information to trade with another company unless clearance has been given by proper authority

- Be aware of company policy as employees make changes
- Company equipment and software may not be used for personal gain
- Computer storage systems should not be accessed without proper permission
- Respect locks and locking passwords; label all storage cases and devices
- Be respectful of fax mail, e-mails, Twitter, and other electronic communications
- Keep back-up records of all stored files; remove old information regularly
- Find out what to shut off and leave on at the end of the day
- Report needed computer repairs immediately to supervisor
- Avoid misspelled words by using spell check and good proofreading practices
- Do not bring disks (storage devices) back and forth from home to work without clearance
- Manage files well for retrieval purposes—pay particular attention to key words

KEEP WORK DESK AREA CLEAN

Whether it's at home or at work, unorganized work areas decrease productivity. Maybe a cluttered work area doesn't affect you. I constantly work at organizing and keeping my work area clean. It gives me more incentive to come back to the work area later. When my desk top or work bench area is clean and organized, I feel more energized and productive.

Years ago, I worked for an owner/employer who had an office area that was approximately 16' x 24'. His walnut executive desk measured about 5'x 8'. It was covered with paper work to a depth of 4"- 7" high over most of the desk top except for a very small notebook area in front of his chair. He seemed to spend very little time in his office. Perhaps he disliked his office. By the way, he would not allow his administrative assistant to touch the desk top. I would venture to say that if he would have cleaned off his desk, I'm guessing his company may have had more growth instead of financial pains and difficulties. In my opinion, there is a direct relationship between success and a clean work area. These simple and inexpensive desk area tips work for me. They can work for you.

- Keeping the most current agenda on top of my desk is like keeping my car washed. When I scan my clean desk top and close proximity, it gives me a sense of wanting to come back to it again and again.
- A couple of your favorite family pictures in the work area are inspiring. Pictures like this can give happy feelings for motivating us at work.
- Having room for a calendar planner available on the desk top is primary. Record things you want to do on specific days. Record telephone calls. Take notes of the time you should call back for response to questions. Mark dates and times when you have made appointments or want to pay bills in advance.
- Check your desk top each time you sit to make sure you have only the important information on the desk top. Throw away anything that is unimportant into a wastebasket which is arms-length from the desk. Be prepared to shred the desk area waste that is confidential at a later time.
- About filing: file the important papers immediately so you don't have to handle

them more than once. Consider using a manila folder stacking arrangement beside the keyboard. When someone calls on the phone, do they have time to wait as you search for a paper with requested information? Probably not. If you're going to look good, you want to know where to retrieve things immediately! Especially take note how your boss files information. Consider using a similar system so there can be more compatibility.

■ Desk tops must be large enough. My desk top measures 1"x 26"x 62" and 26½" from the floor. It is a dark solid walnut with a matching dark Formica inlay, making it real easy to maintain. The top was purchased separate at a second hand store and simply sets on top of a small desk. The desk top could be sitting on top of two 24" walnut file cabinets.

■ Consider surrounding yourself with convenient equipment, computer and printer, T.V., calculator, lamp or light with a daylight bulb, manila folder stepped rack, in-basket, and a file cabinet next to the desk. Many people have a bigger and better desk than me. The important thing is that you have a work area that works efficiently for you.

■ Be proactive with your working habits. Keep clutter under control as a general statement. Start at home and then the same at work. Good luck.

DISTRACTIONS COST TIME

Stay focused on your own task. As a teacher, my job was to help students stay on task. When someone looked at me or tried to get my attention, I assumed it could mean they needed help in some way. It was my responsibility to go see what could be done to help them get back on task.

On the job, hourly employees are encouraged to stay focused on their own tasks because distractions cost time. Employees want to avoid letting other people and other things take them off task when trying to concentrate on doing a good job. It is surprising how much money can be lost when an employee gives in to just the smallest distractions.

Employees on the job do not want to have their boss remind them to stay on task.

KEEP COPIES OF IMPORTANT INFORMATION

Copies of information are important, but which ones do you choose to keep, file and which ones do you discard or shred? All very important documents should be kept in a lock box at the bank with copies at your home office in a safe place. Certified paperwork, wills, one-of-a kind documents, all fall into this category. If you don't have an economical fireproof safe at home, perhaps investing in a lock box at the bank would be the next best plan.

There are many times when dated copies of records become very important, especially when filing taxes. What good are copies if you don't file them under a subject that can be found quickly? Begin giving this alpha order filing plan immediate attention; and you can relax knowing your paperwork is safe and easy to locate at a later time.

ANSWER MAIL IMMEDIATELY

When electronic or postal mail comes in, respond within approximately three days. Some mail will need to be answered immediately, while other mail may be answered later.

E-mail from your boss or colleagues needs to be answered within hours. Use good discretion. When e-mail gets old, it may send a subtle message to the sender they are not very high on your priority list. Answering a note late may change your rapport and friendship with a business colleague. A lengthy reply is not needed and in fact, short e-mails, texts, or briefly written personal notes can take less time for you and the person receiving your note. This is especially true when communicating with persons close to you in the department, company or on your work team!

GET ON KEY MAILING LISTS

Arrange to have your name on key mailing lists that keep you current with events happening in your field of expertise. When you go to a workshop, seminar, conference, technical class, trainee excursion, open house, or exposition, ask to get on their mailing list or e-mail list. In this way, you can keep abreast of changes in your field of interest with new materials, new methods, and the latest technology. There may be times you want to see something today instead of later and, bingo, the information is at your fingertips to get started.

AVOID FOUL-UPS

Here are some ideas to avoid missed appointments, deadlines, or mistakes at home or work. Check the ones below that you may need to give more attention.

___Plan in advance so your project or event can be reviewed before deadlines.

___Use a planner, such as a Franklin appointment planner; make notes each day.

___Set a target as you work and stay focused.

___Find a routine for everything—a check-off list can guide you.

___Tiredness causes greater odds for foul-ups. Additional sleep might help.

___Use spell check. Invite someone to proofread your document.

___Always tell the truth.

___If you don't finish the document, save in designated file and come back later.

___Save copies of everything; place dates on copies when received or worked on.

___Do the preparation in advance, giving times and keeping notes of the progression.

___Does the issue or project meet written objectives, rules, or company policies?

___Give the paper, event, or letter, color for interest.

___Prioritize by checking back with your immediate supervisor for suggestions.

___Write neatly.

___Learn to follow other's successful ideas and read inspirational thoughts.

___Reward your successes with a favorite treat, shopping, or lunch.

___Be upbeat as much as possible—smile at co-workers…they may smile back!!

E-MAIL

Communicating via e-mail is effective and efficient, according to my wife. She suggests these pointers:

- ■ E-mail is a quick way to have a conversation and clarify a question you may have about an important document, meeting, or event.
- ■ Remember that your e-mail may be read by others as well as the receiver.
- ■ If you have confidential information to share with a co-worker, arrange for a time to meet with the person.
- ■ E-mail is efficient; however, if you want to be very sure a co-worker has received urgent information, call them to confirm the e-mail was received.
- ■ Checking incoming e-mail messages often is a way to keep in touch.
- ■ Important e-mail information can be printed and filed for future reference.

NO "I" IN TEAM

Offering to help check each other's work is very much a part of being a helpful, successful person. Develop ways to help and cooperate with co-workers in the workplace. My brother was a CPA (certified public accountant) and mentioned to me he would sometimes have another CPA check his accounting work before submitting the papers to his client. Yes, it's a good idea to team with another employee to have them look over your work on occasion after the work is finished. CAD technicians do the same; they have checkers to look over the print or plans before it leaves the office. People doing inventory, counting pieces in a stack, will often have someone recount each item. Errors are too costly and embarrassing.

There are other good reasons for building teamwork on the job. There are times when you may have a question to ask before you proceed with a decision or project. Other examples that I've experienced: giving co-workers a ride to or from work because their car was being worked on, helping prepare for a celebration at work which would have been very time-consuming, giving others affirmation on a job well done, and listening attentively to colleagues' joys or struggles.

IMPORTANCE OF FOLLOWING THROUGH

Following through is similar to following up. I understand following through with a project as one of the last steps near the end before moving on to another.

A smile to give affirmation is a form of follow-through. A verbal thank you and saying their name is one of the most cherished ways you can affirm a fellow employee, spouse, your boss, children, or someone you're working with daily. A thank you note goes a long way toward building ties, mutual friendships, and good workplace associations. Take advantage of sending cards to others on special holidays or when they do something special for you. This means making it an important priority, rather than just thinking about it.

As an example, small plant seedlings grow into a larger plant, but only after they've been watered. They can grow and flourish into beautiful shapes and sizes from someone following through with special caring on a consistent basis.

Following through with a job is explained here in a number of ways:

Be
A
Finisher

- the project was finished and now you find out what happened
- following up on a sales call immediately so you don't lose it
- sending a thank you to someone after the project was completed
- making a survey and then applying the results
- sending something and then checking to see if it was received
- double checking on an appointment and to remind someone
- checking the rewards for a job well done
- calling your boss to check if he/she received the expected document
- finishing a sweeping job even if it meant working extra hours
- giving something an extra effort by "putting the icing on the cake"
- making an extra effort to thank someone for doing business with you
- asking someone if the delivered item is satisfactory

Learn to apply tips you learned from doing something good the previous time. Sometimes follow-through means taking a few notes to file away for next month or next year's event. Whatever kind of follow-up is necessary, your boss is expecting this follow-up from you!

TRUSTY COMPANION

Have you ever asked someone for a pencil? The answer is probably yes. People carry a pencil because they don't want something important to escape them. Place pencils or pens in key places. These include the car dash, in the garage, close to the front and back doors, next to the telephones, and other key stopping points convenient for visiting with someone. Who knows when you will want to copy something down on the spur of the moment.

Many earth-shaking product improvements have followed on the coat tails of something that was implied. It might have surfaced in the mind from concentration and copying the note down, triggering an association, and bingo—something great is born.

Research has shown us that taking notes also helps us recall information much easier. Additional sensory mechanisms are being used as the mind visualizes the words and also reads and organizes the thoughts into our memory.

I shared with my college students in class that if they use five of their sensory mechanisms as examples listed below, they will have a much higher retention rate of remembering information for later use. I don't know which one should come first, but the five examples are: hearing words being said, using a good pencil or pen for copy work that has been tried, reading information out loud, associating words with something, and finally, using repetition in recopying and shortening the information for use.

You can choose to be a person who is organized and responsible. Try not to depend upon the next person to supply you with a pencil or pen, as I do on occasion in borrowing a pen from my wife. She almost always has a pen available and enjoys taking brief notes.

HIDDEN WRITING SKILLS

People who are able to advance themselves probably have good writing skills. As an employee, send professional, errorless correspondence letters, e-mail, and memos to others. Laura Brill in her 2nd edition book, *Business Writing Quick & Easy*, writes that "Nothing goes on record like the written word, and so every professional who has to put pencil to paper—or fingers to keyboard—should make sure the results represent him or her properly."[2]

A good rule is to be brief and to the point with your written communication. Written agenda either shows an organized manner for responsibility or reflects incompetence. Do you know that feeling of having trouble with writing letters, memos, notes, or recording agenda for your supervisor? Do something about it now, so it will not continue to reflect upon your potential... or your future! In many areas of the country, organizations provide classes offering help in this area. Call the local community college or vocational school and inquire about classes that offer special help with written skills. Even better, ask your employer or supervisor where you could acquire this kind of enrichment.

Make an appointment to go in for counseling. The cost for all this is very minimal compared to the benefits. The local county offices may have someone on staff who could steer you in the right direction. Some assistance programs have monies available that need not be paid back. If this goal speaks to you, I hope you are encouraged to strengthen your writing skills for better communication on the job and in all your interactions with people. Small improvements can make a big difference.

WORKING SMARTER

Do you plan for work, family, or leisure time in advance or do you just do what comes along? Plan for the future, not the moment, when possible—rely on your common sense to know when to remain flexible for important interruptions, such as taking time to be respectful and kind to anyone who calls or stops by and needs your advice or help. To make significant progress toward working more effectively, efficiently, and feeling happy with yourself, planning must precede or happen before hard work. You'll most likely make all the time back with even additional time for enjoyment because of your planning.

How do I start this planning process and work smarter?

- Easy—find a quiet place that looks relaxing. Think about what to do first!
- Second—what does my common sense tell me to write next on the list?
- Third—tell yourself you can make good choices and be responsible with your time. Continue to include all important work and activities that can really make a difference in your life and those you work and live with today!
- Try to be complete, including leisure time and flexibility in your day. Let yourself enjoy the journey, whatever and wherever the plan takes you. You will, hopefully, feel happy with yourself for trying to make good common sense decisions today!
- There will be days we may be disappointed in our decisions—we can learn from them and move on. This is the whole reason for practicing a planning routine rather than just going through life using trial and error. You may want to search

for inspiration and counsel in passages such as 2 Timothy 3:16 and Hebrews 1:1 of the New Testament of the Bible.

As an example, of sketches for a small home, if a project such as this has ample planning in advance, it can add to the financial worth later for resale. Also, a home can be aesthetically more appealing if more planning has gone into it. Some families may unconsciously feel much better about staying home more to rest rather than traveling many miles away to rest and recuperate. For example, one home may have a restful atmosphere, and the other home not as comfortable. Qualified designers can be hired to accomplish this effect for people who work smarter rather than harder. I've heard people say on occasion, I wish we would have done this or that…longer and better planning probably would have avoided dissatisfaction. On occasion, you can hire a specific professional for planning. It will most likely be worth the cost of their fee by adding more equity and/or resale value to the product or project. In the end, the extra value may compensate for the initial invested cost. The bottom line: do your planning in advance.

Choose a time to sit quietly and undisturbed for a planned time during the day. Some will call it a meditation or planning time. Consistency in planning may be helpful so it happens often. It's a time to contemplate or reassess what must be done. More will be shared about meditation on page 138 in the topic, "Allow time for deep thoughts."

My father told me that "by spending money you can make money." He was encouraging me to spend and invest wisely for things that do not lose their value, and to learn that through careful planned spending, it would pay dividends in the long run.

When my wife and I first started a general contractor company years ago, we were dedicated to working very hard, but did not set aside enough attention to planning. As one example, we may have been in a better position if we'd spent more time planning our financial insurance needs. We had not evaluated the situation well. Now, we had to learn from our mistakes. This was a situation where we were working harder, rather than smarter, and had not done sufficient planning in advance.

In conclusion, working smarter could result in different rewards, such as living a more fulfilling life of happiness with family or a more abundant life of financial success or both. It may be possible that you could enjoy more peace of mind. Whatever your situation might be, when you plan and reflect, priorities will likely change. Time to reflect on the past, may bring a stronger faith, realizations, and new wisdom, having the potential of changing your life in wonderful ways!

GOES WITH THE TERRITORY
Even though the contract says one thing or the job description is agreed upon, there is

more to the job description than meets the eye. There are other common sense expectations. Supervisors enjoy simple jobs getting done without ever asking the employee to do them. The alert employee may notice tasks that are unfinished—take the time or offer to complete them even though the task is not part of the job description. There were times in both LouAnn's job and my job when something needed to get done and was not in our job descriptions. All we had to do was to "step out of our comfort zone" and finish what needed attention.

Consider taking this quiz – answer yes or no.

1) You can expect to get paid for a personal postage stamp to mail a company business letter after work in an emergency. Yes or no

2) You can expect to get paid gas mileage for using your own personal car to run an errand several blocks away, picking up coffee break snacks for the 10:00 a.m. group meeting. Yes or no

3) You can expect to get reimbursed from the company for a birthday card that was purchased for the department boss's party. Yes or no

4) You broke your $3.00 drinking glass while taking a business order to a company customer in the company truck. Do you ask for reimbursement for the glass? Yes or no

5) You purchased coffee for a company visitor on the way to taking them to the airport. Should you turn in the $1.35 bill? Yes or no

6) You agree to stop and pick up a co-worker on your drive into work since it will not be too far out of your way. Do you ask for mileage reimbursement? Yes or no

7) Salaried persons need breath mints from time to time while talking with clientele in close proximity. Should you turn in a receipt for the purchase of the mints? Yes or no

8) You spend $100.00 out of pocket money for purchasing a special vibrating seat cover for the company car without getting a prior OK. Is the company required to reimburse you for the expenditure since it stays in the car? Yes or no

My assessment tells me that all the answers are no.

a. If you missed 0, you are probably on the right track.
b. If you missed 1 answer, you might read the question again.
c. If you missed 2 answers, you may want to visit with someone about the questions.

In number 1) above…it probably would not be appropriate to bill the business office for one stamp when it may cost the company $1.37 just for recording an entry.

2) above…if it's only going to cost you the trip, a couple of dollars, be happy that you can help your friends by being able to go after the food for break.

3) above…this is not a company issue. This is a special thing that you and your friends are doing for the person in charge.

4) above…at some places, personal things are not to be taken or used at the office.

5) above…this was a personal decision for the person. The only time the company would pay for it would be if you have an expense account already established for this kind of thing.

6) above…good people do extra things like this on a regular basis free. Use this errand as a way to show a sense of caring for one another.

7) above…it makes good sense to use breath mints on occasion to be at your best with clientele. Avoid bothering the company with one dollar and two dollar items. Just show that you have good common sense.

8) above…don't make expenditures unless it has been approved in advance. And in fact, you'd probably want to have it approved before you paid for it yourself and before using it in a company car.

The mentality of saying, "That project isn't in my job description" is out. The mentality of realizing, "I want to make a difference by being willing to adapt and be helpful as an employee" is in.

Just a few more examples: organizing your supply cabinet if no one is assigned to doing that task…cleaning the computer monitor…updating your telephone directory…and daily clearing and cleaning your work area before leaving the office. None of these may be in your job description. Daily work like this is needed and will probably help make you a better employee for the company. These were only a few examples of things that "go with the territory" for an up-and-coming good employee.

In summary, quite often supervisors or management are looking for persons to promote, those who are going the extra mile, and doing the little common sense things to help the team and organization be more effective.

TIME MANAGEMENT

Oh, what an important topic! Much of my book is about time management. But, I will attempt to list some of the more important ones below that come to my mind. One of my pet peeves is when I arrive late or finish a project late. I will admit I've been late too. It simply is a matter of respect. This means making a big effort to go and finish early. You've heard the saying, "The early bird gets the worm." The person going early and finishing a project early will no doubt experience many advantages. Job-wise, it might mean the difference in making or losing the sale, getting heads up on something before the meeting, being respected and liked by others, the bonus or promotion, or just keeping your job! There are many more reasons why you should go early and/or finish a project early. Following are a few ways, not the only ways, to do better with time management that my wife and I have picked up through the years.

- "Don't bite off more than you can chew," as the saying goes. Give yourself limits.
- Set priorities; give ratings- 1st urgent, 2nd important, etc. Eliminate some things by scheduling later. Simplify your life as you plan, which comes first, second, etc.
- Sub-divide projects or events into smaller manageable work—ask others to help.
- Estimate amount of time for activities. Arrange to finish earlier than estimated.
- Avoid procrastination, letting things go, thinking a better time will come later.
- Don't make decisions too quickly, "haste makes waste."

- Do your fact finding. Think it through first before you act. Make decisions and stick with it. **What** is it all about—budget, profit margin, resources, space, personnel, and other criteria that affects you at home or work? **When** will it happen? **Why** am I doing it? **Who** is going to read it? Must it be done a certain **way**? **Where** is this going? **Will** I accomplish this in two hours? **How** will it align with the goals in the end?
- After you've made your priority list, concentrate working on one thing at a time, avoiding letting others take you off task time. Stay focused.
- Entertain yourself with a break. Freshen up and stay with it to the end.

In an article from the Newton Kansan, Sharon B. Molzen shared this very important fact about time management. She advocated that "working smarter, not harder, is what time management is all about." She also added this very important note about being able to finish a job; it will "boost your energy level, help your concentration and enhance your feelings of personal satisfaction and motivation." [3]

In conclusion, it does not have to be complicated. It's a matter of making the best use of your time each day. Every day you make the best use of time in the workplace, you set up a routine that will please your supervisor and yourself.

TAKING NOTES AT A MEETING

1. Review topics, **A Lesson in Listening**, Chapter 3, page 19, and the topic on **More Than Listening**, Chapter 13, page 139.
2. Prepare the laptop or iPad; and remember to bring a storage back-up. Do a test run if you are not familiar with what you brought to take notes. If you are taking notes on a note pad, check out your pens or pencils—place at your fingertips.
3. Locate yourself in a place where you can hear all those present at the meeting.
4. Handle anything important before the meeting that may be an interruption.
5. Take time to read background information prior to the meeting. Be informed.
6. Clear your mind of all other activities so you can focus on the discussion.
7. Plan ahead how you will effectively save your notes.

In summary, your filing practices may be essential for effectively retrieving notes later. Review your notes later that day while it's fresh in your mind to clarify important details.

SIGNING IN AND OUT

Telling someone you're leaving the office is acceptable protocol in business circles—a matter of respect. One example for using this practice is shared in the following paragraph.

The person who doesn't check out with the receptionist or someone in his/her department may be missed at a crucial time at work. As a way to respect others, share with someone where you are going and when you'll return—you'll develop a better rapport with everyone. Even if you're late somewhere, call in and keep the office or job people informed. It's a courtesy in the workplace. Nothing can be gained by making people wonder where you are or when you'll be back on the job! It's about not turning away potential sales! Have you ever had to wait for someone? Sure, we both have, and it's not a satisfying feeling. Management or the owner of the business is looking for the person who is conscientious and excited about satisfying the customers!

THE THREE RING RULE

When answering the phone within three rings, as they used to say, the receiver signals respect to the caller. Now, with new high tech phones, callers can communicate much quicker. Purchasing new, efficient equipment helps to achieve this goal. The person or business calling will most likely appreciate an efficient, professional voice on the phone. If you are the person being called, you may be the one to give the caller a first impression about the business or organization. Every call is important!

Here's a phone tip I found in a pamphlet called "Communications Briefings" which advocates a positive way to answer another person's phone at work. Have them answer with "class and enthusiasm. Instead of saying, I'm going to transfer you to _____, try this: Pat Gonzalez is the real expert on that, and she'll be glad to help you. I'll transfer you." [4]

The telephone rings and rings. Do you answer your boss's telephone? Depending on prior arrangements, if nothing has been discussed then yes, go ahead by answering the phone and saying, "Good morning, this is Bob and Mr. Mason is out of his office right now, may I help you?" Take good notes and leave a telephone message for Mr. Mason. As soon as he comes in, share the conversation with him. By the way, when you were in his office, you should have avoided looking over his paperwork as you talked. Confidentiality is high on the list to keep your job and advance in the workplace.

And finally, when talking with someone, being polite and a good listener is helpful and important!

THINK AND THEN DO (EFFICIENCY)

One of my employees stood still looking at the ground with a broom in hand. He was not sweeping, just standing there looking down and probably thinking, well if I do I do and if I don't I don't, not very motivated, very excited, not seeing past the dust, well on second thought, not even seeing the particles to be swept! Employees are expected to get something accomplished for the pay they get and to work more than one project at a time.

I've heard supervisors say that "if there is nothing to do, go sweep." Instead of grabbing a broom, there might be stacking, filing, or planning to be done. There is always something to do that is worthy of doing your job well. If you are considering the ranks of a good job or promotion, then think again because the work in nearly all jobs continually stacks up and it becomes a matter of prioritizing.

Even in the classroom, there were a few times I would see a student simply sitting and waiting on me, doing nothing, until I could help them with a question. They should have been pressing themselves to go ahead with another project while the present one was put on hold. If you're someone who has difficulty handling more than one project at a time, you may want to consider some of these helpful hints. As an example, you're puzzled at something or at a stopping point on the job after confronting a problem. There is no one on the job at the time to help you. What could you do?

- Check your return call voicemail or e-mail.
- Organize the counter so it has an organized look and is attractive.
- Check your calendar for meetings or projects coming up.
- Check recorded messages, times, and dates.
- Record thoughts about things to do.
- Look around…what else needs to be done?
- Ask whether you can help another person in the area.
- Look at past projects…record and file brief remarks on each one.
- Prioritize; decide which projects need more attention.
- Analyze how others can be involved with you.
- Review your job description.
- Read an instruction or machine manual to help do your job more effectively.
- Top off the fuel level or instrument to the full mark.
- Shine the equipment, dishes, windows, tools, etc.
- Stack the lumber better so it will not warp.
- Freshen up a bit so you're at your best for another customer.

These pointers have been similar to what you just read in the past topic, **Time Management**. Another similar list shows up at the end of Chapter six under the topic, **Go the Second Mile**. In planning work-related jobs and projects, the five Ws can be used: who, what, when, why, and how it will happen. Try to figure out who should be involved. Just what are the objectives? When is the best time? Estimate the time for whatever. Question "why this and why that" if it is appropriate. Last but not least, put together a suggested plan or procedure on how it might be carried out for the best results. And remember, before all is said, please be courteous in a timely manner to the people you're asking these questions!

There is usually no such thing as being completely done with everything and to go home early because there is nothing else to do. When 4:00 p.m. comes and 5:00 p.m. is quitting time, start thinking about the thoughts above and planning for the next day. "What didn't I accomplish today and what must be finished yet today or first thing tomorrow?" Then again at 4:45 p.m., "Have I forgotten anything that is urgent to be done before I leave and won't wait without causing difficulty for the coming day?" Stay after hours if something has been forgotten and make it right. Record any thoughts or notes to take action on when you arrive the next morning.

In conclusion, find time to be a more effective employee by working several projects simultaneously, sometimes called multi-tasking—so if one project is stalled, you can go to the next and the next.

TEXTING AND SOCIAL MEDIA

As society progresses, our world is getting more technologically advanced every day. A way to stay current is to be informed about the latest communication or social media. Texting is a quick way to stay in touch with family, friends, co-workers, and people in general. Sending a text instead of making a phone call allows you to have a conversation wherever they may be and doesn't put the pressure of having to respond and talk that instant. For many jobs this is how workers communicate, and it may be much more time-efficient. Something that you need to be careful of is that Texting can be saved and read multiple times over, so make sure you do not regret what you send!

Social media is relatively new to our world. The purpose of social media is a public display of people's thoughts, pictures, and what is current to their life. This paragraph highlights the overall concept rather than which form of social media you should be using. At the time I wrote this, Facebook is the biggest and best thing but falling to the likes of Twitter, Instagram, and Snapchat. The danger of these forms of media could introduce a negative aspect which one has to guard against. Some people take Twitter to the extreme. For instance, "This morning I brushed my teeth," followed by 30 other tweets that day, to the point that everyone knows in detail what you did that day. Many people may read that and say, "Why did I waste a minute of my life reading those tweets or posts?" A bigger issue is that of becoming addicted to social media in general. Becoming addicted will negatively affect your time management and face-to-face relationships. The final outcome could become an addiction to staying in the loop with the latest news and gossip, but could mess up both business agenda and personal relationships. Remember, everyone can see what you post and sometimes it could be taken the wrong way, affecting the outcome of actual facts and job security in the near future.[5]

CHAPTER FOUR SUMMARY

I've tried to give pointers about how to be organized on the job in this chapter. Actually, it's not only about this chapter, but information in the entire book. And, I have to clarify that this challenge is an endless effort of developing ways to be better organized for the job.

CHAPTER 5

EMOTIONAL ISSUES AT WORK

Learn to motivate yourself— no one else may take the time to do it for you!

HANDLING CONFLICT

In my opinion, dealing with conflict works best when all persons involved are able to voice their opinions calmly and quietly. As mentioned before, be a good listener. **First**, keep a cool head, even when things aren't going your way. Consider the other person's point of view. **Second**, ask forgiveness for failures or something that is not going well. Give the other person time to come together with you and talk about disagreements. This is high on my list for resolving conflict. When mistakes happen, the way you handle the situation can really make a difference in resolving the conflict quietly and with dignity. Keeping a good attitude is a key.

KEEP A GOOD ATTITUDE

Motivate yourself on a continual basis. You may not be able to count on another person to do what you can accomplish by yourself. Talk yourself into a good attitude. Remember, this is your life! Start the process of consciously motivating yourself in a new way. As problems happen, think about your options. What should you do first? Find probable solutions to problems encountered. Choose the best way to respond. Get positive feedback from close friends. Thank them for helping you meet life's challenges.

I don't know how much you know about golf, but the following golf experience will be used to drive home a point I want to make. My thoughts go back to a time when I was golfing with friends and doing very poorly. I allowed myself to feel bad about missing shots, and not judging the distance correctly. My game went downhill with almost every shot. I was allowing myself to feel like I couldn't do anything right. In fact, I felt like giving up the sport before realizing what the problem was—my attitude! I was not handling the off day well. I felt like doing what the guy had done who was golfing with the group ahead of us. He missed an easy shot and his temper flared. He threw his golf club at the ground. His behavior probably didn't help to make his game better. He needed to lighten up. For me, I needed to keep things in perspective and improve my attitude.

Professionals tell us laughing is good for our health. Virginia Tooper, vice president of

Premier Chemical Corporation says, "Laughing improves your health, your outlook on life, and your ability to communicate."[1]

Finding something to smile or laugh about seems to help me when things aren't going my way. By laughing, my muscles relax and I usually feel like smiling—I no longer feel tension. With positive thoughts, I feel that I'm able to perform better.

Elwood Chapman says, "If you can show an interviewer that you are human-relations competent and that your attitude is positive, your chances of landing the job will be far greater."[2]

FACING NEW CHALLENGES

Whether you're preparing for a promotion or a new job, either one will change your daily routine immensely. Yes, a new situation can be interesting or frustrating: your choice. New challenges bring more expectations. Now you're expected to rise to the occasion or risk failure, and failure is not going to be an option, right? So what may be some of the new changes or challenges facing you when getting a promotion or working in a new job?

First: Working more hours is probably one change. So, don't let fatigue set in. Try to get more rest as challenges arise. Tell yourself to "tough it out."

Second: At all times, keep an open, honest understanding with your boss. He/she probably has 101 other important items on the agenda at work. If you want to talk with your boss, you may want to think about what you want to say for a day, unless the discussion is urgent. Begin with a genuine compliment. Then at a convenient time, calmly lead into what you want to share. Try to stay focused on what you want to share. Avoid talking about some insignificant issue which is unimportant at the time. Share about a good part of your job. Avoid complaining. If the discussion is very emotional and challenging, work at keeping your composure. Share with confidence. Think positive. You want to have your boss see you as adjusting to your new job assignment. Share how you appreciate your work. Even though you may be struggling to find good things to share about, try to keep your conversation short and "don't make a mountain out of a mole hill."

Third: You may be pressed for finding quiet time to focus on the more important issues on the job or even at home, but please prioritize. Pick out what should be given attention first, second, and so on. Maybe it's as simple as needing to get rid of clutter in your life, getting more sleep, exercise, or eating more or less so you are at your best. Whatever your priority is, I encourage you to make a plan and work the plan.

Fourth: As already discussed in Chapter 1, concentrate on working relationships with other employees on the job. Take a genuine interest in them.

Now it's time to work even harder than resting on your laurels. Tell yourself often: the new me is willing to work longer hours and give more of myself. The real test is being able to handle these new job responsibilities. Perhaps your supervisor gave you this job or promotion with the confidence that you could do even better as time goes on. You may have to say to yourself often, "I can, I know I can."

EMBRACING CRITICISM

Pride may get in the way of successes all too often in the workplace and also around friends and family. Think about this—if you choose not to accept criticism, how are some situations going to improve? Next time someone wants to give you criticism, consider their helpful suggestion as an act of kindness or friendship rather than a negative.

Check out these guidelines for **accepting criticism better. Let go of your pride and—**

- **control your emotions and temper.** Don't get angry.
- **set aside your ego** and consider advice from others or their interests above your own.
- **examine yourself** by finding and concentrating only on the good in every situation.
- **seek a positive outcome** out of negative criticism.
- **think about a solution by listening well** with an open mind.
- **calmly share your feelings.**
- **think first about how you're functioning** while controlling your attitude.
- **reflect on how your decision will look to others** before speaking.
- **talk it out constructively.** Do not discourage others from giving you criticism!

DIFFERENCES OF OPINION

Many times in life, there are give and take situations. Right from the get-go, take the position to listen to other people's opinions as they share. Both of you could reach a common ground of understanding more quickly. When differences of opinion are allowed, pleasant, effective conclusions and outcomes are possible. Keep your perspective by feeling OK with differences of opinion. Give the other person a yes signal of confirmation often. Wait until they're done speaking before you begin. Give yourself a pat on the back for being respectful of other people's opinions.

Since being able to have a difference of opinion with someone is so important, consider this scenario if you need encouragement to work harder on this challenge. Arrange for another person to sit in on discussion between you and the person who is difficult to visit with. Invite the person who you asked to join you to give you helpful suggestions privately after the meeting.

People who respect others' opinions may have potential as leaders in the future.

LEARNING FROM MISTAKES AND FAILURES

Have you ever been told that if you're not making a mistake or two now and then, you may be standing still? Without making a few mistakes and taking some calculated risks in doing something constructive, you may not be accomplishing much that's new and refreshing. When the mind is creating new and refreshing agenda, there will be a few mistakes made. Making a positive response to mistakes is what counts. When you find a mistake has been made, consider a quick response in the most positive way you can. Finding great solutions can make a huge difference in your day.

However, that does not mean just any temporary quick fix should be used, like a car repair situation long ago. The exhaust system was not repaired correctly. Some shortcuts were taken. And guess what? Sufficient time and book car parts were not used to make the job complete, and as it turned out, my car needed to be fixed again soon.

Make immediate adjustments that will hold the test of time. If your mistake involves someone, visit with the person immediately. Mistakes are forgivable. Too often though, our human nature wants to cover up the mistake or smooth over the situation; this may not end well. You don't want to have the issue continuing to come up over and over in the future.

The effects of a mistake may gradually worsen if not acted on immediately. Just like installing the wrong bearings in a pulley, mistakes eventually may break and cause other things to break down. Be a strong person and step up with immediate positive attention. Facing the problem head-on may avoid bigger problems and grief later.

Push ahead, find solutions—be courageous and responsible. Don't just sit back and settle for the easy route. Pioneers push into the unknown. Responsible people who push for new experiences may find new opportunities by re-positioning themselves. Avoid setting yourself up for failure by doing nothing! Expect something great and pray for good outcomes.

Consider this: with successes there may also be failures and disappointments. But with failures, the challenges can also bring positive changes for making new personal gains and goals.

As Henry Ford said, "Failure is only the opportunity to begin again more intelligently."[3]

> **When there are failures, take time to apologize.**
> **When there is forgiveness, there comes responsibility.**
> **When there is responsibility, there is growth.**

Additional growth can come by training ourselves to concentrate on the good things rather than concentrating on the bad. If too much time is spent watching and living a bad lifestyle, a person may crowd out the good.

BE FLEXIBLE

A flexible person can adjust to the need without complaining. Flexible people can usually work in a quiet or a noisy atmosphere, whatever the case. They can work in less than perfect conditions. If they're asked to assume a new project, they can ask questions and find the most efficient way to complete a project. A flexible person is ambitious and helps others in the process. This person works on being open-minded. They listen to the suggestions of others. They look at options and realize there might be a better solution than their own. They are seen as a compromising person. They talk and act their part. Yes, this person deserves receiving a promotion when it comes up. They have not given management any reason to doubt how they would perform if the challenges got tough!

Now—for the big question. Do others see you as the **flexible person** described above?

If you couldn't give a quick yes answer to this question, be patient with yourself. Make being flexible a goal of yours in the coming weeks and years!

BE PROACTIVE

Start finding temporary solutions to problems before encountering them. This can be a motivator in itself, because now confidence kicks in as you have temporary fixes to meet the challenges that come your way. Don't wait to become proactive. If you wait to find solutions only when problems occur, you may put yourself under stress if too many problems surface at the same time.

Live your life with energy and anticipation for exciting things ahead. Step back from time to time to reflect and assess how you're using your energy. You might be saying; "I already do that"—that is great! If you're not stepping back to assess matters regularly, you may want to ask yourself on a regular basis, "How can I do it better?" Find people who can help you. Avoid persons who may want to discourage you. Seek out those who want to build you up and give them plenty of genuine praise. Do your planning in advance and commit those plans to God in prayer, asking for His guidance on a daily basis. Isn't it great to know we have a God who will hear us—if we ask? Matthew 7: 7

ACTIVITIES TO COMPLEMENT JOB

There are several ways to become involved in your community. (1) Join a club. (2) Meet and discuss with others who share similar goals and job interests. (3) Get to know a circle of friends who you can confide in and receive feedback. (4) Seek out friends to socialize with after work and weekends. (5) Attend a church or Bible study group of your choice to develop friendships. (6) Attend a luncheon meeting, coffee break group, bus tour, weekend excursion, or breakfast meeting where people enjoy visiting together. (7) Consider developing a similar interest with co-workers, such as games.

Reward yourself for doing some of these activities if you're not already doing so.

DEVELOP LASTING VALUES FOR LIFE

Do you have a good value system to solve difficult problems? I hope so. To me, value is an applied act of using good integrity and reasoning. Without having meaningful values for life, we make not only ourselves vulnerable to making poor decisions, but others around us as well. This can lead to unhappiness.

I heard an educational expert say the best time to learn about values is between the ages of one and five. Other authorities claim that values are learned all through life. As an employee in the workplace, you have opportunities to model good values for others who observe your actions. Often employers want to hire employees who have good value systems and who they can trust for their decision making. Consider taking an inventory of just a few of the values that come to mind for me. Answer the questions in this values exam with a yes or no and then just for fun—grade yourself. Do I try to:

- allow others to bring out my strengths?   Y or N

46

▦ listen well and accept others' opinions?	Y or N
▦ exercise good judgment?	Y or N
▦ help others in their struggles?	Y or N
▦ reward myself for doing well on the job?	Y or N
▦ move beyond finding fault in others?	Y or N
▦ take responsibility in the community?	Y or N
▦ recognize the importance of family?	Y or N
▦ use my time wisely?	Y or N
▦ understand the importance of daily prayer to God?	Y or N
▦ organize my thoughts into positive action?	Y or N
▦ read the Bible daily for spiritual growth?	Y or N
▦ examine my strengths and weaknesses often?	Y or N
▦ please my employer?	Y or N
▦ attend conferences/classes yearly?	Y or N
▦ respect the elderly people in my life?	Y or N
▦ honor my country and the freedom we enjoy?	Y or N
▦ be neighborly?	Y or N
▦ seek out new friends with good values?	Y or N
▦ be a good steward of my finances?	Y or N

Invite your spouse, best friend, or family member to do the same. Test for discussion together.

BULLYING

Do you know anyone who intimidates or makes life difficult for another person? Or a bully who tries to belittle someone while trying to make himself/herself look better? This not only happens to young people, but can happen to adults in the workplace, community, and school. If this happens to you, what can be done?

"How to Deal With Verbal Bullying," on ehow.com, gives some excellent ideas to deal with bullies, such as these four:

▦ Use humor to deflect the situation.

▦ Show no anger.

▦ Record a journal entry on each incident.

▦ Issue a formal complaint following the grievance procedure.[4]

Following is a statement from another Web site called, "How to Stop Bullies." The Web site says, "Bullying is when someone keeps doing or saying things to have power over another person."[5]

Several more ideas that I've picked up from experience that may help:

- Know in advance what your employer's actions are about bullying.
- Keeping your composure, be confident and ignore his/her behavior.
- Anticipate what you are going to do if the bully gets physical.
- Stay away from the area where the bully or bullies hang out.
- Focus in on friends who like you and oppose the bully.
- Pray to God asking for his help in the matter.

"Keep away from people who try to belittle your ambitions. Small people always do that, but the really great make you feel that you, too, can become great"   —Mark Twain.[6]

MIND OVER MATTER (THINKING ABILITY)

What does it mean to have "mind over matter?" To me, this means having a burning desire to motivate yourself, going to great measures to accomplish a goal. It has to do with thinking ability—telling yourself that you've discovered the right thing to do. This kind of motivation may happen best by developing a mindset that is pumped up.

Great things can happen by setting out to accomplish something you have decided to do for yourself!

As an example, if you set out to do something special like wanting a better job, it will probably happen because you are concentrating on succeeding at the thing you so desire. I'd like to think that, nothing will stop you from reaching your goal. Refer to Matthew 7:7, a quote from Jesus passed on to us in the New Testament of the Bible.

Give yourself an edge by concentrating on your next accomplishment and looking for only the good things from situations rather than dwelling on the negative!

DEALING WITH STRESS

By the time you finish reading this section, I hope you'll be able to identify stress more easily. Everyone experiences stress in one form or another. Some people do not call it stress, but may call it something else so it doesn't stress them. The important question is, how well do you handle problems that come up in your life?

Try to identify with one of the following questions. Do you try to "sweep problems under the rug" as the saying goes, or do you act upon them and make a decision? Do you place the unanswered problems on another pile and say, oh well, "I'll make a decision later." Do you allow problems to tire or upset you? Have you had a mountain of bad luck? Do you call in sick regularly at work? Have you moved around a lot while changing job locations? Might you be causing stress for yourself with the way you treat others? All the above could be causing stress! These questions are real!

According to the Compton's Encyclopaedia by Britannica, stress may be an unavoidable part of life because we have new and changing situations regularly. Some of the most stressful causes can be: death of a close family member, divorce, injury, illness, or being fired at work. Other stressors such as: marriage, retirement, preparation for a new family member, financial change, job change, school related expectation, or changes in life responsibilities at home or at work, follow closely behind as 'could be, would be' reasons which may be stressful if not having prepared for them in advance. Even daily activities can cause stress such as a move, a change in recreation, a change in eating or sleeping habits. [7]

Please don't let frustrations that come along in life such as missing a bus, visiting with someone, breaking a plate accidentally, upsetting the glass of water, bumping your arm, or overcooking something for lunch stress you. Treat them as "the things that are happening to nearly everyone." In the end, it's the way we approach matters and life's challenges.

Even a very resilient person realizes changes are inevitable and there will be disagreements from time to time, perhaps chaos, and adjustments needed. We're living in those times. We need to practice conflict resolution. Try to realize that it's how you work out or handle your problems and differences that is important. Even making a decision to not make the decision tomorrow is a good decision. Make decisions soon to resolve those things that may bring on stress. Use humor and give in by allowing change. Don't end the day without forgiving someone who has treated you badly. Ask for forgiveness when appropriate. Do things that give yourself peace of mind and others satisfaction. Surround yourself with people who say good things about you in your presence. Spend less time with people who tear you down. You need a balance in life between your social, spiritual, physical, emotional, and financial life.

I've noticed in my own life that when I'm trying to do too many projects at one time, I feel tension. Too much tension and overloading causes me stress. It could bring on physical discomfort or even an illness if I'd allow the stress to continue and build. I've also learned that stress is less likely a problem when there is a balance of activities in my life.

While preparing to teach a personal management course, I found a list about "coping with stress" from the Hutchinson Community College Campus Bookstore. [8]

The list below has potential to give your life healing and happiness. I strengthened the existing list with additional line items. Here is a passing thought. Just for fun, treat the following list as a $300.00 therapy treatment. Go ahead and circle parts of the following list which you want to refer back to later, which may help you deal with stress better.

COPING WITH STRESS

Get up 15-20 minutes earlier	Don't rely on memory… write it down
Make back-up sets of keys	"Anticipate needs, write in a planner "
Ask for help from friends	Treat problems as challenges
Invite friends to enjoy things with you	Remove clutter in your life
Find things to smile and laugh about	Get enough sleep

Be prepared for stormy weather
Walk with a light step
Say something nice to someone
Say hello to friends and neighbors
Schedule a fun time into every day
Believe in yourself…you are special
Stop thinking about negative things
Develop a sense of humor
Invite someone to Starbucks with you
Create a good name for yourself
Gaze at the stars and moon
Learn to sing or whistle a tune
Listen to a concert or watch a ball game
Find a recliner and read a book
Stop some bad habits
Take time to smell the roses
Take a 10-15 minute power nap
Pay attention to your appearance
"Strive for excellence, not perfection"
Go shopping with a friend just for fun
Maintain weight or lose a couple pounds
Feed the birds… watch them enjoy
Learn a new Bible verse or two
Be responsible for your feelings
"Know limitations, let others know them"
Learn the words to a new song
Clean out and organize one closet
Realize that traffic can be slow downtown

Teach your pet trick commands
Appreciate the finer things in life
Read the Gospels and learn about Jesus
Take a stroll in the arboretum
Soak in the tub with bubble bath
Keep a journal or diary
Visualize yourself winning
"Go to a ball game, scream for your team"
Call a far away friend
Ask a loved one for a hug
Practice taking some slow deep breaths
Cook a meal and eat by candlelight
Watch your favorite T.V. program
Go to Worlds of Fun in Kansas City
Buy a flower for someone dear to your heart
Accept support from others
Do everything in moderation
Watch a movie and eat popcorn
Look at works of art at the museum
Put air freshener in your car
Slow down on the highway
Stand up and stretch your limbs
Memorize a joke
Play a game of golf or your favorite sport
Exercise every day
Get to work early to visit with colleagues
Go on a picnic in the park

CHAPTER FIVE SUMMARY

In conclusion and on a serious note, arranging time for prayer with God has possibilities to fix many stressors. Consider putting your challenges into God's hands and have faith. God is always there to lead us on our journey. He knows what's best for us in His own time period. We can choose to live each day to the best of our ability. I encourage you to try being patient and waiting on God to answer your prayers. With God's help, I believe each one of us can do better in handling stressful challenges.

As for my own experiences, God answered some of my prayers immediately and then answered other prayers after many years. As I look back at my life's experiences, the Lord God almighty knew what was best for me all the time! As my pastor, John C. Murray, put it, "Sometimes the answer to prayer is not to change the situation but to change me."[9]

CHAPTER 6

PREPARING FOR JOB EVALUATION

Create a mutual feeling of respect between you and your supervisor.
It starts at home with family and the people you meet daily!

GOOD ATTENDANCE IS IMPORTANT

Persons looking for getting pay raises or keeping a good job **cannot afford to use excuses** for being late or being absent. Changing your attendance habits may be the hardest of all changes you'll ever make. If you haven't already given this aspect a high priority, it is time. Choose to take pride in your job attendance. Take measures to protect the dignity between you and your employer. Try to have near-perfect attendance! I'm guessing most employers would say poor attendance or tardiness is high on the list of reasons why some employees do not do well. The following are some excuses or reasons encountered during my 30 years of teaching. I'm guessing a few were made up, but were shared with me as excuses/reasons for being late or missed attendance:

- Needed to fix the car bumper
- Went to the hospital to visit someone
- Woke up too late—the alarm clock did not wake me
- Needed a day to pay bills; electricity may have been shut off
- Babysitter didn't show up or was ill
- Roads were too slippery after the snowstorm…car even got stuck when I tried
- I was hurt badly over the weekend
- Returned very late from the baseball game
- Had to work the night shift on my second job—needed more sleep
- Stopped by the hospital for a shot
- Problems with my family
- Worked at painting job so I could pay the rent
- My son came home to visit and it made things very hectic
- Felt sick and didn't want to give it to anyone

The last excuse, "felt sick and didn't want to give it to anyone," is probably one of the good excuses. Most employers do not want you to give a sickness to other healthy employees. Part of the job requirement is to find ways to stay healthy and not get sick! A bit of advice:

when convenient, find out from your boss what the company policy is about missing work if you feel sick.

Health authorities tell us to avoid shaking hands with everyone, because the hands may be spreading germs. Other ways germs spread to others are from coughing or rubbing the mouth. Touching your face with the hands is another way to spread germs.

If you're going to have excellent attendance, consider developing a back-up plan so you will not arrive late or miss work. Old habits can be changed! What kind of problems can develop? Poor attendance causes mega problems, leading to passing up pay raises and job promotions. Following is a story that someone once shared with me— "An employee was coming in about 10 or 15 minutes late quite often, both mornings and afternoons. A client had been trying to reach the sales representative at those times. The customer was having trouble reaching the employee. For whatever reason, the customer quit calling." The story ended with the customer taking his or her business elsewhere. The company lost thousands of dollars by losing this account.

Additional problems may develop from expecting others to fill the gaps for the person coming in late. Many times, the first thing management wants to accomplish is having a meeting to set the tone for the day. Now, maybe the person who is late could have benefited from this input, also. Misunderstandings and problems occur from missing this agenda, which may be a key point for the company to operate efficiently.

All the loss of income or misunderstandings within the company could have been avoided by one employee coming in early rather than late. Poor attendance can contribute to some of the lack of happiness on the job.

There will be exceptions when managers excuse lateness or being absent. There may be times when missing work is excused because prior arrangements have been made. But for the most part, the best choice is to avoid missing work! Go out of your way to go early, showing how grateful you are and how important your job is to you.

BODY LANGUAGE TALKS

Non-verbal language contributes much to conversation between individuals, as most of us already know. Try to show your undivided attention at all times by picking up on what the other person is sharing. Avoid pretending you're listening. Good body language can show others you are trying to hear everything they're sharing.

Start now to consider what your body language may be saying to others, even if you don't have a job at the present time. Pick out a desired job position and start preparing immediately for the appointment, interview, or evaluation.

Employees cannot be preoccupied with their own problems, but can focus on being at their best in meetings with others. As you go to the next job evaluation, the employer wants to see someone fresh and ready to carry the workload expected of them. A person coming to the job site, who is obviously struggling with too much baggage, may not have the ability to carry any more workload. An employer wants to see someone anxious to get started. They want a person who carries his/her self with an attitude that shows, "I can get it done!" Remember to wear a happy face! However, there may be times when you want to be more serious and sensitive to the other person's difficulty and stressful situation. A smile on your face, as you talk with others, shows them you want to be their friend. A cheerful attitude with a smile shows confidence. My theory is that even dogs can tell what kind of mood the person portrays.

In the next couple of paragraphs, I want to focus on dress, stature and how it relates to non-verbal body language. There is a saying that "looks say it all." Well, I suppose that's true many times but not true all the time. Sit and stand tall, showing "I'm interested in everything you say." Show an image of "I care" by not slouching. Look energized with good posture. Pay attention to your stature. The way the body sits or stands sends a message, such as posture, that may give a signal the person is preoccupied with problems or lack of self esteem. Unless you are experiencing back problems, you'll probably want to stand up straight to show your confidence. Dropping your head down too far may show a sign of sadness or being preoccupied. The opposite side of this is lifting your head and chin too high, and showing a sign of being overconfident or arrogant.

Some time ago, two persons approached me outside the front of my home to ask whether I would be interested in hearing about a good insurance plan. The sun was shining and it was about 90 degrees that day. The one person was wearing casual slacks and light colored shirt—dressed OK. The other person was wearing an over-sized shiny dark striped suit, white shirt and tie. As they talked, my concentration was on the person who was hot and sweating. I wondered if he was on his way to a formal dinner or wedding. His clothes were a negative distraction as they tried to give their sales pitch on insurance.

Another example of dress is the color and combinations of clothes we wear. Using good judgment in choosing clothes for the interview or the job evaluation is very important. It tells who we are without words being spoken. Think about what your present or new employer would prefer.

Consider asking for advice from friends about dressing for the present job or preparing for the next job. This is an excellent choice to begin paying more attention to the way others perceive your stature and the way you dress on and off the job. To save money, consider buying clothes at a secondhand store. Perhaps exchanging clothes with a parent, aunt or uncle, brother or sister may be a good option. Make sure the clothes fit. Also, what's good for one job may not be OK for the next!

Find a way to observe what the employer prefers. Many jobs demand manicured fingernails. Notice what others wear on the job, in advance. Look over trade magazines for clothing styles that fit the occasion. You may want to dress a little out of style, rather than wear tattered or dirty clothes. Even one bad spot matters.

In non-verbal communication, the eyes are a giveaway! Many people are trained to read non-verbal expressions just by studying the eyes. Eyes that appear to be shifty, blood shot, half awake, not focused, or staring off in space could send a message you are tired. Train your eyes to focus on the person speaking to you. Show a smile of affirmation for taking the time to share a conversation with you. Employers are looking for individuals showing kind respect for one another.

Also, hair styling is important! Hair stylists can give us helpful advice. Just like the other categories of body language, hair styling can send the right or wrong message in seconds, distracting or adding to the conversation. Consider hair styling similar with the employer's preference for the workplace. For example, what hair style do the majority of other employees wear on the job? In addition to the right kind of styling, hair needs to be cared for daily to give that "I'm ready look." It may show much about your interests and priorities without someone even asking about ambitions for the job.

Jewelry and apparel can complement clothing styles. Observe how other employees handle this issue. Too much jewelry can be a distraction or a safety issue in some jobs.

When fingernails are trimmed and clean, it is another plus for the employer and the clients to observe. Even plumbers and painters can still try to keep their hands clean before and after the job is finished. Many jobs demand manicured fingernails. My wife rubs a small amount of lotion on her hands to keep the skin and cuticles healthy and looking good.

Look your part. The way you take care of yourself may indicate to an employer how well you'll take care of your job, as well.

Just tell me why I'm not ready for an interview!

A Person's Image

It is a goal of many dentists to keep saying, "Brush your teeth regularly." Perhaps there is also a correlation between taking care of the teeth and a signal about taking care of your job. I decided my dentist knows his stuff. Taking care of the teeth makes great common sense! Clean white teeth and a nice smile can give a friendly first impression to those we meet on a daily basis. There are very few jobs where this isn't important.

In summary, you may want to find out how people visualize you as a person. As I've been advocating, this business of body language or non-verbal communication says something very important to those we meet daily, even though there may not have been a word spoken. Count the number of things that many employers may not appreciate about the person pictured opposite page wanting to interview. Find the answers on page 197.

1 _____
2 _____
3 _____
4 _____
5 _____
6 _____
7 _____
8 _____
9 _____
10 _____
11 _____
12 _____
13 _____
14 _____
15 _____
16 _____

MAKING SUGGESTIONS WITH QUESTIONS

Build a working relationship with your lead person or supervisor by sharing good ideas and things that happen. Avoid talking only about problems or an unnecessary question with him/her. Raise a variety of productive questions the boss can help answer. Think it through well, so you don't always know the answer already to the question.

Here is one example of measuring a thought (asking for an opinion) on your boss if you worked on an assembly line putting together seats for a golf cart. This may or may not be the best example, not knowing your situation, but here's the question: "May I ask you a question that occurred to me today about gluing the front seams together?" And he/she says "OK." And you respond, "We have been doing it this way for nearly five years. Could there be a better way that can be done more quickly and will cost the company less money?" I'm sure the rest of the conversation would be very interesting.

Keep in mind—the past example is only one of hundreds more approaches you could use. Be ready to use your boss's suggestions! Don't measure something on your boss or lead person and then go ahead and do it your way even though he/she didn't like your idea.

IT'S THE BOSS'S BUSINESS

Keeping one eye on the boss may be an unknown weakness for some people. In one work situation, an individual seemed to be watching my every move. At one point, I shared with him that I was the one to supervise what he was able to accomplish. I shared a theory with him that goes like this: "When someone looks at me constantly, it may mean they need help. It then becomes my responsibility to see what I can do for them." It is also disrespectful and unprofessional to monitor the movement of your supervisor or anyone else. It could be a red flag that you are not focused or concentrating on the work at hand. In fact you should be concentrating on your own assigned task for the day. For the most part, well maybe it's a known fact, you'll accomplish much more when you're able to focus primarily on your own tasks rather than trying to figure out someone else's business.

When someone is talking about something within a small group setting, try to decide whether it's confidential or just general talk. Watch for non-verbal clues that can be considered when trying to make a decision on whether to enter into the conversation.

Consider this—you are at an informal luncheon. Everyone is standing around visiting. Your boss has pulled a co-worker to the side and it looks like they're really talking about something heavy. Maybe it's connected to a job evaluation. Who knows? You may want to avoid interrupting their conversation. They may not want anyone else to be involved in their important discussion. Try to mingle into another group to talk with someone where the discussion looks inviting and light hearted. In conclusion:

Avoid placing yourself into difficult situations.

DAY PLANNER

Do you own a calendar book organizer or day planner? If you do, is it being used for recording appointments and important reminders on a day-to-day basis? The size is not the important thing. The way you use it is the important matter! A small $6.95 calendar notebook which can be kept in the pocket or purse works well. It's a matter of convenience. Whatever the size, even if it's an electronic device, it could be referred to on an hourly basis so it's easily and quickly accessible.

I want to point out the use of an organizer every day, every hour, regardless the size. It will not be any more effective than how often you conscientiously choose to refer to the organizer. Some ideas for your daily organizer:

- ■ Organize notes from all present phone conversations
- ■ Keep names of people and dates on the day you talk with them
- ■ Record notes, upcoming events and appointments
- ■ Log phone numbers in a directory

- Write down ideas about conversation with acquaintances
- Project ahead on days to meet with someone or complete a project
- Record birthdays and special occasions to send a card or message
- Save ideas that pop into your head about something
- Document mileage or names that can be used later
- Write down referrals and names of important ideas for later
- Save the daily organizer or planner pages for future reference

Some time ago, a friend had made plans with me for a meeting together. The meeting time came and went and he did not come. I have been guilty of the same in the past. I needed to apologize and remember the next appointment! I've learned an organizer or planner helps me avoid missing engagements.

As every year goes by and your life becomes more involved or perhaps more hectic, I would guess you might not remember everything without some kind of an organizer to record important thoughts. Even if you think you don't need some kind of a daily calendar book, small spiral notebook, electronic organizer, try it and find out **how much more efficient** you can become with a planner.

AVOID "I CAN'T"

Any time a person says it can't be done, the possibility of having it not happen may be right. It is gone! On CNN recently, a guest on the show made a statement to the effect that "If you say you can't find a job you won't find a job." How true this can be.

If a person can say in their own mind that it is possible, it makes finding a job much more possible to happen; not that it will definitely happen. We must train the mind to think positive! The aggressive, sought-after employee has learned almost anything may be possible if one sets the mind to it. Positive thoughts can lift our spirits and give us hope and encouragement in reaching fantastic opportunities.

Just a little negative talk is enough to change the whole situation. It is no different than putting spoiled apples with good ones. A bushel of shiny, red, delicious apples can be turned bad soon with only one apple that is not good. The whole team must be thinking "We can" while working together. Otherwise, one person could jeopardize the whole team effort. Employers cannot afford to have someone who may affect the whole team adversely. With only one or two persons on the team thinking that "it cannot be done," as an example, it may be enough to prevent the whole team's success.

WORKING CHAIN OF COMMAND

Follow the chain of command. In almost every situation, **it is not** advisable to go around the boss! Do not bypass your immediate lead person or supervisor with questions and problems that come along in the course of the day. I have heard adults talk about their work and going around their boss on issues when answers were not satisfying them. This could be one reason for losing a job. I would suggest handling matters directly with a supervisor in a professional manner.

57

I've put the following list together, **communication mistakes to avoid** with the boss:

- Interrupting others' concentration unnecessarily when the boss is busy
- Calling the boss at home because he/she was in a meeting at work
- Talking negatively about your supervisor with other employees
- Forgetting to thank the boss for little things he/she does for you
- Asking for special favors too often
- Coming late and leaving early from work
- Rationalizing to yourself by calling in sick when things aren't going well
- Sticking up for yourself no matter what or when something doesn't please you
- Telling the boss that you do not like working overtime
- Showing anger when he/she corrects you
- Walking out before a conversation is finished
- Blaming the boss for making you look bad when things don't go well
- Showing no kindness or thoughtfulness for upper management
- Showing indifference when called upon to do special projects
- Turning down invitations and not attending company events
- Walking into the boss's office unannounced when troubled about a situation

If there are differences with the boss, try to solve these differences as soon as possible. But find a time to calmly think of reasons why you have difficulty working through misunderstandings. Problems must be solved with your immediate supervisor regardless of the circumstances. You may want to pray to God for understanding and direction so you can be forgiving. There must be a mutual feeling of respect between you and your supervisor so there can be a relaxed exchange of conversation, free of tension. When the cardinal rule of communication is not taken into consideration, how can problems be resolved without causing both needless stress and wasted time? Problems may never surface until too late if you're not communicating well together. Periods of unproductiveness or indifference will probably affect your job tenure or promotions.

Find times to share with the boss about things that are exciting and productive. This will be music to his/her ears. Open up conversation by sharing accomplishments you've made for the department or company when time or opportunity permits.

Here is but one example as you are visiting with the boss: "You probably remember last Friday when we couldn't get the company car started in the morning, and we were late to the appointment. Well, I did something about it right away on Monday. I called maintenance, where the car is usually parked, and asked what they would recommend so it wouldn't happen again. They said they could install a frost plug in the car block so it could be kept warm even though the temperature dropped to freezing. The repair worker said it wouldn't cost over $75.00 for that model of car and they could install the plug immediately. All I need now is to get an OK from you."

Be sensitive to your boss's needs. "Bite the bullet" and give your boss the credit for things done and don't worry about getting the credit yourself. Again, visit with your immediate supervisor regularly about exciting things that are happening in the company. However, avoid sharing so much that it becomes an annoyance problem.

As you practice keeping the lines of communication open, you will be able to resolve problems more quickly when problems surface.

WHAT IS CLEAN CLEAN?

What does it mean to keep things sanitary and clean? What makes clean, clean? What is clean to one person doesn't always mean the same for the other. There are many meanings to keeping things clean. There is shiny clean, dusting clean, sterile clean, just plain clean, mirror clean, spotless clean, hygienic clean, sparkling clean and more. Find out specifically what is expected of you.

It also means keeping yourself clean. A clean-cut look might give you confidence.

Do you want a job in a clean environment? Most office jobs, for instance, have all the clean perks like a shiny clean wood-topped desk, computer, clean looking hardware, drapery, and clean glistening windows with rays of light coming through. Drawers are organized inside and out, giving a feeling of productiveness.

If you are cleaning and waxing long hallways in a high-rise building, ask about the expected ways you should do your cleaning. Have your lead person give examples of expected cleanliness. If not, find out who can answer your questions.

Even if you are working in an auto service area, customers do not want someone with grease on their clothes or hands touching interior car upholstery. Clean company outfits may be furnished. Most environments are expected to keep things clean, even in some machine shops and aircraft hangers.

You may take a break and eat popcorn with others. Some workers may be reaching into the sack and helping themselves to a handful of popcorn. Should you say anything about this practice? I wouldn't suggest making a big deal of this in front of everyone. You can pour or scoop out some popcorn onto a napkin. In this way, germs aren't transferred from hand to hand. Even though you wash your hands often, that doesn't mean others are keeping their hands sanitary and clean.

Here are a couple of other practices to deal with—show others the respect of not touching the top edges of the Styrofoam Cups while you pass the cup or loosen one from the others. Also, there is the issue of touching the other stirring sticks or the toothpicks before taking one. Hopefully, the toothpicks are wrapped in clear plastic.

Employers would basically like to see their employees practice cleanliness daily, everywhere in their living standards, through good hygiene, mannerisms, and dress.

BE ADAPTABLE

Roll with the punches and adapt to changes expected in the workplace. That's probably an understatement in regard to the enormous amount of resilience expected of persons in the workplace. Employees are expected to follow the lead of their boss even if they change their mind from one hour to the next. If an employee can't handle the employer's change of mind on issues, they just may be saying goodbye to a better job offer, wage increases, and promotion. However, many lead persons, managers, and supervisors appreciate employees who question things from time to time while using good discretion. As stated earlier, be adaptable, as one of our family members recommends; this may be one of the top character traits to develop as an employee.

Persons able to adapt quickly to change are very valuable!

Be willing to compromise. Sure, this can be difficult in the workplace. Help make the decision-making process easy for the team to reach conclusions. Practice patience with people who have differences of opinion in the group. I have experienced that patience may tip the decision in your favor "after everything comes out in the wash." As an example, just one color change can make the picture look different. Or, another beam of sunlight can change the whole outcome of the color. So it is with decision making—how you allow for new ideas contributed from others can affect the dynamics of the total outcome.

Do you have to know why the final decision was changed in the outcome? Probably not! Yes, sometimes it would be good to know why a change was made. It would be nice for management to share the reasons for the change. But there should not always be need from you to know when and why a decision was made!

The flexible person can adjust to changes without complaining. This person can work in a quiet or noisy atmosphere. The carpenter's helper can transfer 2"x 4" lumber off one truck and put them on the other truck without asking why. You may be expected to dress a certain way or wear a company uniform and not ask questions why, unless it's against your convictions, and that must be dealt with in a very sensitive manner.

REVIEW YOUR JOB DESCRIPTION

How can you possibly do well without knowing the expectations of the job?

If you want to advance in your job, and if it's convenient, find out more from your employer about the job description. Some companies have this written in a brochure or manual. Be courteous in finding out about those specific job responsibilities. Otherwise, try to compile a list of your responsibilities which are expected of the job. Don't blow it off and later regret not taking time to follow up.

Please don't be so concerned about the title of the position. I've seen persons who were only interested in their job title. In fact, job titles can do more harm for a beginning employee than what they're worth. The person you are working for may not even have a title for your hourly job. That's OK. No matter what your job is, nearly all jobs have a common denominator. The bottom line may be as simple as helping the customer find a solution to their needs. This may mean breaking away from what you're doing and giving the customer your undivided attention. Many times it's as easy as being a good listener. The person coming to your business or company is probably seeking help from you! Be the kind of person that goes out of your way to give customers some kindness. It may be as easy as giving them a smile.

What comes next if you learned something more involved in the job description? Make a decision of how to put it into practice. If it's no more than deciding to table it for now or dismissing it for the time being, or how fast you'll introduce it, you've made a decision. Just a side note, others may or may not want to hear what you have learned!

Take your time to think about unclear job expectations but do not procrastinate. You've probably heard how some people cannot get good sleep. It's been my experience that if I don't do something about a fact, it may come back to me in a dream. The dream would then keep me from getting good rest at night. It's like I hadn't found a parking place for the car for the night and must keep steering it in different directions.

Perhaps you learned more about a big responsibility of your job description. Ask your employer for additional details. A second criterion may be; how will this added responsibility in the job description affect my family interests? I'm sharing this because an employer may ask how you will handle or are handling the added responsibility in a job review evaluation.

In everyone's job description, there is an unwritten part that implies, work together to find the answers. So as you learn about things, develop an understanding with your co-workers. Rise to the occasion to help others. Be accountable, reliable, and trustworthy in your actions. Probably the most neglected part in some people's lives is following through with agenda to the finish, which has been delegated for us to do.

Put into practice the things learned from day to day which affect your job description visibly and invisibly.

WITH MORE KNOWLEDGE COMES MORE RESPONSIBILITY

The Peter Principle tells us there can be people who go up the ladder so far and fast they cannot handle the additional responsibility that comes with the promotion. When a person acquires a new job promotion or additional knowledge, the question that comes up—what are you going to do about this change?

There are many motivational courses and seminars out there to help lead a more structured change. I would encourage you to attend one professional motivational conference every one or two years, centered around acquiring new knowledge for new job expectations. Personally, I like to hear a motivational speaker every few months in one form or another. Your excuse may be that you can't afford to go hear a motivational speaker. Attending services at a church event of your choice may be a start in finding a motivational speaker—the services are free. Many times, my pastor's sermon becomes my motivational talk. Your employer may even have a course or book in inventory to let you read. Many employers would pay you to attend a workshop of this kind. It boils down to this—if you have the desire to seek out this need for your job, you'll find it. No one can motivate you more to learning everything there is to know about doing better in your job but you!

There is much more in Chapter 9 to strengthen your job knowledge in preparation for your job review with management. As you continue in this book, there will be many more ideas to choose from, and then you must decide what to do or not do with this additional knowledge. As I've already said, prioritizing is just part of becoming more successful.

Here is something powerful to think about. Have you heard the statement, "We are God's keepers?" To me that means, with additional knowledge we are responsible to carry out the things we know are right in God's sight. How would Jesus want us to handle additional responsibilities as more knowledge is acquired?

GO THE SECOND MILE

I think preparing yourself for advancement means doing an outstanding job in the position you have. When opportunity comes along, you may be the one to receive more benefits, a pay raise, or be promoted to something better. Are you aware most supervisors keep a file on their employees? To my surprise when I retired, my boss returned the file folder of letters and notes written about me from my past employment.

All employees will want to have a good working relationship with their supervisor or lead person. Supervisors will invariably want a "yes" answer even though they give you choices such as, "Can you stay an extra hour and help finish the mailing?" And your answer should be, "Yes, I'll arrange to do it." You must take a position of being proactive for your supervisor. Otherwise, get a different job in which you can take that position. Not really—you may find the next employer feels the same way. I do not recommend changing jobs just because there is disagreement. Most employers have similar expectations. Changing jobs may not be in your best interest. So think twice, think long, before you change jobs. What I really mean is to keep a perspective! As an employee, whatever you do or wherever you work, you must realize you've been hired to carry out and do the work planned by management. That's what becoming a middle class income wage earner is all about. That may be precisely why they have hired you. They know you're a hard worker! So keep a perspective of why pay raises happen. Be patient with your lead supervisor. By the way, it may take several years of hard work as you position yourself to deserve advancements.

Quite often your work will go unnoticed, so keep some specific notes as a record of the day-to-day significant accomplishments and file them for a rainy day. Don't show the notes to anyone unless the day comes when it is asked for—maybe in a job review. I suggest showing big accomplishments in the resumé. Refer to the resumé form in the Appendix. Also, see Chapter 10 for more ideas to strengthen the resumé.

When the supervisor or lead person is away and you are caught up, you will still want to be productive. The following list is much like both topics, "Goes With the Territory" and "Think and Then Do," at the end of Chapter 4. All three topics address a very similar work ethic for employees who find work without being told to do so.

I'd suggest when you work ahead with projects, remember two things: First, make sure the extra little effort you accomplish is not just busywork. Second, ask yourself whether your boss would support what you are doing.

- sharpening or improving something
- filing and stacking things into an acceptable order
- emptying or filling containers
- reading up on some new tool or instrument
- pulling out or storing seasonal things
- working with inventory or identification labels etc.
- roughing out some paperwork, material or project in preparation for the next day
- asking a fellow employee in the same work area if you can help them
- fixing and repairing
- working on your filing of paper work
- cleaning up, dusting, sweeping
- preparing packages for mailing
- oiling or greasing mechanisms
- reviewing new instructions
- restoring some instrument or piece of equipment

With some companies, it is not unusual for the boss to be called away repeatedly. That leaves time to make some very important decisions to show your boss or lead person you know how to go ahead with important things rather than sitting down on the job. When your boss is there, expect to be called away from your work assignment so he/she can give you work ahead. Quite often, a supervisor will give you more than you can do so you'll have more than enough work to keep busy for a number of days, if necessary.

CHAPTER SIX SUMMARY

As you may have already figured out, if every employee isn't giving their very best, every day, and all day long, the company or establishment is probably not going to be as successful. Most likely, you are there to do productive work and given a wage by the employer to make a good profit; otherwise your job may not be needed.

CHAPTER 7

OFF WORK AND AT HOME

IMPORTANCE OF FAMILY

Family support can make a huge difference in our lives. Father, mother, stepfather or stepmother living together with their children brings closeness and comfort to children. Family includes grandmothers and grandfather. Family includes aunts and uncles, great-uncles and great-aunts, nephews and nieces, all having an important place in the family. Adopted children and half-brothers and sisters, brothers-in-law and sisters-in-law, great-grandfathers and great-grandmothers all hold important places in the successes of one another in the family. Family members have opportunities to give care and affirmation whether they live in close proximity or communicate via e-mail, cell phone, or other means from a distance.

If you aren't close to someone in your family at this time, then do the next best. Try to fill the void by developing a friendship with someone who is dependable and trustworthy, like someone in your "Confidence Circle." Refer back to Chapter 1, the paragraph on "Building a Confidence Circle." Don't miss out on opportunities that may have come quicker if you had received advice and encouragement from a very good friend. Good friends can be like family; they can be there to help in times of celebration and through times of difficulty. Many times, we can have more potential to get along with others while having a support group to share our ups and downs in life.

What can you do if some ties with family or friends are not working out? If possible, find a distant relative and strengthen those family ties now. If there are family problems, step up to work at healing those differences. Try searching for forgiveness in your heart to make family connections right again. Find issues that can pull your family together. Make it a practice to unite and compromise with family and friends, rather than focusing on differences of opinion.

Another way is to find a support group. Large cities have a community health coordinator located in one or more of the city offices to give you counsel at no charge. Some small cities have organizations like Circles of Hope in Newton, Kansas, which offer help for struggling persons who are reaching out to people who will help them.

When friends and family members give encouragement to each other, self-esteem and confidence can increase. Recently, my grandson gave my granddaughter encouragement for an upcoming game. This, no doubt, gave her a lift in being able to perform better as a basketball player. The same can happen as family members support each other in studying for exams, job searching, or special projects.

COMMIT TO AN EXERCISE PROGRAM

Many jobs do not offer the exercise one needs on a continual basis. For that reason, a special effort to get plenty of exercise can be part of your life commitment. I was told that sometimes doctors may go swimming or jogging before they perform a surgical operation? By exercising the body, the blood warms up and flows through the veins and arteries, helping the body to function much better. The body performs better as a result of exercising. That, too, is why some companies have set aside times for exercise.

Can we afford to avoid a good exercise program? My answer would be no. New, fresh oxygen can come from exercise. Exercise tones the muscles. Exercise can make you feel invigorated and more efficient. Yes, you know the rest of the story—this helps to make an energized you!

"Most of us eat too much and move too little," suggests Lisa, my half-sister. When she was wellness director at Showalter Villa in Hesston, Kansas, she advocated developing a good exercise program, maintaining good extracurricular activity, and eating right. She encouraged people to set up goals each year and keep a record of exercise every day by writing it on a calendar. Lisa cites a great source for more information in the book Real Age, by Michael F. Roizen, MD. What does Lisa say about eating right? "Most of us are emotional eaters. Your stomach will tell you when you are truly hungry. When your stomach is satisfied (not full), stop eating. This is easy to say and hard to do. Many of us have been conditioned to clean our plate and to eat at certain times of the day. Try to be more in tune with your body and only eat when you're hungry. This takes a lot of discipline when food may be free, when you eat out, or when you are at someone else's house. Also, try to avoid using food as a reward or as a stress reliever."[1]

Here's an interesting twist for a good exercise to stay healthier shared in a presentation by Al Schmidt found in "Bits of Wits," entitled, "Lettin Go and Holdin On: Finding the Humor and Courage to Live Well:" "Laughter is internal jogging."[2]

Oh sure, you can over-exercise and make the muscles sore and tired, especially if you are not consistent with your exercises, overdoing, or doing the exercises incorrectly. As a past coach and athlete, my theory is to exercise thirty minutes, three, four or five times a week. As I said above, it is important to have consistent periods of exercise to keep the muscles toned and fit. Some people will want to do some type of exercise daily. That is good, also. We can constantly work on this challenge! This can be a win-win situation.

LEAVE PERSONAL BUSINESS AT HOME

Would you say you are on top of things at home? Off-work planning for extracurricular things should be handled at home so you as an employee do not have to make calls at work for personal matters. I covered this topic earlier. I'm covering it again because it's being broken so often.

Some employees may have seniority, own the business, or be assigned by their boss to make some personal calls. Either way, you'll be better off if you choose to take care of your personal business on personal time, not while you're being paid by the employer. Go out of your way to avoid doing this at your employer's expense.

It may be possible that if you're happy at home you'll be a better employee at work. Reflect on how to get refreshed at home—maybe it's about finding meditation times for yourself. Keep your home relationships from getting strained. Plan ahead as a household. Stay on top of the bills coming in by having a given time each week to arrange payments to creditors.

Protect your valuable time at home. Don't share too much personal business at work with other employees. Guard against doing things that don't build up your personal business at home.

FREE TIME

When you put together a resumé (read about resumés in Chapter 10), it would be good to have a paragraph to include leisure activities. Leisure activities are a great way to relax or exercise. This may include bicycling, jogging, walking, tennis, basketball, baseball, softball, football, badminton, croquet, horseshoe, sewing, art, card playing, knitting, swimming, boating, and other activities. This helps the employer to see you as having a well-rounded personality. If you can't think of any leisure activities that you presently like to do, please give this some serious thought. Employers want someone with good social skills and who enjoys taking part with others in leisure time activities.

It takes an employer much time and resources to find a new hire. They may be looking for a long-term employee, so why not allow them to think about promoting you in the distant future? They want more than someone who only knows the technical side of the job requirements. What may be their rationale? If you can enjoy visiting with people in leisure activities off the job, you probably will enjoy relating to others more while on the job. Most of the time, it is essential that others are involved with your job decisions. The better you can dialogue with friends on and off the job in leisure activities, the better you'll function and fit in with most employment positions.

PLANNING PERSONAL GOALS

What are your ambitions or goals in life? Do you make daily goals? Have you given yourself incentives for working in a good job? Do you have short or long range goals written down? Do you have aspirations for the type of job you want or what you desire in the future? This gives purpose in life! This gives a person rationale and reasons to be motivated and find work in a good paying job.

Aspiring to be the lead person on the work shift, a policeman, a supervisor of the crew, or finding a job can be goals for you. To own a small home, obtain a specific degree, become a youth leader, auto mechanic, marry a wife or husband, help put your spouse through college, or become a parent, could be goals for you. Dreams can come true after goals are identified and given a chance to develop. Some people may have the goal to "keep up with the Joneses." Consider doing your own thing. But try to fit in without making a big deal of your differences. Set your own goals while allowing others to have their own goals. Lead your life trying to get along and treating others with respect—be yourself. There will always be others who are more successful; that's OK. Be genuinely happy for them! Remember, they may have chosen different goals and that is OK. Success is only as much as the beholder views it as a success. The point I'm trying to make is, develop goals and purposes in your life that you can manage and get excited about. Zig Ziglar in his book *Top Performance* says that "one of the greatest problems faced in society today is the problem of unrealistic expectations." [3]

We must set goals that are realistic for ourselves! Be the captain of your own ship, but make sure the ship is not too big, can be kept in good order, and steered in the right direction. Nor do you want your boat to be too small and be unsafe in rough waters!

If you're expected to carry out a request for the company you work for, treat it as a high priority! Another way to think about it…treat it as your own personal project and give it your all. Take ownership in what you do.

After reading the following sample goals, I'd encourage you to make a list of your own personal goals. Save your goals in a convenient place and then modify them as time goes along. Do this to strengthen organizational abilities and experience greater happiness! Use the same structure or make more or less categories, whatever fits your preference. Give thought to dreaming things that you hope will come true in your life time. I really encourage you to do this, you owe it to yourself. If you do this, maybe in 5 to 10 years, you might be able to look back and thank yourself again and again!

1) **Examples of Daily Goals:**
- Purchase a lined pad for doing daily planning (something like a diary)
- Take a multivitamin supplement tablet daily at breakfast time
- Set the alarm for 6:30 a.m. and shower each morning
- Eat 3 times daily in a relaxed atmosphere so the food digests well
- Pray and thank God every day for food and the blessings he provides
- Update your planner daily
- Check the final plans to see if everything is ready for tomorrow

Daily goals can be accomplished easily by simply purchasing a lined pad for a dollar and using each page as a day planner. Save each dated daily lined list in order of the previous day and put it into a manila folder for reference later to pick up things that haven't been accomplished or lined out. Each day or two, transfer the ones that did not get done and lined out to the current day being planned. I go back from time to time and bring back a daily goal that was not accomplished because things changed and now it can be used again on the present day priority list. Write telephone numbers to the left of the vertical red line. To the right of the vertical line, place either a last name or a company so you can scan the lists faster at a later time. Use the remainder of the line for very brief notes or telephone conversation. Abbreviate as much as possible. Quite often I get two lines of notes into one space by abbreviating.

Remember, keep a prospective what I have to offer, these are only examples.

2) **Examples of Weekly Goals:**
- Fertilize the indoor and outdoor plants with fertilizer
- Call my parents and let them know what's going on in my life

- Study for my Sunday school lesson coming up next Sunday morning
- Plan next week's grocery list so it's ready when I go to the store
- Fill the car with fuel next time we are close to a service station
- Remind the neighbor boy to mow the grass on Saturday
- Make final plans for next week's dinner out with friends

Week by week goals may be something like having a list for next time you go downtown or to the city. It may be a note to write, or e-mail you want to send to someone for doing something. Perhaps there is a ball game you'd like to watch. Update weekly goals much like updating daily tasks in a planner. If you haven't used a planner, go ahead and use a simpler form of planning for now. Most planners come in the form of a calendar with space to update information regularly. Maybe after you're making more money, you'll want to work toward using something more like a Professional Franklin Planner.

3) Examples of Monthly Goals:
- Pay the rent three days early before the 1st of the month so it's not late
- Pay all the bills by the 26th of the month
- Get tickets for the Rio concert next month
- Clean the bird bath. Check the health of the fish
- Plan ahead for having photos taken this fall for the church directory
- Call to get tickets for the KU basketball game next month at Kansas City
- Mark the calendar to attend the neighborhood party in two months

Check your planner and record important dates and meetings in advance to help remember details. Changes are hard to make immediately; people need time. Remind someone ahead of a deadline. Write expected goals; this is your log record to document important agenda. Bills can be paid on time by including deadlines ahead of the monthly due dates on your calendar to avoid those unwanted interest or late carrying charges. This also promotes a good credit rating. My wife and I compare our monthly calendars and special things we want to do, watch, or attend together.

4) Examples of Yearly Goals:
- Use the credit card more wisely, make some notes for change
- Plan to attend a seminar suggested by my sister or friend
- Save more money per month for savings account
- Read one self improvement book
- Review qualifications to get my job promotion
- Plan vacation
- Find a probable home to buy as an investment

These are like New Year's resolutions! Do you need to attend seminars or college to improve your effectiveness? What are you planning to buy in advance for the children, grandchildren, or special friends? If these ideas are written down and you just happen to be at an estate sale or mall somewhere just browsing…that is the time to buy. Having written those things down in advance and having the chance to buy in the off-season can sometimes save money. The person who plans to buy a car and begins saving up money early can save a staggering amount of money. Avoid paying those high interest rates or carrying charges by paying in cash. Just a thought, sometimes one has a better chance to buy for less with cash because you have more leverage to name your price. Planning ahead with your income tax consultant, such as the H&R Block agent, will pay back dividends in tax savings. And also very important, who are people you want to learn to know better? Find some good books to read. What do you want your resumé (a sample resumé is included in the Appendix and explained in Chapter 10) to look like as you move in the direction for meeting your dreams?

How about planning for a two or three week trip? Do you need to vacation far from home? One summer when we were younger and short on extra cash because of paying back college debts, we made a decision to vacation by finding something in our own locale. Each individual day for four days, we traveled out of town either north, south, east, or west. Each night we would come back to sleep. That was more fun than we ever expected and we had a good experience as a family.

5) **Examples of Five-Year Goals:**
- Arrange to take classes to improve job evaluation review
- Strengthen family ties and be there when the children need me
- Change my hair style
- Find an insurance company that offers better service for less
- Update my wardrobe and coordinate clothes that I now have
- Find a way to car pool to work

What kind of college degree do you want to aspire to for advancement? What level of management can you handle or be content with? Should you be buying a home instead of renting? How about planning for the purchase of a second car? What kind of family do you desire? What is your philosophy about morals or having a religious life? It is not too early to start a savings account and to put away money for later even if it's only a small amount. Do you have a group to meet with once a month? It can be challenging to take time to learn new friends or it can be exciting. How about starting a dinner group to associate with monthly? We have a dinner/cards group—the friends are great! Sometimes wishes happen because they've been planned in advance.

6) **Examples of Mid-life Goals:**
- Improve relations with my friends, spouse, and children
- Do better at putting away money for retirement
- Get more serious about reading the Bible in a small group setting
- Start a garden to help with the grocery budget and eat healthier
- Review my personal goals

- Start a second retirement IRA plan
- Arrange for a living will

Do you have a retirement plan started? Are you putting away money for retirement? Have you made a will for yourself? Are you satisfied with where you are? It's not too late to make changes in the routine you are living! Personal assessment is important! What is your purpose in life?

Is it time for a personal image change? Evaluate your wardrobe…is it outdated? How about some house cleaning…getting rid of things that haven't been used for some time? Re-evaluate your past goals and sit together with someone to evaluate plans for the next decade.

7) Examples of Retirement Goals:
- Update the will and power of attorney
- Review my net worth
- Get a physical from the doctor
- Arrange to see the children or past friends during special times
- Consult an organization to help plan for retirement
- When will I size down to a more affordable income
- Join the senior center
- Support my children and grandchildren in special ways

Have you checked the status of your Social Security account or your savings accounts? Where do you want to spend the rest of your life? It's not uncommon to spend twenty years in retirement. Buy the things you want for retirement before retirement because you want to be debt free in retirement to enjoy those senior years. After some people retire they are lost and have little to do or show for themselves. They have no purpose in life after retirement. Those that have set retirement goals early will probably enjoy themselves more. Is there a plan to down-size or move to a house with more efficiency? What things will you want to do before retirement? Do you have dreams of traveling…putting away a nest egg in advance so you don't have to make a draw on the principal? It may be good if you planned retirement in the community where you have been living and where past friends can be a support group so loneliness doesn't prevail. You need friends during retirement. Perhaps that is why birds and animal pets often become more important during this time. The fact of the matter is, planned goals will increase the odds of helping all this to happen in a more orderly manner.

8) Examples of Life Goals:
- Review living will
- Help the grandchildren, close relative, or friend
- Study the saving grace of Jesus
- Do things on my journey that are heaven-bound
- Review the plans for happiness in retirement
- Think about assets for humanity and God

How do you want to be remembered? What kind of a person are you? Have you lived the kind of life where you can be content and feel you can eventually go on to live with Jesus in the eternal heaven above? Some people write their own obituary. What will be the emphasis in your will? Have you planned a legacy where your siblings or wider family can continue to build on what you have started? Will you have a "Confidence Circle" of friends who care very much for your welfare and your family because of the love you've shown during your years of friendship? What's important for you and your God?

READ THE NEWSPAPER REGULARLY

Reading the business news is something I look forward to doing each day. I hope you have interest in this also. It becomes a high priority for the person advancing in the workplace. A heads-up approach means keeping up with what is going on around you. Local, community, regional, and "USA Today" gives valuable support information for your day-to-day decision making. This is not normally something that your boss tells you to do. It's assumed you know it comes with the job or as the saying reminds us, it just "goes with the territory." It normally takes only a short time to scan the headlines. Some do it while they eat. Some do it while they watch television. Others do it on the way to work if they are commuting. But, please do not read the news on the way to work if you're the driver.

What constitutes business news? It will take time to develop an eye for scanning the paper for related job news. What should you be looking for? It might be a new company that started, a new ruling for the working class, an automatic raise for the person in a certain income class, or a research project that proved that people that read a certain comic are happier. Good reading might be in the sports section if your company is sports-related. In any case, news may affect your job, budget, taxes, company sales, or who knows. Read the news with a passion to strengthen your job security.

WATCH AREA JOB OPENINGS

Even though you may have a job, it may still be good to keep your resume updated. It might be interesting to read about job openings which are similar to your job. One can learn to appreciate more about your own job by comparing it with others. Perhaps the business you work for could benefit by knowing something about the competition. By watching area job openings, you may be able to see subtle things which could be in your best interests.

With the emphasis upon having job descriptions written more thoroughly, it may be helpful to watch how other job openings are worded. Perhaps you could do a self analysis, on your own time, to see how many ideas you can come up with to enjoy your present job more.

APPRECIATES NICE HOME

As I was driving through town today, I couldn't help thinking to myself, I need to write about places to live. If you're earning a small income, then consider renting an affordable place to live. It's important that your home doesn't work a hardship on your budget. If you can, find something that you can be proud of…painted nicely, has an open out-of-doors area with green nice shrubs and clean windows. Make it a place you can call home, not just a place to live.

Try to find housing that gives you comfort and enjoyment. Our first rental was a downstairs apartment, approximately 500 square feet. We were poor. The important things were (1) we could afford it, (2) it had clean fresh paint, (3) the apartment landlord lived upstairs and cared about who we were, (4) the premises were taken care of with green mowed grass and trimmed bushes, and most importantly, (5) my wife and I were comfortable and happy in our small basement apartment that felt like home. We felt good about telling our friends where we lived.

After a year and better of planning, we increased our income and this allowed us to move into a larger ground floor apartment.

Later, after finishing college and getting my first teaching job, we moved into an upstairs two bedroom house apartment in a nice neighborhood, close to work. It was quiet with shady lawns, many trees and hard surfaced streets. After two more years we found a larger, comfortable two bedroom house with a fenced-in yard. This allowed my wife to take care of our first child along with a friend's child.

After two more years we purchased our first home. This would allow us to build equity as a home owner rather than only paying rent. It was an old two-story brick home with lots of character in a nice neighborhood. The home needed tender loving care and much improvement. But it was home to us! Home was a place we could come to get refreshed and prepare for the next day. The neighborhood and the people living close to us shared the same philosophy of wanting home to be a quiet place of warmth and rest, free of crime and carelessness.

As you plan ahead, consider buying something which after the project is improved by you, will be equal in value with other housing in the neighborhood.

EATING HEALTHY AND STRETCHING GROCERY DOLLARS

Eating healthy three times a day is probably best unless your doctor tells you otherwise. My doctor told me that eating three smaller meals and eating routinely more often, such as a morning and afternoon snack, is better for me. For others it may be different than what I need. Eat right and think better. Give yourself an edge by eating foods that are good for your body. Eating a balanced diet, eating regularly, and drinking plenty of water are all keys to eating right. There are many books out in the bookstands on eating right.

Would you put the wrong oil or too much oil in your car or starve it for the right level of oil? The answer is no, you wouldn't. Don't cheat your own engine (body)! It's much better to choose better foods to eat than pinching on your budget to save a dime. A friend told me just lately that "some things coming through the window of your car are not good for you." I thought that was an interesting comment. My wife and I try to work at eating healthy foods rather than spending the dollars taking medicine. You wouldn't put diesel in your auto gas

72

tank if it is supposed to run on regular unleaded fuel. As we hear from experts, the body is the same. It needs nutritious foods in the right amounts to run right.

Sources remind us that breakfast is very important for getting a good start each day. You probably eat breakfast; if not, please do. Eat something for breakfast, for your sake even if it's only cinnamon toast and tea. There was a time when I had only coffee in the morning. That was not good. About 25-some years ago my doctor told me I was drinking too much coffee. He also said that for every ½ cup of coffee, I should add ½ water. That was good advice. Give yourself rest time when you eat. I'm trying to eat my meals more slowly now. Maybe our body doesn't digest and get the value from food as well when one eats on the run.

What could some meal suggestions look like? A good breakfast could be oatmeal with 1/2% milk with a few craisins and raisins on top the oatmeal, wheat toast with non-cholesterol spread and natural strawberry fruit preserves, water, coffee, and a small glass of fruit juice. Or another breakfast example, hot Lipton Herbal Cinnamon Apple Caffeine Free Tea with fried wheat bread topped with light syrup, 1/2% milk, a little glass of tomato juice, and water. Sometimes, all I fix myself for breakfast is a dish of Quick 1-minute Oat Meal. I pour out about ¾ cup of oatmeal into a dish, add some water and microwave it for one minute. I add a sprinkling of dark brown sugar and 1% milk. I add a small amount of one kind of fruit, whatever we have available, such as blueberries, apples, blackberries, or peaches. I try to have a ¼ glass of juice or hot coffee and then make sure I've had my one glass of water for the start of the day. During breakfast, I take one multi-vitamin.

For lunch, have a tossed salad, spaghetti and meat sauce, home made cracked wheat bread topped with Smart Balance Buttery Soft Spread, and low sugar-natural berry fruit jam, cooked fresh green beans, Natural Unsweetened Applesauce, milk, and water.

For dinner, you might want a tossed salad with a few carrot slices, celery, vegetables, and green lettuce with a nutritious topping served with cracked wheat bread. Add a baked potato (with edible skins), baked chicken (brushed with 100% pure olive oil), and a small amount of mushroom low-fat gravy over both. Top off the meal with a fresh cut fruit salad. Have a couple glasses of water.

If you want to snack early in the evening, have a bowl of bite-sized Wheat Chex or your favorite healthy cereal with milk and some pieces of fruit on top.

Obviously, there are thousands more appetizing recipes and food combinations than what I've given above. Many cookbooks, magazines, and recipes found in the marketplace or even from friends, give good ideas for breakfast, lunch, and dinner. My thoughts are that I could pay more attention to the quality and quantity of the food I eat everyday.

If you have a job where you burn off a lot of calories, then eat more, but try not to overeat or have junk food in between the three main courses. And before you go to bed, get your body prepared for the rest mode by not eating and drinking heavily just prior to turning in for the night.

Be proactive and conscientious about drinking enough filtered water daily. You may need to remind yourself to drink more water sometimes even if you're not thirsty.

The following are only a few ways that my wife and I have learned to stretch our grocery dollars:

■ Scan local grocery store sale ads for buying more for less.

■ It's OK to use coupons, but would caution you about buying something you don't need.

■ I try to buy foods that are grown closer to home.

■ Buy in larger amounts that already come in smaller containers to save money.

■ Check the expiration dates.

■ We have learned to read the labels for more nutritious foods.

■ Plan the main dishes in advance so the grocery shopping becomes easier.

■ Keep leftovers on one specific shelf of the refrigerator with the freshest food to the back so there is a rotation of the things to eat sooner at the front.

■ Make enough for more than one meal, saving the rest in small freezer bags or small, clear casserole dishes.

■ Food preparation can be mixed and combined with the foods on hand so it does not have to be thrown out.

■ I was told in a jobs fair seminar that you can find better food prices on the lower shelves. I don't know if that holds true, but I do know that you may want to guard against quick impulse buying off the easiest most attractive shelf.

■ Good food is expensive. Medicine, lost time at work, and sickness can be more expensive.

■ Buying fresh fruits and vegetables are good for our health. I just returned from the grocery store where I picked up 1% milk, a box of whole grain cereal and bananas for break. I forgot to buy frozen blueberries for breakfast tomorrow morning. Plan ahead, right! A half dozen berries would have been good in my cereal or wheat grained pancakes tomorrow morning.

■ Listen to friends or family for ways they are saving dollars on their food purchases. At our last family get-to-gather, conversation led to buying groceries, and we learned some good tips from each other.

DEVELOP PRAYER LIFE

In Matthew 6:6-15 of the Living Bible we can read about the kind of prayer life God wants us to have. Ponder these words spoken by Jesus himself and then passed on to us in written form by Matthew for our happiness and fulfillment. [4]

You might consider inviting His presence into your heart!

One of my editors asked why such an important topic is so short? My answer is, God doesn't need long, drawn out prayers. In my opinion, He just needs to know that we are thinking of Him as we grow spiritually.

VACATIONING

Vacations give time for relaxation and meditation. It gives the body healing time away from the challenges of the work schedule. It is a time to get away, rest and recuperate from the daily work expectations. The body needs special attention just as your job needs special care and attention.

Here is something you will probably want to consider. Let's say you've been putting in long hours of hard work and now are eligible for a planned vacation. If you've been working very hard, it might not be good for the body to make such an about-face to only sit quietly and do nothing on vacation. I ask you, is it possible a person can overdo a good thing by doing absolutely nothing for a week or two? It would probably be advisable to get involved in swimming, walking, or some kind of planned exercise during vacation along with entertainment, rather than just sitting around for such a long period of time.

Try to go into vacation more gradually. Vacations are for giving the body and mind a time to process and catch up with the past and to think of fresh new things in the future. It is a time to see things differently in a more restful mode; to do more meditating and reprocessing of objectives and goals in life; and a time for laughing and enjoyment. It's easy to lose sight of our goals when busy daily routines push out quiet times of relaxation. Vacation time is a time to reflect and find the good in nearly everything.

SPORTS TALK

Do you attend sporting events occasionally? If you do, you probably talk to others attending—this is a very good time to converse with friends and others in the community.

My daughter and son occasionally ask me whether we're going to the football or basketball game on Friday night. Each of their families enjoy athletic events as an integral part of family life. My wife and I used to participate as players and now we're spectators for enjoyment. It's a time for having popcorn or a soda, making new friendships, seeing old friends, encouraging players—an enjoyable, inexpensive way of mixing with people.

When you're close to athletics you learn dynamics which may also be helpful on the job. If you can appreciate athletics and competition, you'll probably have a greater appreciation and tolerance for workplace competition. Athletics have the potential for building character. There are many experiences in athletics that can be used for job and personal growth. Athletes are told and learn that good exercising programs and athletic training demand disciplined minds. Triumphant employees need an edge to having their bodies in the best possible condition to meet the mind-boggling workplace pace!

The motivated employee welcomes competition, because where there is competition there is lots of activity and that's good for personal growth and business!

GETTING BETTER SLEEP

Some persons get along with only six and seven hours of sleep a night. But maybe you, like me, need at least eight hours of sleep per night. Can you sleep all night or do you awake during the night sometimes after a dream? As for myself, if I don't clear my mind of unhappy thoughts before going to bed, my mind may want to work overtime trying to find solutions.

Any one of the following may be reasons for not getting the kind of sleep you deserve. Compare the following 10 issues with possible solutions:

ISSUE ONE: I'm afraid of crime in my neighborhood
POSSIBLE SOLUTIONS:
- Lock doors and windows at night
- Try not to be outspoken to anyone and only give encouragement to others
- Move to a safer neighborhood and develop friendships with neighbors
- Pray to God for your safety

ISSUE TWO: I'm not getting along with my spouse or best friend
POSSIBLE SOLUTIONS:
- Ask to make things right…ask for forgiveness
- Say only good things to your spouse or friend
- Get help from someone who would not share this with anyone else
- Pray to God for understanding

ISSUE THREE: I don't know how to solve my job problem
POSSIBLE SOLUTIONS:
- Set new goals to help yourself find new solutions
- Ask to discuss this matter with your lead supervisor or boss
- Go to your best friend or family member to help you
- Pray to God for help

ISSUE FOUR: I don't know how to fix my financial problems
POSSIBLE SOLUTIONS:
- Prioritize…spend your money on things you need for the most part
- Develop a friendship with someone you trust to give sound financial advice
- Perhaps this is as easy as reviewing your budgeting daily
- Pray to God to help you be a good steward with your money

ISSUE FIVE: I feel uneasy about how the move to my new job will take place
POSSIBLE SOLUTIONS:
- Plan and arrange with others for a temporary date to move
- Make a list of options for moving, and then prioritize; 1st thing, 2nd thing, 3rd, etc.
- Discuss the move with your circle of friends
- Pray to God that the move will take place smoothly

ISSUE SIX: I have trouble getting along with several people at work
POSSIBLE SOLUTIONS:
- Decide to go to your co-worker(s) to resolve your differences and apologize
- Ask for advice from someone in your confidence circle of friends
- Turn the tables. What would you do if the problem were reversed?
- Pray to God for forgiveness if you offended them

ISSUE SEVEN: I don't think I have the right kind of medical health insurance
POSSIBLE SOLUTIONS:
- Ask advice from insurance counselors, health clinic, or company health agent
- Go to your closest friends for suggestions
- Discuss this with your doctor
- Pray to God for his direction and to keep you safe from injuries and sickness

ISSUE EIGHT: I'm desperately wishing to afford a better car and rental house
POSSIBLE SOLUTIONS:
- Start a savings plan, depositing small amounts each week
- Work more hours in the day putting away more savings
- Spend less. Save more!
- Pray to God for His leading in this matter

ISSUE NINE: I want my children to obey me, but they choose not to
POSSIBLE SOLUTIONS:
- Discuss alternatives with each other
- Agree to enforce and follow up on your decisions
- Ask a close friend to share with you how they would handle discipline
- Rationalize with children about why and what their feelings are on obeying you
- Pray to God, thanking Him for your children, and to help you be a good parent

ISSUE TEN: I want to advance myself at work but do not know how
POSSIBLE SOLUTIONS:
- Read and try applying reminders and suggestions learned from this book
- Don't give up on believing in yourself
- Encircle yourself with friends you can count on to give you help at any time
- Pray to God that he will show you how to advance yourself at work

Notice how each of the problems above started off with the word I. Even though I worded it that way, in today's society, too much emphasis is placed on me, I, and myself. Use words like him, her, they, them, his, she, you, yours, etc. Place the emphasis on the other person.

Might that be something you want to give more consideration to? If this is your situation, place more emphasis on allowing others to counsel and help you—this may help you sleep better.

In general, pray to the Lord...taking all your concerns to Him before you sleep rather than trying to solve all your concerns immediately by yourself.

Other ideas for consideration about getting enough good sleep are: Power naps during the day for 10 minutes are worth nearly an hour at night for me. Maybe the mattress or pillow is not right for you. Many people tell me that a bedroom that is a little cooler is better. A darker quiet room works best for me but I strongly feel that a person can program their mind to sleep under diverse conditions. Probably the biggest culprit is just plain not getting enough consistent sleep! Some people are hard to get along with when they don't get enough sleep. Still others probably make more errors or are not as effective on the job when they aren't getting enough sleep. How about the grouchy parent who doesn't get enough sleep and takes it out on fellow workers or worse, their children? The bottom line is to be at your best by arranging to get enough sleep!

And to summarize these thoughts, I could not recommend sleeping pills or power up drinks to take the place of sleep. Our bodies need ordinary sleep to stay safe, productive, and healthy.

HELPING HAND FROM SPOUSE AND/OR CLOSE FRIEND

I have a jewel for a wife. A good spouse can strengthen you as a person. If you have a spouse, significant other, or close friend who is thoughtful, cooperative, and kind, she or he may be able to have a positive effect upon your effectiveness in the course of the work day.

Think what the potential might be if you were married to a spouse with whom you could bounce off new ideas every day and function as a team! Or, sharing ideas with your closest friend!

A challenge for you: if you are married, strengthen your marriage while strengthening your job potential. I would suggest that keeping your spouse actively involved with your interests can be very helpful, especially when changes are taking place at work. Invite your spouse to be involved in the decision making and avoid shocking decisions that were made days or weeks prior to an announcement.

If you are married or have a close friend, take time to have discussions that center around how each one can help in the other's advancement. Respect each other's feelings. Keep in mind that we can meet our spouse or friend halfway in discussions. Mutual trust and mutual sharing of time is very important. If one arranges to attend a seminar, workshop, or class, why not allow some time for your spouse or friend to do the same? Bring them along with your employment growth to avoid going in different directions or creating down time for the job.

There could be a scenario where husband and wife or close friends are both working long hours in different diverse working proximities for the whole day, and then do not share enough about their jobs and changes taking place. I can't stress enough the importance of sharing and sharing alike! Stay on the same wave-length so neither one takes the situation for granted! Assumptions can cause misunderstandings.

LIMIT SCREEN TIME

We can most likely agree television, computers, smart phones, ipads, and other hand held electronic media devices can be a means for people to advance themselves. We are experiencing the "electronic information knowledge explosion" where we are bombarded with graphic information. The old saying "a picture is worth a thousand words" applies in this situation. Graphic images have so much to offer for processing information, even more than ever before. One can be updated quickly, listening and watching the news from the Internet, newspaper, television and with so many other devices.

Take the 6:00 p.m. news each day... the news comes on and immediately you can be learning more than just news. You can pick up on the latest clothing colors on the market by observing his/her colors and the way it's put together. Other information can be learned such as expressions, advertisement, hairstyles, word pronunciation, background sounds and set arrangement. Non-verbal subliminal graphic messages which may be consciously or unconsciously recognized is all part of the information blitz. Learning to process the best and the most from watching graphic presentations is challenging.

Watch selected television shows and or movies. Have you ever sat through a TV show or movie and then said, "Why did I ever waste my time watching that?" Sure, perhaps we've all done it; so—maybe you'll want to ask yourself that all-important question about avoiding the feeling of emptiness for making a choice of that kind.

Choosing to make good use of time may open up possibilities that make a big difference. You'll have more time for laughing, smiling, and looking at the positive side of life. It is important that you keep a perspective on the amount of time you watch the graphic screen. How much time should be spent on watching the electronic picture screen? What's good for one person is not necessarily good for the next, so, as always we can use our common sense. For me, an average of two hours per day is OK (day job not included), providing it is educational, entertaining, refreshing, sometimes humorous, and worthwhile. So before you get involved with too much multimedia programming, computer surfing or social media, think about whether the selections will help enrich life for meeting your full potential.

Looking back in time...I watched the Kansas City Chiefs football team on a quiet afternoon. The following day, I wore my Kansas City Chiefs tie to work. Several persons asked me whether I saw the game on T.V. Sunday. As we talked, we had some very good conversation before returning to our offices. Having similar social interests with others at work is one of those key elements looked for in effective on-the-job discussions.

In summing up these thoughts, you may want to consider spending more time meeting personally with friends and others than using the electronic media. The time may be coming, if it's not already here, when a person must evaluate whether too much time is being spent in front of the electronic screen. Will our effectiveness of dialoguing with others be socially impaired? One of my granddaughters already says that she prefers to see a friend's facial expressions in person more than using Texting for important conversations. Next time you are using a multimedia electronic device, take a minute to ask yourself—is this the best way to enrich my life?

UNEMPLOYED YOUNG ADULT

If you're living at home, then this topic fits you. William Damon, one of the nation's leading authorities on teens, starts his article in the U.S. Weekend paper by saying there are too many young adults living at home. And I would say, "Is this OK?"

Damon is quoted by saying, experts claim it "ranges from lack of money to lack of motivation…parents can prevent their children's failure to launch by encouraging them to find and explore their passions and by helping them to expand their horizons when they are young." [5]

Many young adults probably have not been given enough encouragement and direction in their quest for making a good living for themselves. If you are a young person, what is it in your case? Have you launched your career and own life to live? What do you have as a burning desire to be? Are you following your dreams?

Damon also says the ones who have purpose are the ones who can "navigate through this complex world." [6]

And my response is, if you are living with a friend, parent, or guardian—do you have some ideas about the kind of work or service you'd like to do. Sit down with your parent(s) or the person(s) you're close to and discuss your ambitions. Share with them how you want to pursue your passions and expand your horizons! As I've said before, it's your life. There are so many opportunities out there just waiting for someone, perhaps you!

CHERISH THE MOMENT

I like the quote found in Tony Dungy's book *UnCommon* about doing better. He writes, "I wonder if we all need to do a better job of listening to that gentle whisper from a God who daily reminds us to enjoy the sacred moments with those we love—with dear friends, with those who need us, and especially with our precious children." [7]

What a profound statement!

Perhaps you don't have children, so, then those persons close to you!

CHAPTER SEVEN SUMMARY

As I heard a teacher tell his student one time when he entered the classroom, "come on in, we're glad you're here but leave all your personal baggage at the door!" There is a lesson to be learned from this for the successful employee, take care of all your personal business at home and come to the job fresh and ready to put in a good day's work.

CHAPTER 8

FINANCIAL PLANNING

Do your financial planning well in advance because "windows of opportunity come and go!"

DEVELOP YOUR OWN BUSINESS PLAN

When the term business plan is mentioned, most people think of this as a plan describing the process for starting your own business.

I want to give you this challenge: make it your business plan to know where you're going with your job and finances. This can be compared to making plans for a trip. You plan ahead well, checking all the necessary travel routes, hotel accommodations, and connections on the journey. Handling the small details before the trip can result in a more stress-free, fun time.

Why do we check the route on GPS or map before leaving on a road trip? This is done so we can find our way and save time. The same should happen with a job situation. Even as you continue on course with a job, it's similar to driving a car. You don't just let the car move on its own. You're looking ahead for curves that come along. No passing zones or waiting for a red light, all play into this scenario. Just like reckless drivers on the road, we must plan ahead so we are not reckless on the job or with our finances. We can allow for speed limits that slow the progress in the course of a busy day so we are safer and have security of knowing there are limits. We may check for lane changes just like there are change orders on the job. There can be road blocks just like in business. Drivers keep track of the number of miles and employees monitor hours put into a project. There are tailgaters to be aware of just as there are competitors in business. Looking for the unknowns is like defensive driving. You watch for business employment signs much like watching the indicators on the car instrument panel. Planning ahead carefully can make the difference in achieving your goals.

Set aside times for monitoring the progress of the plan. You decide where your landmarks are to review and stay informed. The more often you check the progress, you may discover a more satisfactory outcome of reaching the goals in your plan.

There are some of the same questions in starting your own business as there are for doing better on the job. Pretend you are an entrepreneur (owner of your own business). Only, this will be **Your Job Business Plan**. Put yourself in a position to understand where you are headed. Briefly read over the line items below and then use lined paper to plan. Consider jotting down some of these thoughts in your own words. Call it: **Your Job Business Plan to Become a Better Employee**.

- Describe the position, or the work you hope to do and desire to have.
- Does your mental and physical make-up handle this work? Is this your passion?
- (1) Are you a self starter or

  (2) do you like to have another person plan the work?
- How much would you like to earn per hour? Or, per month?
- How many hours will you need to work on the job to make this happen?
- What are your work objectives and reasons for doing this?
- Who or what might help you strengthen your objectives?
- Make a list of probable people who would step up to advise you.
- List and break down the steps for these planned objectives to be successful.
- Set a tentative timetable when you can finish this proposal.
- For what will the extra income be used?
- How much is needed to break even, after expenses are taken out?
- How much more is needed for increases in the future? How will this happen?
- What is your history? (Put together a resumé using the form in the Appendix.)
- What is your net worth? (Use the financial balance sheet in the Appendix.)
- Make a current inventory of the things you own now. Use the inventory list in the Appendix. Add and subtract from it as you wish. Find a $ total by totaling each list. Then put your inventory hard copies in a safe or a second location.
- How about benefits like health insurance, etc.? How will this factor into your plan?
- Be prepared to do more paperwork and set aside more planning time. As you reflect on doing it, you'll probably think, wow, that exercise was great!

CREDIT CARDS

When I was a teenager, I knew very little about a credit card. Only after starting college did I see friends using them occasionally. We just didn't use the cards then as we do today. Then, after my wife and I were married, it didn't take long for us to realize we should apply for one or two credit cards. We wanted to (1) build up our credit rating by paying on time and (2) have a quick loan mechanism for making necessary payments when we didn't have enough cash at the moment. Our policy was then, and still is, to pay off the card in less than 20 days. This helps to avoid paying high interest or carrying fees.

The process of charging to the credit card can be a good thing. The flip side is that it can become time-intensive and expensive for the convenience. Sometimes we hear about people running up huge amounts of debt on their cards. This cannot be good unless there are savings to offset the expenditures. If accounts are paid by credit card and you have a given dollar amount listed on the monthly budget sheet (see budget form in the Appendix) to cover the purchase, then it is probably OK. I'd say you would then be using the credit source wisely. Some credit card companies offer an incentive cash refund or merchandise from earning points for spending X amount. The reward points can be cashed in for cash or traded for service or merchandise. We use our reward points as payment sometimes at hotels for overnight lodging when traveling. Some of our friends have chosen to get cash back.

INCREASE YOUR CREDIT SCORE

Life will be less complicated if you have a good credit rating. Practice paying your bills early and avoid late fees. By paying bills, and especially your credit card bill early, creditors become friends. Paying bills on time may influence people quietly and without notice. The ability to make large purchases may be easier with a good credit rating. If the credit rating is not good, it is much harder to correct it than establishing good credit initially. Maybe you have experienced losing your good credit rating because of a job loss or another reason. There can be hope in this situation by paying on time, but this requires hard work. Here is a good tip: be conservative in a loan request. Is your loan request for an investment need or something you want?

A loan is easier to obtain from a financial institution if you've had a consistent good pay-back practice with the people you deal with regularly. Poor credit ratings affect you in ways you're not even aware. Remember, lenders will review payment habits and credit score before approving a loan.

Many years ago, I asked for my Credit Score Disclosure. At the end, it gave the value of my credit supplied by the consumer reporting agency with a numerical value. It gave categories of key factors designed by some organization disclosing my score. The particular printout had 47 line items of defined reasons about my credit score. From this they determined the risk for the amount of credit (money) I was asking for in the application. In the first paragraph of the paperwork sent to me of the "Notice to the Home Loan Applicant," it read, "In connection with your application for a home loan, the lender must disclose to you the score that a consumer reporting agency distributed to users and the lender used in connection with your home loan, and the key factors affecting your credit scores."[1]

In conclusion, position yourself in advance! Ask your banker where to get a complete list of entries affecting your credit score. I would hope your local banker or credit associate would work with you to explain the results. You'll find it most interesting! I sure did! Credit ratings can be your friend or foe.

TOO MUCH DEBT?

If you don't have a debt problem, count your lucky stars that it hasn't affected you yet. Even so, suggestions in this topic, chapter, and entire book could give you a heads up on having more money to use for things you'd simply like to enjoy. Too much debt can negatively affect your job success. It can also make it rough on family life. If you are struggling with this type of situation, you may be asking yourself what to do next. I emphasize too much debt can negatively affect our job success. So, that is precisely what we want to concentrate on, getting cash flow turned around. Wouldn't it be helpful if everyone in the same household could be involved with helping to keep debt in check, no exceptions? A pamphlet from Prairie View in Newton, Kansas, by Faith and Life Resources, entitled "Dealing With Overwhelming

Debt" says, "Across North America, household debt had been growing much faster than incomes for several decades."[2]

So, give yourself time to control debt. Controlling personal debt is often linked with overspending. Is it possible to avoid impulsive buying? If we are spending for things we definitely need, and not just want, we are learning to sacrifice and be happy with our decisions!

Consider using the monthly budget form and financial balance sheet in the Appendix to plan for correcting your growing debt and becoming more self sufficient.

Joe Dominguez and Vicki Robin in their book *Your Money or Your Life* advocate reducing the consumption of resources to save money. They recommend saving money by using "words that start with re, recycle, reduce, restore, reuse, repair." [3]

Maybe it's time to find a good trustworthy licensed debt counselor, successful business minded friend, or a pastor with a business background. If you have a debt problem, meet with someone to visit about your debt and budget soon. If you're deep in debt, maybe it's time to consolidate all bills (debt) with the lowest interest rate, then arrange to have bills paid one week before they're due.

Whatever you do, please don't give up on controlling debt. Study and apply ideas in this Financial Planning Chapter, that fit your situation. It probably will not get turned around immediately. It will take patience and determination for months and months, maybe even years, but imagine what it will do for you and the generations to follow if you can "get a handle on your debt." You might want to visit with someone you trust to give you good, sound advice. It can help to keep a perspective. Avoid accepting any self-defeating thoughts that may cross your mind or that you hear from others who are loaded down with debt, and perhaps "in the same boat." You may want to tell yourself, "I will work at this and can get it done."

FIGURING NET WORTH

Following Chapter 18, in the Appendix, there is a very simple financial balance sheet to figure your net worth. That is like telling you how much money you have.

There are many reasons for using a financial balance sheet. Quite often, banks want to know what your assets and liabilities look like before giving a loan. Banks usually want you to fill out a similar form if you're asking them to give you a personal loan or for some business endeavor. Go ahead and copy the financial balance sheet in the Appendix as practice to give you an idea of how much you're financially worth. I had a family member help me the first time. If you don't have a family member, find a very close friend you can trust who would be willing to assist you.

Start by filling in the **Current Value** of each of the categories and then add the same column to find your **Total Assets**. Do the same for **Total Liabilities** (debts owed) in the second column.

As an example, one particular asset entry is about your personal property, such as household items. I've put together a personal inventory listing you can use in the Appendix. Find the inventory list and complete the value worth (actual estimated worth of what it would sell for) of each, add all entries together and total. Transfer the total dollar amount to the line marked **Personal Property** under the first column called **ASSETS**. Personal property is everything you own that is not connected permanently to the wall, floor, or ceilings, as part of the house real estate. As I said before, use the forms in the Appendix in the back of this book as a start. I use this method to inventory our personal belongings. Take pictures of your possessions. Photos can be used (1) in case of fire or (2) for renter's insurance, if you rent, or (3) to see if your personal property can be covered within the homeowner's policy, if you own your home.

Continue by doing the same for the column labeled **Debt Owed** at the upper right. List all your debts and add them up to find your **Total Liabilities** from money currently owed. At the bottom right of the work sheet, recopy your Total Assets from the left side to the bottom where it asks for Total Assets under the heading, Net Worth. Finally, subtract your total Liabilities or Debts Owed from your Total Assets to get your current financial net worth.

As a challenge each year, see how much your net worth increases. You'll be amazed at how much you can learn from this experience!

MAKING LIFE INVESTMENTS

In the book entitled *Ernst & Young's Retirement Planning Guide*, in Chapter 4, the co-authors write, "The step from saving to investing is the largest step you can take on the road to long-term financial success and making your retirement dreams a reality." [4]

First: I'd say the most important investment would be giving back a portion of the money you earn to the church or other worthy institutions. Start with small manageable amounts. As you start to earn more, check into using the long form of doing your income tax work to help reduce your taxable income.

Second: My second priority investment happens with people. Give of your time when you can help someone by doing a good deed. Build friendships wherever and whenever possible. Strengthen your confidence circle and as you increase numbers in your networking with people.

Third: Do a good job for your employer. Treat your employer as a first priority. Or, if you don't have a job, work hard at finding a good job and stick with it. Avoid job hopping.

More education can bring opportunities

Fourth: Start with a high school diploma. Check out your possibilities, one at a time. Some communities offer GEDs and give help in special ways like reading and other special classes for a minimal dollar amount and sometimes for free. Other communities have both day and night courses in continuing education. This would be worth your time to check if there are free classes offered in your community. Ask for counsel to talk about a vocation which is best fit for you.

If you need assistance, community organizations are good sources for inquiry. Just recently, Casey Jacob reported a number of Harvey County organizations in Newton, Kansas, teamed up to help struggling people who aren't making ends meet. Agape Resource Center,

Peace Connections, Mid-Kansas Community Action Program (MidCAP), and the Harvey County Extension reported offering free classes that taught marketable job skills and skills to make life easier.[5]

Following is an interesting statement from a Web site under the name, "Vocational (Trade) Schools Worth It?" I think the unknown author of this has shared what it means to be well-qualified for a good job. The author says, "Well qualified means that you have a good education, work experience, and a well rounded personality. Having one without the others is minimally qualified or unqualified. Don't think, like some of your peers may think, that just getting a diploma will get you the good jobs."[6]

In the spring of 2014 I was given a flyer about Machine Drafting from Hutchinson Community College which had a sub-title of, **"What Can I Earn in this Field?"** And, I quote from the flyer for someone who earns a 2-year Associate Degree; "Recently the Kansas Wage Survey reported average hourly earnings of over $19.00 for Architectural/Civil, Electrical/ Electronic and Mechanical Drafters." If you worked 40 hours a week @ $19.00 an hour, my calculator gives me a total of $760 a week gross pay. Working 48 weeks a year, I find it totals $36,480.00 for a year. This does not take fringe benefits into consideration. In the same flyer, it points to finding additional information in the "Occupational Outlook Handbook (www.bls.gov/ooh) and through the Kansas Department of Labor (www.dol.ks.gov)."[7]

I chose a career in college which paid back one-half of the college loan amount in a ten-year period, if I stayed with that profession for a given amount of time.

After graduation from high school, a local veterinarian visited with me, and offered to pay all my college if I would work with him for four years. I decided not to pursue becoming a vet, though. There may be some employers who will pay part or all of your tuition or even all your college expenses.

There are grants available that you are not required to pay back. College scholarships are available for those who qualify. College admissions departments are available to work together on affordable packages for potential students. Ask about an educational package tailored to meet your needs.

Fifth: Start investing your earnings early. Open a savings account to deposit small amounts at a time. That's key to investing. Invest in something that is not as risky, like a savings account, a CD protected by F.D.I.C., a Roth IRA, or in stock with the company where you are employed. Real estate has been good for some people. There are many more investments you could buy that hold their equity rather than losing their value. Get advice from a banker or someone close to the type of investment you're considering.

A car's value usually goes down (depreciates). There are exceptions, such as one I learned from my Dad. He purchased a brand new John Deere tractor and put it up for sale after two years of use on the farm. When he sold the tractor, he received more than he paid for it in the beginning. It was a model in demand because of its past performance.

Sixth: When you are ready, start planning to buy an affordable starter home in or very near your community where you work rather than renting or leasing. When I say affordable, my local banker at the Citizens State Bank told me, "Your monthly payment for the home should not be over 28% of the gross amount of your income." Your monthly payment includes the PITI—payment principle, interest, taxes, and insurance(s). Just make sure it is a good fit with your budget. Give yourself some wiggle room for the unexpected. Consider buying in a good neighborhood so it will appreciate (gain in value) faster. Take advantage of being a first-time home owner with a low-interest loan.

My wife and I, after five years of marriage, purchased our first older two-story home that needed TLC—tender loving care, through FHA. We did most of the painting and fixing up to make it feel like home sweet home. Three years later, we sold it for a nice gain to purchase a small new home. Our first starter home turned out to have been a very good investment to gain equity for the down payment of the new home. Following are ways you may be able to buy into your first starter home if you show need and have a limited but reliable income.

"Self-help housing programs" are examples of how partnerships make housing opportunities happen. Rural Development – USDA, the Federal Home Loan Bank of Topeka, the Housing Assistance Council, and Mennonite Housing have been able to provide funding and operations for eligible families wanting to own a home and willing to help build it.

Mennonite Housing recruits families from all walks of life, willing to work together during an eight-month operation of building houses for each other. Normally, work groups are the size of six families; no family moves in until all houses are complete. As the families will tell you, it's hard work, battling the elements and other challenges, but at the end of the day, it's well worth it. Families that qualify for funding, have to contribute a minimum of $1,000. Their sweat equity down payment contribution in building their own house can equal up to $20,000. The average house is 1,000 sq. ft. with three bedrooms, two bathrooms, a full basement, and a two car garage. Mennonite Housing acts as organizer, coordinator and, most importantly, instructor for all participants in their effort to build a quality affordable house. Make sure these facts are correct about the program conditions by contacting Mennonite Housing in your area.[8]

Habitat for Humanity, an international organization, works much the same way. It offers approved families a chance to buy into an affordable home with zero interest rate. The total out-of-pocket money is $1,000. The buyer works on their own house or someone else's with the help of a trustee. The applicant puts in sweat equity hours of labor, which accumulates up to 500 hours of work on the job. After that time, they work out the closing plan for the home and ownership begins. Again, make sure I got it all right by calling your area or county Habitat for Humanity Office for more information.[9]

DEVELOP AN ORGANIZED BUDGET

I hope you are budget-oriented in one manner or another. Do you use a budget? And if you do, is it realistic? Do your small bills add up so fast that you wonder where all the money went? If you can have a calm or good feeling about your earnings and spending, it will free your mind to deal with more important challenges of life and your job. The mind does not work as well when it's cluttered with the financial woes of money problems. Also, financial problems often create bad relationships with family, employers, social groups, creditors, and others. Money problems tend to pop up in unexpected ways. As you find the time to do so, gather those financial plans together and follow through with developing a budget to use faithfully. Following Chapter 18, in the Appendix, is a very simple example of a budget form. You may copy it if you'd like. There are many other sources and forms for making your own budget. I would encourage you to first tailor your own budget after an existing plan.

Strengthen your ties with a local banker or credit union so you can feel on top of your money matters. Ask someone you know well to share a person's name who they recommend for you to see at the bank or credit union. When you go in to share with this person, tell them who recommended their name to you. This is important! Do all the things you would normally do at an interview. This may be a wise starting point.

The book called *Organize Yourself*, by Eisenberg and Kelly, is another good source of strength toward getting more organized. In chapter 16 of their book, the authors give five budgeting categories: "Setting Goals, Establishing a System, Identifying Trouble Spots, Charting Monthly Expenses, and Keeping It Up." Eisenberg and Kelly say, "A long-term goal may help give you a reason for sticking with budgeting." [10]

Establish personal goals, as you read about in Chapter 7 that appeal to lifelong ambitions and commit to them. Write them down into workable dollar units. Study the effects of whether these goals are financially feasible. Ask yourself where your interest will lead. I hope your goals are in sync with your monthly budget.

WATCH FOR WINDOWS OF OPPORTUNITY

Take advantage of honest opportunities that will give you good fortune. Try to think about where the other person is coming from as they relate to you. If another person with whom you work or your supervisor calls you to do something, try to give them a yes in response. Another option could be that you'll check your schedule and let them know. Say it with enthusiasm! Try to accommodate them even if it means canceling your own plans. Sacrifices like this may be hard, but it is necessary to build mutual camaraderie or goodwill toward building strong workplace associations. Be genuinely courteous. Important areas in life center around being respectful to everyone and helping the other person feel important. Windows of opportunity open themselves if you allow yourself to be helpful to others.

Windows of opportunity come and go. This may be a defining difference to help those who are successful. Windows of opportunity could close if we are not open-minded. This is similar to running a business. The doors of the business must be open for people to buy from them. There is a time when you may need to allow others, including parents or family, to help you! This may be your opportune time in life as you graciously accept help. It is just as important to be a gracious receiver as it is to be a gracious giver.

Here may be some additional examples of how opportunity knocks at your door:
- Someone asks you at work to join them for a lunch meeting and you decline… you may have just closed a door to being part of a new, interesting project, for instance. If someone asks to meet with you, that may be their way of saying, "I want to visit with you about something important." Consider canceling any routine thing you had planned and accept their important invitation.

- When meeting and working with other employees or your supervisor, consider remembering to treat others as you want to be treated—which is most likely with respect and professionalism. "What goes up, comes down, and what goes around comes around" as the sayings go. Consider becoming known as a friend to all.

- You may be investing all your extra dollars in education as you push your career plans ahead, and someone or an organization wants to give you $1,000 just because you have a reputation for being responsible. I suggest you let your common sense guide you. You can be modest about it and ask if they're wanting to give this to you for a special purpose. You'll want to find out whether there are strings attached. If it's legitimate, you should immediately affirm them for their kindness and that you really appreciate what they are doing! Independence is good, but not to the extent that you are not able to allow others to share with you. This same person may be testing you about handling an offer of this magnitude. Who knows, it could possibly lead to a desired job or promotion in the workplace.

- You were walking down the heavily crowded street downtown and you dropped your wallet, not knowing you did, and another person took time to give it back to you. Use this as an opportune time to really show your colors. Show your gratitude for their act of kindness. What if the person giving the wallet back to you especially liked your courteousness? What if you needed a job and they were looking for a trustworthy employee? One good thing leads to another many times in life.

- You give much effort and a lot of pride in paying your bills on time. One day you ask for a loan and the banker sitting across from you says, "you have reached your $5,000 credit limit. However, since you have such a good record of paying bills on time, the credit ceiling will be raised to meet the amount you were asking." Here is a case where you took special effort to pay bills on time, which paid off. Opportunity is not always luck! Opportunity often comes to those who consistently open doors rather than going around with an unhappy look.

- You have been given a good promotion. Now it's time to work even harder—not resting on your laurels. You're ready to work longer hours and realize that by getting more, this also means giving more. The challenging test is whether you can handle the bigger challenges of being promoted. If the opportunity relates to a pay raise or promotion, please realize management may have given you the pay raise hoping for an even higher level of expectation.

VALUE PERSONAL CONTACTS

How can one create more business for your employer? Make good people contacts. Quite often, making more money for yourself and others with whom you work comes through people associations, as you read about in Chapter 1. The more doors of opportunity you can open, the probability of earning more increases. Good relationships are passed on to other people and these people pass it on to more people. However, customers and associations with new people may only give you a one-time chance.

Representing yourself well is primary to selling products for the company. In my lifetime, I've seen more people be successful in an interview, or make a sale, because they represented themselves well. Try to keep a good rapport and treat others as you want to be treated in all associations with people. Following is an important thought on making investments.

Maybe you're saying, "I've blown the chance with too many people already." So, consider changing now. Become the person you can feel good about. Treat everyone with genuine kindness. Consider apologizing for mistakes. You'll be amazed over and over. Making good associations with people brings amazing results. Sometimes the financial gains are immediate, then other times one must wait years for the pay-off.

ENVISION MORE FOR YOURSELF

What do you envision God doing for you in your lifetime?

Ivan Friesen, writer in our church winter 2010-2011 Sunday School Adult Study Quarterly entitled "Assuring Hope," wrote, "It is sometimes said that the prophets in the Bible are predictors of the future. But is this what the prophets do? Not really! What they do is to give the people of their times and later readers such as ourselves, insight into the mind of God! This insight is based on God's personal revelation to them, often in visions." He continues, "When I open the Bible in the morning and turn to one of the prophets, I do not expect predictions. I expect a word from the Lord through the prophet about God's intention for my life, and for all God's people." [11]

Toward the beginning of Joel Osteen's book, *Starting Your Best Life Now*, he writes, "Enlarge Your Vision. We serve the Most High God, and His Dream for your life is so much bigger and better than you can even imagine." [12]

I truly think that God intends us to dream bigger and have faith that He will answer our prayers to make us all that He intended us to be.

Joel Osteen's thoughts, in his May 21, 2013, TV message, left me with the same conclusion as his quote above. We expect too little of God.

How do we program our minds so we can envision more for ourselves? I believe we can by learning to know God better, praying to Him, and reading from the Bible daily.

GUARANTEES IN LIFE

Put all consumer warranties, guarantees, and rebates in one file folder for review when needed. Consider recording the expiration deadlines on your calendar.

Are there any guarantees for life? I can think of one that is like a promissory note. Some guarantees are for one month, six months, one year, three years, but this one is for life. A friend told me he has a bumper-to-bumper warranty for the life of his car. But, there was a catch. If he sold it, the warranty was over. There is a warranty or guarantee that lasts for life. This guaranteed promise is for your life, not concerning a car. It is something that makes one feel good in our heart. There are many who have vested in this guarantee in the Bible. Jesus tells us that all we have to do is believe in Him and He promises us eternal life. That message comes from John 3:16. What better investment can you make in all your life?

INVESTING LOCALLY PAYS BACK

Do you make it a practice to buy locally by supporting your community area? Here is a story about a person named Joe. Joe lost his job and now is searching to find something that pays well and will be interesting. It's Monday morning, and Joe knows he can't afford to wait too many days, because quite frankly, he will run out of cash soon and the unemployment paychecks may stop. So he decides to start the week by going to the donut shop to have a donut and coffee at 7:30 a.m. to find out whether he can learn about any employment openings. He thinks, "Maybe a person at the donut shop knows of someone hiring." Joe finds out the local grocery store needs a person to stock the shelves. "That sounds like a possibility," he thinks. "I'm trustworthy and would know how to do that." Joe calls the local grocery retailer where he learned of the opening.

Joe makes an appointment to interview for the job. During the interview, the owner mentions he wants someone who has been coming in to buy groceries from him often so they have an idea where things are found. Joe thinks, "That fits me." The grocery store owner also says, "If a person has been buying and doing business with the area retailers, they may understand the community needs better." Joe was lucky he made it a practice to shop in the community area. The story ends with Joe getting the job.

Retailers and dealerships buy merchandise for us to buy. We trust they carry good things for us to purchase. These community area retailers appreciate hearing from their customers. Find appropriate times to give them a thank you. This can have a mushrooming effect upon your success. These same retailers likely have a strong network of people that work together closely. As you shop and trade together, a pattern of camaraderie begins to happen. This has the potential of opening doors of opportunity.

Community people need your supportive efforts just like you need them.

SUCCESSFUL PEOPLE LIKE SEEING OTHERS DO WELL

What are some ways that we can encourage others when they are doing well? My philosophy is that successful people love to see others doing well.

It's a mind-set which has to consciously start by the person saying, "I will begin to enjoy seeing and helping others be successful." A trap that some fall into is thinking they must be given the credit for everything they do. Build up your boss and give him/her the credit. Be happy with building someone else up often, and you will be the benefactor, the real winner! You may not realize the rewards of this theory immediately. The way you treat others is a sign of the progress you may well experience yourself.

On the other hand, there may be occasions when the supervisor, maybe even a father, is difficult to work for and you will need to grin and bear it. They may be preoccupied with important distractions and it may just take time for them to see things differently, even a few years. On the other hand, it's been said that hardship can build character. Count this period in your life as a time of growth. There will be ups and downs. If you are one of those who have a boss, who gives you credit for doing well, be very appreciative. Realize you have a good situation where the stage is set for you. Simply stated:

> **When minds are working together for the good of all, there may come great stories to share about a higher level of achievement by the total group.**

TIPS TO GETTING A LOAN

- Start out only with a small loan to give yourself a good payment pay-back record.
- Visit with your local banker before you actually need a loan.
- Have a financial balance sheet ready to show the loan officer (see Appendix).
- Point out to the loan officer your savings account on your financial balance sheet.
- Be ready to prove how you will make regular payments on time.
- Compare interest rates and other charges from a second or third source. Please do not cave in to a loan shark who charges absorbent interest rates.
- Ask whether there are any hidden costs in the process of getting the loan.
- Ask to have them give you an example or two so you understand the process.
- If your loan is for $2,000, what is the total cost including everything in the end?.
- Ask the loan officer what he/she thinks is the maximum amount you could borrow, but do not max out your potential.
- Don't sign the paperwork until you've taken it home and had someone else review it.
- Don't take out a loan if they press you to sign it immediately, this is a bad indication.
- Ask a friend about their loan experience with the company. Were they satisfied?
- As I shared in the first suggestion, start out with a small loan and payment plan so you can build up a good credit rating with the financial institutions.

HARD TIMES BUILD CHARACTER

Time has told me that many people have gone from having very little to having very much in their lifetime. America offers freedom and opportunity. In our great country, a person can start out with very little and end up with remarkable wealth from sacrificing years of dedicated preparation for something better.

We attended an area church service to hear Gracia Burnham of Rosehill, Kansas, speak about her and her husband Martin's year of captivity in the Philippines. During their time in captivity, she shared how she had time to reflect on a number of things. She said, "We have a God who gave us Jesus who can give us all things if that is the desire of our heart." The beautiful thing about God is that he is interested in taking care of the needy. God wants us to hand over our needs to him. About midway through her book, *To Fly Again: Surviving the Tailspin of Life*, she says, "When life spins out of control and we can no longer manage our circumstances, we are forced to become more long-suffering, less demanding, more serene." Also, in writing to a deeply troubled man, Burnham said, "Your situation sounds very sad and hopeless. But that is exactly the kind of situation that God specializes in... making good come out of hopelessness..."[13]

In a study guide entitled *Ephesians*, by Faith Walk Bible Studies, the author, Bryson Smith, reminds us in lesson 3, Ephesians 2:1-22, that Paul, one of the greatest authors and disciples of all time, reminds us that we can achieve all things through Christ who strengthens us.[14]

START SAVING SOONER

Do you have a savings plan? If you don't have one, start immediately, even if it means depositing only a few dollars a week, as I've advocated earlier. Yes, only a few dollars a week!

Whether you start saving in small amounts or larger amounts, starting to save now is the most important. I will give you two examples, the first from one of our granddaughters and one from a friend about fictitious people like Tom and Tim below.

First, a story shared with me by one of my granddaughters who started a savings plan leading to larger amounts later: "a year ago, I had a bunch of crumpled up one-dollar bills and thought of them as a hassle. Then, I thought, why not start saving them? Every dollar bill I got in change, I would stuff in my gallon jar in my room. To my amazement, within two months, I had collected $200. It was exciting to have a new challenge of finding how quickly my savings grew." You might try something like this.

Most banks will not charge anything for starting a personal savings account. Everyone needs a small nest egg to borrow from in an emergency. A savings account can also act as a good credit reference when you need to borrow a larger amount from a bank or credit union. Savings accounts add credibility to making applications for credit or making purchases. Please allow it to grow. Savings accounts indicate you are disciplined.

The following example of Tom and Tim's savings practices were prepared by a retirement income planner and long-time friend. It is an example of how two people started putting away money into a retirement savings plan, one early in life and the other later.

"Two friends, Tom and Tim, are both 20 years old. Tom decides to begin right away saving toward retirement. Tim on the other hand feels that he has many years before he needs to begin worrying about this, so he is going to wait till later. Here is how their decisions turn out.

Tom begins saving $25/week in an account that earns 4% interest. He does this for 15 years—from age 20 to age 35—and then makes no additional contributions to this account.

Tim waits until he is 35, and then decides he better start saving, so he begins saving $25/week in an account that earns 4% interest. He does this for 30 years.

At age 65: Tom paid in $19,500, and his account is worth $88,738. Tim paid in twice as much as Tom—$39,000—yet his account is worth only $75,430."

Here is the conclusion: "Tom contributed for half as many years as Tim, but ends up with over $13,000 more, just because he started early." [15]

Also, by starting early you add to your net worth, allowing you to have more borrowing ability for buying a house or another type of investment.

I met a man lately who did not have either a savings account or checking account. Both are helpful and essential to advancing in the job world and building your own retirement funds. This is one of the smart things to do as you are making a plan for yourself or your family. Go in and meet with a bank representative. Plan in advance what you want to say to get the conversation started on the right foot. As the saying goes, "First impressions are lasting impressions." Keep this first-time meeting very brief, maybe 5 or 10 minutes. Do some of the same things you would do in an interview. Listen to his/her advice very closely. Be sure to thank the people you have met.

FILING INFORMATION

A good inventory of all monies, software, hardware, equipment, supplies, household holdings, cars, real estate, investments, insurance plans, agreements, and contracts can give a better sense of organization. You'll need this if you figure your net worth (see Appendix for a net worth form). Without a sense of retrieval ease, filed information becomes almost useless to make good decisions. Your potential for becoming successful is minimized. The organized person can make much better decisions for each situation if the total picture is better known and studied before a decision is made and put into action. A good decision-maker is born by having more facts at hand in a moment of decision. Knowing where all your records are is just another piece in the puzzle toward climbing the success ladder. Know the facts. Avoid guessing at making important decisions. After studying the facts, decision-making becomes more efficient.

An adequate record-keeping system helps save time. Our self-esteem probably gets a shot of adrenalin by knowing where to find a file or important document immediately. Take charge and know what you have at your finger tips.

The following two paragraphs will give many hints about hard copy filing. Even if you were to use a computer to organize your files, it may still be best to keep a place for filing important paper copies also. This is only one of many ways to do it. There are probably as many ways to do record keeping as there are people doing filing.

A used two-drawer file cabinet can be easily purchased for a reasonable amount. Next, find a comfortable, well-lighted place in the corner of your apartment or home. Decide where the filing cabinet will be best located, within reach of your desk or table. Also, find a comfortable office chair. A chair with wheels works best in an office area with a vinyl mat, if it's on carpet. Get a box, basket or tray to keep all your incoming mail, a second basket or tray for bills to be paid, and a third for the mail that needs to go out immediately. Find other places to put all other mail such as magazines and newspaper for reading later. Determine a set time to pick up and sort through the mail daily. Avoid sorting the mail over and over again; this can waste some of your time and may cause you to lose or misplace papers!

You can choose additional items you want in your office. Some suggestions, along with your computer and printer: telephone, a 4-6 tier manila folder rack for filing paper work quickly, address books, and area phone books. Arrange a place for storing all your office supplies close to the well-lit office center. You will probably use and like this area more if it is equipped with items you like, such as your favorite framed photo or small plant.

What about your state and federal income taxes? It is a good idea to keep given categories of receipts and information together for completing your income taxes even if you aren't itemizing yet. Ask for and save all receipts whether you pay by credit card, cash, or check. This practice could be used for strengthening your budgeting. If manila folders are used, start with printing key words on the tabs with a med-point black marker. Make manila file folders for things such as: **Bank business, Church, Insurances, Inventory, Investments, Medical, Receipts, Utilities, Vehicle, Warranties**, etc. Be very careful not to misfile papers. Continue to place paperwork into the front of the folder each time. By doing this, you end up having the most current in the front and the oldest paperwork in the back. Reuse folders by putting on new sticky strips.

Take an inventory of everything you own. You may use the inventory list from the Appendix and then add or subtract from it as needed. Be specific about the items and estimates of worth. Take pictures of things and place them in a bank safe box or at another location. This list could help for personal property insurance planning as well.

Choose a place out of the office area to store old and inactive business so it doesn't clutter the active business going on during the current year. I do this at the end of each year as I prepare to do taxes. Each box of old business should be marked on the edge so information can be retrieved at least for seven years back without a big loss of time. Consider this aspect very important! The above arrangement is by no means the only option, but it is a start toward getting a filing system in place and then it can be improved each year.

BARTER TO SAVE CASH

Bartering is trading services or items with someone instead of using cash. When bartering, cash will be saved for something else and the budget will go further. Basically, this is what bartering is all about.

Here is an example of bartering. A friend has chickens that lay eggs and you want to buy two dozen. You don't have cash for eggs, but have a strawberry patch. Your friend likes strawberries so you tell them that if they give you eggs, they can pick strawberries out of your patch for the same amount you owe for the eggs. You're saving your cash and trading the strawberries for the eggs. Almost everything can be bartered, including labor.

Persons who barter are required to report their income value received when they do their taxes. Let's say you spend $200 bartering for paint from another barter member. You pay with a barter check. The barter bank deducts $200 from your barter bank checking account. The paint may or may not have been lost inventory, but was still in good shape. Another party gives you a $300 barter check for the labor you charged them for services. You deposit $300 into your barter checking account. Now you are $100 to the good, less some barter banking transaction service charges. Your trading does not have to be equally the same or with the same party. It is as easy as running a checking account through an ordinary bank, except the bartering is handled through a "bartering banking organization."

More **strengths** are that barter members can afford to open up new transactions without having large cash expenditures. Many times I would buy for less with a barter check and then sell to someone else for a cash gain. We used the restaurants sometimes and did not spend a dime for the service or food. Being in the carpentry and painting business, it seemed there were more barter patrons wanting us to come work for them than working for cash paying customers. Therefore, it was easier to build up barter dollars. There are companies in some metropolitan areas that have groups of people signed up to do bartering among one another. The bartering establishment (barter bank) keeps a running balance of all the trading, then gives you a monthly statement just like the bank would do for your cash trading on your checking account. At the end of the year, the bartering organization sends you an income/expense statement for tax purposes. When I was in the remodeling business, I could sell used or small amounts of material at the Barter Auction for good prices, again increasing my balance of barter dollars in the account. For instance, it was easier to sell some stuff, cut offs, items of very little cash value, and things I would have normally had to sell near junk price at a garage sale.

Some of the barter **weaknesses** are: do not relax the need for having a contract or hard copy as evidence for the exchange of everything. Don't spend your barter dollars just because it seems free. Sometimes you would have to go more miles to buy or sell. Watch out for outdated or defective merchandise. In my opinion, barter works better in a metropolitan area. There may not be a barter organization in your area. Also, I found there may be less supply needs in some categories such as buying groceries, medical availability, buying gas for your vehicle, buying a vehicle with only the options you want, or buying insurance, as examples. For that reason, check out how many barter members there are in your buying and purchasing area and what they want to barter.

You can check the Barter Bank charges for their services before you start an account. The bartering company, acting like a bank, charges X amount for the services rendered to you, and bills you with a monthly statement for all the transactions as a servicing fee.

As a precaution, start off on a very small basis the first few times or months, "to get a handle on things," so you can have a good experience.

MAKING SMARTER PURCHASES SAVES CASH

If you're involved with buying products or parts for your employer, this section may be of real importance for you. If not, perhaps some of the ideas could be applied to buying for your own personal uses.

We all know choosing between products is sometimes difficult to get the best buy. Better material in a manufactured product usually lasts longer. Quality material may look better and will probably perform better in the long run.

BUY TO GET MORE VALUE OUT OF A BUCK

Spend your dollars advantageously. If you pay 10-25% more initially and it is guaranteed to last three times longer, that is good. This reflects upon your ability to make good financial decisions. A good money manager invests for the future. This may result in more equity income as time goes on.

BUY WITHIN THE BUDGET

Buying a lower quality product may reflect upon one's judgment in the eyes of observers. Buying a less expensive product may be OK. Who knows, one of the observers may be your future manager. I'm not saying this will happen, but why take a chance with the unexpected. I'm a believer in advocating that you spend within your budgeted means. Whether you're buying for yourself or the company, it involves good judgment to stay within the budget.

BUY BEST VALUE

Let's pretend you have a $500 line item for furniture in your budget on the job. You work as a crew chief on the production line in a factory. Your boss recommends you buy a desk for filing your paperwork. You can probably buy a used desk for as little as $100, made with a particle board core, versus $200 for a desk made of solid lumber or metal. In several years, the particle board desk with a thin plastic film covering will look tattered and be worth very little. Most likely, the solid lumber or metal desk will not only last much longer, but will continue to look better into the future. I would suggest purchasing the one which will last much longer. This purchase reflects upon your ability to make good judgments.

BUY RIGHT AND VALUE INCREASES

As an example, my wife and I purchased a piece of oak furniture at a family silent auction. I'm sure we paid much more than our grandparents did many years ago. The piece has held its original beauty. It has probably appreciated (gained) in value by more than 50% of its original value. Presently, we could probably get more than the value paid for it at the sale.

My dad did a similar thing on the farm by purchasing a John Deere 3010 tractor. After the purchase and using the tractor for a couple of seasons, he sold it for more than he initially paid. How could he get more for it after using it for two years? He took very good care of the tractor those two years. The tractor held its value because of the brand name, reputation, quality, performance, popularity, and demand.

BUY TO SAVE TIME AND MONEY

Just one more example—I was painting our house and caught myself going away from the principle of buying quality material to achieve better results, as I'm advocating to you. To my knowledge, the inexpensive paint had no plastic polymers in it, and it shrank, dried too rapidly, and left hairline cracks. After making the discovery, I went to buy a better quality of paint. I needed a paint that would not break apart, would stay flexible, and would have good covering ability. This better quality paint job would probably last five to ten years rather than three to five years.

BUY RIGHT CHOICE

As for making choices to purchase different products, there are probably more choices to consider than particles of sand on a beach. This takes into account formulas, textures, shades, colors, qualities, and more. More is said about this in the following paragraph. This complicates the purchasing of merchandise! Do your research well before making the final decision on a product. Run it past another person to get advice and find out what works well for him or her. If the product is for a client or an employer on the job, review the successful procedures used in the past.

Following are additional considerations for making product choices. How well is it accepted within the circles of people you know? Who will use it? How about comparative costs? How about compression and tensile strength, texture, color coordination, and overall appearance? Durability to last in extremes of hot or cold temperatures, elasticity, and ductility are very important. How will the weight, shipping, and handling factor into the purchase? Service to the customer, availability on demand, recommended life span, replacement ability, and cost of installation need to be studied. What about convenience, design coordination, beauty, environmental and green application, moisture resistance, and fading resistance? Does the size and shape of the product fulfill the need? Will the product prove to have investment potential? Is it competitively priced? And finally, is it safe and how long will it hold up to the demands of the customer?

BUY THE NEXT GENERATION OF MATERIALS

Synthetics and composites are becoming a way of life in material use. The plastics or synthetics industry offers a large part needed in the material industry. What will be the next generation of materials? For anyone working in purchasing, it's helpful to become aware of the latest materials. Composites and special carbon materials are becoming more prevalent. I'd encourage you to do your research and study the options available to stretch your dollars, as this can result in buying more for less.

BUY SMARTER, USING GOOD RATIONALE

So now—do you purchase the better merchandise or the cheapest? A better way to phrase the question is, should you pay more or settle on the less-expensive product? The more expensive product choice may likely be the best in the end. Yes, many times it follows this pattern of "what you pay is what you get," **but that is not always the case!** Take into consideration, the better product may be priced down a good percentage because:

- the retailer has an over-supply
- an old model needs liquidated, clearing the inventory for new products
- business needs quick cash flow, so certain things are priced down to sell quickly
- the product does not have the marked-up sales potential the newer one will have
- the product has a small weakness that does not affect its performance
- it does not meet the new trend of color(s) or style

- there was a mistake in production and too many were produced
- the season is finished for the product and the in-season stuff needs to go on display
- the merchandiser is sizing down inventory to enable paying less income taxes
- the business is selling particular merchandise to get it into the hands of customers
- selling at much less may help knock out the competition in the same market
- the merchandise is being sold out to finalize a bankruptcy
- someone is retiring and they can't continue their business
- a product is discounted as a loss leader to bring in people who may buy other products
- they may want service or sell it fast before the competitors' sales begin
- the product may not have sold earlier because it was not initially displayed correctly.

Becoming smarter in buying merchandise reflects upon your ability to know how to handle money better. This may have implications for better employment.

BUY AFTER CHECKING INVENTORY

On the job, you would probably want to check first whether current or old inventory can be used before ordering new. Check the condition of the old material, where and how it's been used, versus the current need. Then you and others must evaluate whether using the present and/or past inventory is best.

BUY AFTER YOU'VE WEIGHED IN ON ADVICE

Perhaps you should engage someone who is more knowledgeable. Or, perhaps there are people who would help you if you ask them. Companies hire consultants to help make good decisions because they know the payback can generally outweigh the consultant's fee and most often produces better results in the end. So it may be advantageous for any success-driven person to become more knowledgeable or check with other people regularly about product selections.

THE PAYCHECK

So what about the paycheck? Some employees say the check is everything, but others see job benefits as equally important on the job.

Here are two important considerations:

First consideration: I like the quote given in the book *Successful Living: A Study of Bible-Based Economic and Lifestyle Principles*, by Luke Weaver. He says, "It has been said that we should live by the 10-10-80 formula, meaning that we should give away 10%, save 10%, and live on the remaining 80%."[16]

We try to set aside the first 10% of our income for the Lord's work, as learned in Genesis 28:22 and Proverbs 3:9.

Second consideration: prepare to increase your paycheck potential by strengthening your portfolio. That means your interview application and resumé have the potential of becoming more convincing.

As you receive more and more money on the paycheck, you may want your employer to invest some of your earnings into a tax shelter plan. Depending on the tax bracket you're in, it may be to your advantage to defer some of the cash income presently to pay less taxes. Start out with small amounts.

If you're working for a large progressive company, maybe it's as simple as investing a small portion of your paycheck in the company who employs you. Ask about the tax advantages and the long-term security and growth of your probable investment.

I've heard from sources that each year of college education may be equal to a potential increase on the paycheck. Go see a college admissions counselor to check what you can earn with different career paths. Of course, I must be first to say that college is not the only way to get pay increases. I've met many successful people with a high school diploma and many more successful people with only one year of college. This may bring us right back to soft skills and interpersonal social issues on and off the job that earn increases for the paycheck.

You have been reading suggestions to increase your monthly paycheck. This is the time in your life which can make a big difference. Take charge now. I wouldn't suggest you wait till later. Maybe it's like Tom and Tim earlier in the chapter about "Starting to Save Sooner." Tim waited and Tom took charge by acting early. Also, by planning early to make interpersonal social changes in your life now, probably would equate to experiencing comfortable raises in your paycheck sooner than later.

INSURANCE

Find an insurance agent who has been recommended to you by a friend in your own community. Call the agency to make arrangements for an appointment to visit about all your basic insurance needs. Share with the insurance agent that you have questions and need good counsel. At this time agents do not charge a fee for this. It is free.

The following paragraph is some basic advice by Harms Insurance Services in our community. I hope this is enough to get you started with questions for insurance.

"If you own a vehicle, you must by law, have auto insurance. If you have a loan on your vehicle, the bank will require you to have full coverage on the vehicle. If no loan on the vehicle, you might want to carry minimum liability limits on the vehicle. On the other hand you want to have liability limits high enough to protect your assets (vehicles, home, personal property, land, etc.) in the event you were liable for causing bodily injury or property damage to someone else or their property. Cost of the insurance depends on the number of cars, the limits of liability, the deductibles for comprehensive and collision, age of the drivers, the driving records of the drivers, and your credit or insurance score. Another consideration for insurance is to protect your personal property or home if you own it. A homeowner policy will include coverage for the house, your personal property, and personal liability. There will be a deductible, which is what you will pay if you have a loss. If you do not own a house, you can get coverage for just your personal property." [17]

Perhaps you own a mobile home rather than a house. As long as you keep the mobile home in repair and tip top shape you'll probably get your money back and have gained some equity. That's good, you are investing, rather than losing it in rent money. If so, you still want to be prepared to cover a catastrophe like a fire or a major storm so you don't lose your investment. A fire or storm could exhaust your savings and/or cash flow. Also, without insurance it is harder to budget for the unexpected. I recommend you build in some security for yourself for peace of mind.

You can learn much from visiting with insurance agents. Maybe you can find a friend who could recommend some reliable person from an insurance agency. Otherwise, find helpful insurance agencies in the Yellow Pages. Also, another place to get answers to your questions about insurance is to use your favorite Internet search engine and type in "insurance commissioner" to get more information on insurance(s).

CHAPTER EIGHT SUMMARY

What are your financial goals in life? This is a very important issue in the success of following your dreams. It's about allowing other trusted friends close to you to be involved in surrounding and supporting your endeavors. The bottom line is, how much do you want to earn and how hard are you willing to work to reach these goals?

CHAPTER 9

DOES MANAGEMENT CARE?

THE COMPANY POLICY MANUAL

Nearly every company has a company policy. But not all establishments have booklets in written form for all employees. Usually, if the company has an employee manual or booklet, they give it to you when you're first hired. If you've been given a company manual, read it well! It's even more important as you read the policy manual, **to consider its implications**! Information can easily be misunderstood, so read it twice and three times again. Allow your supervisor to help you become informed.

As an employee, your work is much more impressive if it meets company guidelines and aligns with the company mission statement. In my life time, I took things like this for granted too often. Management may assume you know company policy and all that is expected of you. Not knowing policy may be the reason an employee goes off in the wrong direction on occasion. It is wise to align your hard work with company objectives so your efforts will not go unnoticed.

Back in chapter 4, I discussed the topic, "Goes with the territory." Not all your responsibilities will be in writing, word-for-word as explained in the company work manual. Maybe you will want to review implied expectations.

During my years of counseling, some adults shared with me about failing to know the company policies. One example was a business that did not approve overtime, unless approved in advance. So the challenge is—try to follow company policies.

BE LOYAL AND SUPPORTIVE

Company policy drives the impetus for the organization. The president or CEO carries out the decisions made by the board. Your boss makes decisions based on the directives handed down to him or her. Management makes choices to put these decisions, systems, or regulations into practice. Many of the decisions by management end up in company policy manuals.

Management may not be able to tell employees all the rationale or confidential information used for decisions. The timing is usually very important for announcements within a company. However, the project or plan could be misunderstood. That is one reason why some decisions aren't always immediately shared with employees. As an employee, meet the challenges and aspire to do the work to the best of your ability and have confidence in the managers, supervisors, and upper management.

When management does ask for input, go ahead and share, but choose your words well. Make it short and keep an upbeat attitude. Show confidence and a genuine smile. Try aiming to please! Let your supervisor see your true colors.

Following is a short list, I put together, to help you support company policy:

- Make your own detailed list of the changes going on around you to think about.
- Go with the flow; making the best of each day without a lot of unnecessary apprehension.
- Do not speak badly about the management or the company.
- When bulletins are posted and new data comes your way, be serious about studying the content and then try to decide how it positively affects your job.
- Attend meetings planned by management to be a well-informed employee.
- Pray to God asking for guidance in your efforts at work.
- Offer to work with new projects.
- Surprise your co-workers with new enthusiasm.
- Step up to your potential—**be genuine and supportive of the boss.**
- Search for your best. Be a hard worker, showing a good work ethic.
- **You may now have positioned yourself for opening up a whole new level of loyalty to the boss and others in your work area.**

AN AGREEABLE PERSONALITY

You will make many choices on a daily basis at work. You can make the choice to support people whether you're off the job or at work.

At work, when your boss is looking for feedback suggestions, he or she will most likely look to those who have listened, shared, and tried to be agreeable. Consider the old cliché— put on a happy face from when the sun rises until the sun sets. When we're thankful and choose to be agreeable, our face reflects enthusiasm and appreciation to those around us.

Smiling Won't Cost A Dime.
To Not Smile, May Cost You Your Job Or A Raise!

The challenging economic times experienced during times of recession, required people to be even more agreeable in handling expectations everywhere. Supervisors, selected to lead others, have the goal to be aware of skilled employees who are **pleasant team players, cheerful, and solution-oriented**. Lead persons are always looking for these persons to hire and promote when times are good or bad.

WORKING A SECOND JOB

Second jobs might cause some challenges with the primary job. I would recommend, if possible, do well with your primary job. If you need to earn more, try to be sure your second job is flexible. Maybe that is not possible for you presently. Every job requires concentration, dedication, presence, and energy. We must consider these requirements when choosing how to spend our time. When people have second jobs, overtime may become an issue. The bottom line is: allow your employer to feel they are taking good care of you with your primary job.

Another challenge can happen while working a second job: You've been asked to come in to do a special project with your primary job and you decline because of the second job. This may cause your primary employer to raise questions about your dedication to your first and primary job. You will want to focus on priorities.

If you must work at more than one job, decide which job takes priority. Which job may have the best options to turn into a better full-time job? I would encourage you to work the secondary job only when the primary job has been taken care of well. Work the second job as a supplemental income even though both jobs may be half-time. In conclusion, avoid jeopardizing your primary job with a second paying job if you must work at more than one employment job.

ENTREPRENEURSHIP

Would I recommend starting your own business as an entrepreneur? Would your employer care? I can't give you a yes or no. Most businesses want your full undivided time as an employee. It's much like working a second job, as talked about in the last topic. If you are absolutely sure of wanting to try this, you must have more than average drive and dedication. Working as owner of a business takes excellent planning and vision. I'd strongly recommend you listen carefully to a friend or supporter about whether they would encourage you to start your own business. Those that have started and succeeded most often have had the support of other individuals. Then, after they started the new business successfully, they continued to receive support about financial planning and counsel on a regular basis. More is said about entrepreneurship at the end of Chapter 17.

"THAT'S OUR POLICY!"

When sending a message to a customer about a product, and they seem to be unclear about it, I suggest you explain why it is, in an easy to understand manner as you also share the phrase, "That's our policy." However, do not overwork this phrase. Share the company's position with your customer in a pleasant, courteous voice, being very respectful and to the point. Try to make your communication satisfying for your customer or visitor to hear.

SHOW APPRECIATION FOR GIFTS

A verbal or written thank you must always follow a gift given to you. Following up with a thank you is an expected courtesy.

Come to think about it, my neighbor helped me scoop my snowy walks off, and I will let him know how much I appreciated his help. I should not procrastinate.

What has been your experience? Have you had a person help you lately or give you a gift? A thank you in person is usually better. The face-to-face recognition is usually more personable. Which ever do it ASAP (as soon as possible) so they will know their generosity was appreciated.

Perhaps you enjoy creating your own thank-you cards, or shopping at retail stores for notes. By all means, try to follow through with some form of thank you appreciation. Expressions of thanks are remembered!

WHAT IS TOTAL QUALITY MANAGEMENT?

I've included this topic, Total Quality Management, because many companies take this very seriously. As an employee, you too must see TQM as a way to increase production efficiency and profits for the company you work for.

The website www.answers.com gives several definitions for TQM that I particularly like. First, from the Britannica Concise Encyclopedia: "Management practices designed to improve the performance of organizational processes in business and industry."[1]

Second, I also like the definition quote from the Accounting Dictionary which says: "Approach to quality that emphasizes continuous improvement, a philosophy of **doing it right the first time** and striving for zero defects and elimination of all waste. It is a concept of using quality methods and techniques to strategic advantage within firms."[2]

Here's how I think TQM could affect you: You may be working in some type of a support job and must realize the people you support or work with are held responsible to meet a certain measure of excellence to keep their job. I can't emphasize this enough! If the company is part of a TQM program, your performance is tied to this effort also. As a result, you may need to be even more sensitive to co-workers, the company's needs, and your job requirements.

RESPECT CLIENTELE VISITS

Visitors can sense if they enter a business and are not recognized and welcomed. It's important to treat visiting business clientele with nothing less than the best. The way employees treat others can reflect back upon the whole business. **Your visitors could be "here today and gone tomorrow" in a global economy. Treat your visitors, clientele reps and customers like they are your only customer! Many employees may have worked themselves up the employment ladder because of the way they treated people, especially visitors.**

Sales are increased by showing respect to visiting clientele. So, it is my rule that I simply treat everyone as if they will be giving me my next paycheck.

People want to be treated with respect. One of my highest goals is to try to be respectful to others. Very successful businesses know their customers want to be recognized and appreciated for coming to them. Sometimes actions speak louder than words.

STAY OFF THE GRASS

The sign reads, "Stay Off the Grass." Considerable hard work goes into keeping a lawn looking good. A beautiful stand of manicured grass as part of the landscape is expensive, and says much about the employer. Perhaps the employer will take care of its employees the same way. In retrospect, people that come and go should respect the company efforts to keep a beautiful landscape looking good.

A new lawn for the landscape takes many hours of planning even before the grading and contouring stage. Checking to make sure the lay of the land will shed water is important. After the contouring ends, large stones and clods are removed. The kind of new soil is considered. Next, testing of soil acidity is a good investment of time and money. Some put in sprinkler watering systems before the seed is sowed. Seed is very expensive. Crisscrossing the sowing pattern to avoid unplanted strips gives assured coverage. Research takes place in getting a name brand fertilizer. If the ground is hard, lime or gypsum can be applied. The soil is rolled if the ground has half-inch and larger clods. If a sprinkler system is not put in, preparation of a temporary watering system of hoses and sprinklers is needed to avoid the need to move hoses from spot to spot, making it easy to turn the water off and on regularly, keeping the top soil wet at all times. When the seed is kept wet, it won't dry out and stunt growth or prevent germination of the seed. All those things take a lot of time and money.

Maybe you have done lawn work and know the hours of hard work and expense that goes into the planting of lawn grass. Next time you are tempted to walk across the grass at a workplace, remember the story I shared with you today.

Also, there could be a remote chance someone is watching to see if you follow the sidewalk, after applying for work at the business. They may be deciding whether you'd be a good employee prospect.

MAINTAIN CLEAN WORK VEHICLE

I would guess a clean vehicle says something about our attitudes. Have you ever heard someone say, "Your attitude is showing?" A clean vehicle, just like a clean dress or pants, inevitably may tell others whether we have a good attitude. Even the inside of the car speaks louder than words. Avoid allowing things to get messy. Whether it is your personal room, the inside or outside of your car, wherever; you never know when someone will see and perhaps "read you wrong," as the saying goes. There are exceptions to the above statements, but people form impressions about others. What happens if the person hiring for a job or job promotion focuses on this? The person hiring or giving the promotion may be the person you saw yesterday.

I knew a very successful construction firm which focused on hiring a worker simply based on whether the applicant kept his or her tools clean and neatly organized. The person in charge of hiring would go all the way through the interview and later in the discussion would subtly manage to see the inside of their car, and you can guess the rest of the story.

So I remind you to not only keep yourself clean and organized but all your possessions as well. You don't know what an employer will pick to focus on.

YOUR LIFE AMBITIONS

Do you want to be a shift lead person, become a city employee, own your home or business, receive a college degree, construction worker, lead man or woman on a manufacturing production line, day shift manager at a fast food place, sales person for some automobile dealership, work for the county assessment office, marry some day and raise a family, teacher, be a cashier, or maybe be an assistant to a department manager?

My suggestion is to **set your own realistic goals while allowing others to have different goals.** Try to fit in without making a big ordeal of your differences. Lead a life of trying to get along with others, and try not to out-do them. All of us can set our own goals and try to achieve them. Try to write about your ambitions and review them occasionally.

COMPANY EXHIBIT

Some day, you may be asked or volunteer to help with a company exhibit and perhaps get involved with planning before the event. I hope you can have an opportunity of this nature.

This is a time to show your colors, a time to show your employer how valuable you are as an employee. It is an honor to be invited to work an exhibit for the company! Working the exhibit will allow you to meet people you didn't expect to meet. It will strengthen all your skills so you can do even better in your assigned job.

Building an attractive exhibit has potential for both you and the company. I'm not an authority on putting together a display, but have arranged many displays and exhibits. A good exhibit takes time to put together. Preparation is done far in advance. The preparation involves targeting a certain audience. What will they expect to hear and see? What will attract the attention of guests and make it presentable for guests coming to the exhibit? When are the best hours to see the exhibit? How can it be placed in the path of people, realizing the attendees may see it well in advance of getting to the display? From what distance will they see the message you have for them? How large should the exhibit display letters be to give a message you're trying to emphasize? Keep the words to a minimum. Give the viewers one to three eye-catching things to bring them closer to the exhibit and to become inquisitive. Striking colors are necessary that go together tastefully with rhythm and balance. Build the theme around a goal so the client will not go away confused. As the client comes by, give them a warm reception. The team must try to give the same message. Learn how to close the sale if it's sales you're after.

The appearance and words in the exhibit are so important, initially, because you have only seconds to make the right impression of communication.

BE MORE PROFESSIONAL

Employers notice the mannerisms and habits of conduct in people's daily lives. Especially for middle-income employees, employers are looking for hard working, good thinking, and trustworthy help who present themselves well. Whether you're working in a job now or are looking for a job, I encourage you to evaluate your mannerisms and habits of conduct that could be standing in your way. Consider becoming more professional in your dealings with people.

Being professional is defined in my Webster's Improved Dictionary and Everyday Encyclopedia as "one who makes his living by his art, as distinguished from an amateur." Amateurish persons are "superficial; shallow." [3]

If you're a person who may raise doubts for the employer, being insincere about how good of a worker you are, determine how you want to be more than just an amateur. We have many choices in life every day. We can choose to do things that will help us be the kind of employee the employer is looking to train for the long haul.

I've made a list of some **things that may need re-visited.**

- Show kindness even in tense situations.
- Avoid interrupting others when they're speaking or concentrating.
- Have a conscience to avoid stealing, even small stuff.
- I will not to chew my fingernails or crack my neck around others.
- If I'm using drugs in the wrong way, I will try to get help.
- If I find myself getting intoxicated, I will examine what is going on in my life.
- Am I avoiding the use of derogatory remarks?
- Am I willing to strive for errorless quality work, sales, projects, or products?
- Do I strive to show a good personality through a soft, quiet demeanor?
- Avoid getting attention in the wrong way, at the wrong time and place.
- Guard against losing my drive to enroll in classes or seminars.
- If the discussion does not suit me, I will be patient and leave when appropriate.
- Care enough to look my best at all times when out in public.
- If I see another person being bullied, I will help correct the problem.
- I will not try to get away with things the easy way by letting others do it.
- I will spend my valuable time reading and looking at appropriate stuff.
- Use body deodorant, toothbrush, and comb or brush once or more daily.
- Work to keep good company and hang out with the right crowd.
- Be aware of facing someone and looking in their eyes while speaking to them.
- Avoid taking advantage of other people.
- Pay bills on time, go places on time, and meet deadlines.
- Try to live my life by avoiding carelessness and trouble with the law.
- Work at having good credit.
- Do I talk too much and miss valuable, helpful information from others?
- Even though I may struggle with inadequate spelling, verbal skills, writing skills, reading skills, or math, I'm trying to correct these issues.
- Do I ever try to cover over with untruths to make myself look good?
- I have a code of ethics which will help me accept help with my weaknesses.

- If I have no high school diploma, I will work toward that equivalency.
- I have given time and energy to get my resumé right.
- I've developed a good outlook on life and can wear a smile all the time.

Everyone has weaknesses which must be worked on for improvement, including myself. Make your own list for improvement. You and I both know we have it within our power to be more than we are! The important thing about it all is that you act upon these matters with diligence. Does management care? Yes they do! Most lead people and management in general, care enough, wanting the best to come out in their employees. You're no exception.

Maybe I should be asking which comes first, "the chicken or the egg?" We do not need to answer that question, but in the matter of which comes first in a job setting, increased wages or your increased performance, your increased performance most likely comes first.

CHAPTER NINE SUMMARY

Management individuals do care about employees. I would guess that they work hard to encourage employees to do their best, so the business or organization can do well. It is important, as an employee, that you trust their decisions to manage affairs. On a daily basis, you can develop your own daily personal goals to do your part in the business and workplace. When every individual carries their load, the workforce can reach higher company goals. You may want to continue reading about more than just the tips in this book. There can be hope for all of us, if we work hard to become a more trusted, reliable long-term employee.

CHAPTER 10

ENABLING RESUMÉ

Your daily diet of interests will potentially add or subtract from accomplishments for the resumé.

PREPARING YOUR RESUMÉ

How can you put together a resumé that shows you will be a valuable employee?

If you do not have a resumé, you could prepare one. For your convenience, find a sample resumé form following Chapter 18 in the Appendix. You have permission to copy and use it. If you do not use this resumé form, look for more examples in business books and other resources.

During a job interview, the interviewer may ask whether you have a resumé. Be ready to give a completed resumé to the interviewer. Very few persons can prepare a good resumé in a rush situation, especially when times are difficult or during busy days. Resumés tell a complete story of your accomplishments.

Will you have ample information to enter into each of the categories to land the right kind of job? What facts can you include that say, "I am the best candidate and person you want for the job." Find someone to help you prepare and edit your resumé, such as Workforce Centers or an organization attending the jobs fair, so the language is more convincing and enlightening. Even if you must spend a few dollars, this would be an excellent investment to have another person look at your resumé to build on your strengths.

Before you fill in the final resumé form, make blank copies so you can add changes again and again. When everything has been finalized, produce the final copy in type or ink, resulting in an errorless final document. If you make only one mistake, it's worth the time to correct it, even if it means starting over. Avoid misspelled words. Stay with single spacing. Use good grammar and punctuation, without blemishes. Remember—this resumé represents you.

EXTRACURRICULAR ACTIVITIES

Following are more ideas that could strengthen your resumé. Think about each entry closely. Perhaps one or more of the ideas below could be very valuable in giving you the opportunity to hear the news, "You're hired!"

- Join a professional association that publishes a magazine for reading.
- Involve yourself in a club or user group with others to exchange job interests.

- Become a volunteer.
- Join a community sporting events group that meets for fun weekly.
- Seek out friends and acquaintances who have similar interests.
- Find friends who have the same age children or the same enjoyable hobbies.
- Make a wise investment purchase that may help you meet new people.
- Go to the coffee shop with the idea that you will build friendships and learn more.
- Go on a weekend excursion with your wife or friend to some beautiful place.
- Listen closely to things your boss likes and then try it out if it's appropriate.

THINGS AROUND US MATTER

Put yourself in a pleasing mood as much as possible! By surrounding yourself with pleasing objects or atmosphere, you may place yourself into a productive and ambitious state of mind to accomplish more. You need a mostly constant, positive attitude with a yes mood, "Yes I…did." This kind of character mind-set has the potential to lead you into many positive life experiences. Set the stage for accomplishments leading to items on the resumé.

Appropriate art forms can be subconsciously refreshing and uplifting while poor art forms may tax the mind and body negatively. Poor art forms may de-energize the mind in such a way that you are preoccupied. As a result, you may have less time to spend on the pleasing experiences leading to accomplishments you can enter onto the resumé. If you have an area where you spend most of the day, surround yourself with pleasing art forms such as exciting décor, wall hangings, family pictures, attractive work outfits, valued objects, nice furnishings, colorful tools, and things that align with the company or institution initiatives. Memories of past success stories, exciting pictures of company events, and company products follow the same pattern.

Along the same train of thought, well-maintained surfaces, tools, and equipment can make your job something you look forward to continuing day after day. Arrange to keep the surrounding job area pleasing. Even the clothing you wear should be in good taste to help you feel energized and not de-energized.

This applies every time you leave the house! Dress yourself for success. Appearance is not everything but says much about your personality. By putting yourself in a positive, energized mood, you may encourage others to "catch the positive energy." This can have a good, mushrooming effect. Employers want to see positive, energetic dispositions and moods in employees.

I must caution you: there can be a problem of cluttering your life with clutter and things you don't need, thinking you'll make yourself happy with it all. The majority of the time, quality of things is more important than quantity. Consider continually removing the clutter in your life. This will allow room for the stuff which can add value to your life.

Another form of art appreciation happens in the art of conversation with people. Your communication with others is continually telling a story of what's in your heart. The game of charades demonstrates this concept. Persons use signals, body movements, or sketches to add to their verbal effectiveness. If you are time conscious, and I hope you are, you'll probably describe something with the facial expressions, arms, and finger motions. This can make conversation more effective. Our body's non-verbal movements, shapes, and positioning can send very important messages quickly.

Plan daily to put yourself into a positive, energized mood. As an example, you might want to think about the TV diet you surround yourself with daily. Are the shows you watch time effective and uplifting for strengthening your personality or are they usually the 'shoot-em-up' and the 'tear-em down' type of programming?

BALANCED LIFE ADDS CHARACTER

It is important to show that you have a balanced life for your interview or resumé. What do I think it means to have a balanced life? Too much time spent in any one of the four areas of life—Spiritual, Mental, Physical, and Social—could cause imbalance, creating weaknesses in our personality and character. How will you know when you don't have a good balance? I will try to answer this in the next paragraphs.

Consider staying in tune with the people close to you. Listen closely to advice they offer you. Others may give you subtle hints about not measuring up to their expectations. Listen for remarks from fellow workers on the job. Ponder these remarks during quiet times. Ask close family members and friends for feedback about remarks that don't add up to you— but, don't ask if you aren't really willing to change! Usually family and friends will be honest with you, if they feel you are open to it.

The following may be one way to accomplish a good balance. Arrange to go visit casually with your supervisor or boss. It probably is not necessary to make it a formal meeting. Ask if you can measure something on him or her.

As you may know, measuring something on someone means asking them to spare a couple of minutes to hear you share something important. If you have a lead person who agrees to hear you out, then proceed to run your thoughts past him or her for a reaction. Do not over react if you feel you're receiving the wrong answer. Just listen without interrupting and affirm what you're hearing. The rest of the discussion can be very interesting. After the discussion, it would be worth your time to jot down a few notes, evaluate and analyze the reactions shared during the time together.

> **A level-headed person strives to create a good balance for themselves in life.**

The following paragraphs are a continued attempt to share what I feel might help us to have a more balanced life. And by all means, please remember to keep a perspective, my comments are not scientific, only suggestions from experiences in my own life.

■ SPIRITUALLY

A balanced spiritual life can be cultivated with spiritual meditation, prayers to God, reading the Bible, active church participation, spending time visiting with Christian friends, sharing your blessings with others, and strengthening your ability to sense the Spirit's leading in your life. I advocate putting more emphasis on continual growth of your spiritual life! A good diet of reading the Bible can be fulfilling. Reading and hearing enriched stories and testimonies from other Christians leads to a more complete understanding of our heavenly Father's mission for all of us.

■ MENTALLY

Start by making it a practice to remember things, especially names of people. Once a good friend said to me, "Use association to remember names." He said, "My name is Bandy, you know, similar to the name for a type of rooster." I'll never forget his name after he gave me a lesson in association. I've heard that reading good magazines and books helps to strengthen our memory. Press your mind to memorize like persons exercise their body physically, to keep the mind tissues toned.

Try to feed your mind with the good and not the bad—listen to that little ticker close to your heart or your conscience. Press yourself to be involved with people interests.

Socialize by attending people events and enter into active wholesome discussion with them. Read, if you like, the paper, magazines, books, and keep your mind active. Singing and playing instruments invigorate the mind. Often it's how our mind perceives something, such as, is it "half full or half empty?" Obviously, the half full is the positive approach. The mind can be trained to see oneself as young and useful or old and grumpy. It's a matter of continual mental conditioning.

■ PHYSICALLY

I advocate having a good exercise program. Some of the statements following may be repeats from Chapter 7, "Commit to an Exercise Program," but the more important things in life could be revisited again and again.

Exercise no less than every other day until the heartbeat is raised significantly. Some say this means exercising for about 20 to 30 minutes so the heart rate can readily beat faster. Through regular exercise of this kind, the body has a better chance of keeping healthy. It may help to prevent colds and germs that could make us sick. It will help boost our energy level if it's not overdone. Exercise will help keep us thinking rationally and logically. My father shared with me that he attributes the recovery of his health partly to taking 20 deep breaths after awakening in the morning. Try taking a deep breath and holding it for a couple of seconds, letting all the air out and then repeating the same. Doesn't that feel good? You have the potential to bring in lots of fresh oxygen for the heart and mind by doing this. His exercise was a little bit like isometric exercises; stretching parts of the body, holding that position for awhile and releasing it. Try stretching out different parts of your body and then holding the different positions for a bit. This isometric exercise activity does not take expensive equipment. You don't have to go to the gym or sports health club and there is very little down time. With isometric exercises, parts of the body can be stretched to a stopping point and held in that position for approximately 5-10 seconds and then relaxed. I advocate that persons whose jobs do not demand a lot of physical walking and who have been concentrating immensely on detail for long periods, take time for isometric exercises if there are no provisions for getting up to walk around or take adequate breaks.

There are many books and magazines on physical fitness and body building for sale on the bookshelves in stores. I challenge you to find good articles about exercise and body conditioning.

▪ SOCIALLY

Strive for a good social life by learning to know friends. Treat them with respect and kindness as you would a brother or sister. As you learn to know them as good friends, you can laugh, share, and ask for their advice. You can meet together to exchange exciting things that are going on in your lives. This gives the mind a chance to let go and relax while dwelling on things that are worth living and working for. Without a social life with friends, life could become stagnated and dry. Our health depends on a vibrant experience with friends and family! We could easily become self-centered if we didn't mix and care for family, friends, and acquaintances. Our cares and our thoughts could turn to mostly ourselves, setting us up for the possibility of big disappointments or sickness.

Sometimes when someone says, "You've got to socialize," it is taken mistakenly as attending a big party with too much booze. How we act away from work is very important too! Consider being careful what you drink, since it could dim your senses (that is one reason why they say don't drink and drive) and cause you to do or say things that are embarrassing or disrespectful, maybe devastating. What happens if you said negative things about the company or management in your weakest moment? It wouldn't add points to your portfolio. Making good decisions are important while socializing with others. Summing it up—my definition of socializing is centered around the enjoyment of doing things with friends that help us develop character.

For instance, my wife and daughter went to Applebee's with me to enjoy lunch on my wife's birthday. Across from us were about ten working people probably from the same office area, who had arranged to meet for lunch and conversation. They seemed to be having a very good time. The following are some thoughts related to this.

If your supervisor or lead person asks you out to lunch with several others, it would be an opportunity for you to accept the offer. When appropriate, accept an invitation to do something special like enjoying leisure time together as a department, or attending a work-related dinner. If you decline an invitation, the person inviting you may think you don't want to take the time for the event. This may signal the wrong thing. Trying to work at being socially acceptable is expected in workplace circles. Many companies work toward keeping their employees a long time, hoping to see leadership potential develop as one of the team. If someone doesn't try to find time to socialize with others, there is the stigma you may not have potential leadership qualities as an employee.

If you're not making new friends occasionally, consider that change now. You may live a more exciting personal life, enjoying the friendship of others.

OPT TO SERVE AS A VOLUNTEER

Consider serving on a committee if given the opportunity. Promotions could happen when a supervisor, for instance, observes you as a committee member. They will know you want to contribute in different circumstances as an employee or in the community in which you live.

Yes, it may mean volunteering with others on a committee in the department, company, or community in special ways. Committee work often happens in clubs and civic groups.

Community service is a way to volunteer our time. Usually we cannot expect to be paid for community service work. This is our gift of time and goes with the territory. But on occasion, pay for serving on a committee may happen as part of the extended job assignment.

There is a place on the resumé for listing volunteer experiences. Be sure to include all your volunteering achievements on the resumé. Employers may be looking for people who have done volunteering for one reason or another. This has the potential to move you into being third, second, or maybe even first place in line for a better job or promotion. Yes, you've heard it before: along with other qualities, companies are looking for persons who reach out to help others without pay as a volunteer.

WHAT'S YOUR HOBBY?

The saying, "All work and no play makes Johnny a dull boy," has relevance. One important item when trying to help students put together a resumé in class was to check into what hobbies the person enjoyed. We worked together identifying and suggesting hobbies for them to start or continue enjoying while at the same time strengthening their resumé. Many students had fun realizing they have good hobbies, but were not listing them on their resumés.

Management likes to see resumés that have a variety of interests, which indicates the person is active and invigorated. In my opinion, without a hobby or extracurricular activities, you stand to experience burn-out much sooner at work. You may want to choose a hobby that is different than that of your working job. The mind needs a change of pace, time, and rest away from the responsibilities of the job so you can be refreshed again and again.

JOIN PROFESSIONAL ORGANIZATIONS

Professional organizations give the employee an edge to stay abreast of the latest changes and advances in the workplace. Without keeping up with new improvements, job security might be jeopardized. If you are not taking advantage of professional trade magazines and meetings, the competition may be doing it. This could mean trouble for you down the road for keeping a competitive edge. Ask your lead person which trade organization(s) would be good to join.

As an example, a person using AutoCAD software daily on the job could consider being a member of an AutoCAD user group. This allows the user to pick up new ideas shared at the meeting about software usage. Other discussion about hardware setup, compatibility, shortcuts, and day-to-day fixes for problems can be learned in this type of meeting. By meeting together with others at professional association meetings, your job position is strengthened every time! It is a chance to meet new and past acquaintances. It strengthens social skills needed in all circles of employment. As a fringe benefit, you may even find out how much better your job is than other people's jobs!

Many organizations have additional benefits such as mailings, including magazines to keep you informed, showing changes to happen in your job. Sometimes the employer will pay for joining an organization which supports your job interests. If the employer doesn't pay for the dues or subscription, they are tax deductible for income tax purposes, if the taxes are itemized. You will find opportunities to attend conferences and seminars to learn more and also have a lot of fun, if you make a point of looking for them.

Please consider joining at least one organization. Instead of asking yourself, "Can I afford it?" the question should be, "**Can I afford not to join**?" I can't say enough about strengthening the resumé by having these experiences recorded and under the correct headings. Joining professional organizations has many more advantages that I haven't even touched on. The advantages go on and on.

ATTEND CONVENTION OR SEMINAR

How can an employee or new hire keep up with all the latest things happening on the job without attending workshops or seminars regularly? You can't, and still be efficient. Plan ahead with your boss by asking what you need to be looking for and the kind of workshops that he or she recommends you attend. This could be done during your next evaluation, or sooner if convenient. Listen for things the department or company needs and plan ahead. It might be learning about new methods of work routines, safety, software, equipment use, tooling, supplier agenda, employer/employee relations, customer service, new equipment coming on the market, work ethics, parts supplier, all adding to the strength of your resumé.

The important thing is:

> **Keep updating yourself to the new changes coming down the pike.**

ENROLL IN CLASSES

If I've said it once, I'm saying again—if you haven't received a high school diploma, consider making that a goal, attaining your GED or high school diploma. Next, if you do not enroll in college, try enrolling in classes at a trade school or vocational school. Start with small steps. I encourage you to learn or improve your standard English. Sometimes this means you must work and go to school at the same time. But try to work at continuing your education!

Develop an interest in the exchange of information from meeting together in an educational setting. Ask yourself, "What information do I need to continue my expected goals, dreams, and aspirations?"

You may be thinking, "But I don't feel good about going to school." You may not be able to afford not being more educated. Consider classes for your future. I encourage you to give it your all.

"Hope for the future lies in education."[1]

More education is your best investment! But this will take initiative. Schedule a time to visit with the closest educational institution of your choice. Educational institutions have money to loan, special awards, and assistance of all kinds if you show need. There are scholarships, private loan money, grants, incentive payback plans, work study, part-time jobs, co-op, and more.

Opportunities are out there for those who take time to search for them. But you'll have to work hard to find what's possible for you.

Sure, more education generally takes time and money. However, it may be like my grandfather said to me before I went to college: "Roger, you need college for a good education leading to a better job."

Develop a plan, if you don't have one, to become educated. Use discretion. Rough out a simple plan soon. Study it more and prepare to work the plan. Go see a counselor at the closest higher education institution. Work out something that fits your budget and time schedules; modify it, if needed. Ask for a second opinion from another institution, employer, or close friend. Consider not procrastinating for your own sake. Prepare for a job that fits your goals in life.

UPDATE YOURSELF

Years ago, the Wichita Eagle's Business Plus publication published a list of classes held by local colleges. By reading and enrolling in classes and seminars, the success-driven employee can keep up with business trends. Without updating yourself, a person may lose an edge in the job market. One cannot depend upon the employer to tell you about everything you should be learning in the work place.

You must take charge of your life by training beyond high school mentality to upgrade your intellect for the job. My guess is "the knowledge explosion" is nearly doubling every couple years. If this is happening, what kind of change does so much new knowledge bring about? It's mind-boggling if you think about it in these terms. For that reason alone, you must improve yourself often by involvement with many of the following: seminars, exhibits, special shows, workshops, fairs, business invitations, tours, demonstrations, open houses, conferences, reading and watching the news, reading magazines, attending expos, hiring tutors or consultants, and attending classes. How many of these have you involved yourself with lately?

I've seen people who have attended two years of college and were hired for a good job. After working several years, they were no longer able to advance any higher on the pay scale until they took more college. What will you do if that were you? So it is with some jobs; one needs more knowledge to move up on the pay scale.

Many books and resources give advice on how to be a better employee on the job. Think about asking yourself, what information can I get from some source to advance my effectiveness on the job and in the field of my interest?

At a convenient time, it may be good to ask your boss how he or she thinks you can advance yourself.

In conclusion, to have a good chance for advancement, you need (1) convincing job reviews and referrals, (2) strong educational entries showing on your resumé.

COMPUTER SOFTWARE

Strengthen your resumé. Stretch your mind. If you don't already know, learn how to use advanced iPads and laptops to help do your tasks more quickly. Computers can work in your favor, putting together facts and figures quicker than a flash. When I authored this book, I was told that by giving a few simple commands, the computer can edit the manuscript in many different ways. It's amazing if you think about it. It's incredible to think about how computer CPUs are downsizing from the size of a large cereal box to being the size of a cell phone.

I predict companies will soon place advanced nano-sized computer chips into many of our mechanisms, and perhaps our bodies, to do huge mind-boggling operations as the norm. Nano-sized computer chips cannot be seen by the human eye without the use of special instruments. Will we be ready for these changes?

The resumé reflects your interest in meeting the times we're living in today. This computes to job security.

If you're a painter, you will find software presentations showing processes, gizmos, and materials you've never heard of when you attend a paint seminar. If you're a bridge builder, you may learn mechanized technology techniques you've never heard of by attending. If you're an employee at a fast food establishment, learn about new technology coming down the pike at your company. If you want to be a bus driver, computer software will play a bigger and bigger part in the job requirements, just like many other vocations.

Workshops and classes to learn about new software technology are readily available. Watch your local newspaper for ads announcing software offerings. Ask people in your field of interest or computer dealers for advice and arrange to get yourself on their mailing lists.

Give yourself an edge. Learn more about new mechanisms, hardware, software, equipment, processes, and new techniques in your field of employment so you can add this to your job strength.

JOB FAIR

I attended a job fair lately, and to my surprise, two long lines of job seekers were lined up to have their resumés reviewed. As much as I could tell, two businesses were looking at applicants' resumés to strengthen the content and appearance at no cost.

Resumés can be your means to open the door to get an interview some times. A sign at one of the job fair booths read, "95% of positions are either hidden and or filled by referrals.[2] Why is there a hidden job market?"

What was my take on this? This might be happening in your area, but you can develop contacts in your community to help you find a job. Employers are likely willing to hire in today's marketplace if you have strong referrals in your resumé. Seek out a competent employment counselor to give ideas of who would best serve your needs as a referral for the resumé.

The resumé is one of the ways to get someone interested in you as a person.

Your education, past employment, accomplishments and interests must be listed in the resumé as it portrays the real you, willing and ready to work hard for that employer. The resumé becomes your lifeline to moving up the ladder to better paying jobs.

Job fair booths are attended by the companies' best personnel to visit with applicants. Will you qualify as well as your resumé describes you?

CHAPTER TEN SUMMARY

An enabling resume would possibly allow some interviewer to learn if the job you're applying for is a good fit for both you and them. Without providing a good resume for the interviewer, you limit your chances of succeeding down the road in doing well for the company in the long run. This is about you. This is your future, so take time to think about it. Record strengths in your resume about every avenue of your life.

Choose to list people in your resume who could give you a high mark of recommendation. Before listing them, contact them. Ask whether they would be able to send you a letter of recommendation and also their current phone number so they could be reached. By giving past references and current telephone numbers, this could place your resume ahead of several others. In that way, you help the interviewer to see that you are efficient in your work. Again, select your reference people carefully who would be pleased to give you a good character reference.

By the way, an excellent resume could "be useless" if you don't go out of your way to make yourself available for someone trying to reach you.

CHAPTER 11

GOING THE SECOND MILE

EMPOWERMENT ACTS AS FUEL

What does it mean to empower another person? I've come to believe the answer to this question lies in the New Testament of the Bible. Jesus tells us that all we have to do is to turn our life over to God, ask for forgiveness, and pray, committing ourselves to the teachings in the Bible. This change in one's life has possibilities that will empower you to empower others. We can choose to care about other people in ways that radiate from the heart. Encourage others to be the most they can be on a daily basis! There will be people who will become inquisitive about your positive outlook on life. They may wonder what gives you this inner peace of character and ask what gives you inspiration. You may also find many challenges as you live your faith in God. As always, we want to treat others (everyone) as we would want to be treated.

I believe this new faith and inspiration is available for any one. Empowerment may develop when you choose to be all that you can be. As has been said, "Leaders are made, not born." That is also what it means to be born again. As an adult or young person, you will have set a whole new lifestyle in motion. You may become more interested in the welfare of others. You will have put away the things of the past and have time to concentrate on helping others with whom you come in contact daily. Additional thoughts are said about this in Chapter 18.

Continue to build upon your commitment by further studying and learning from the word of God, such as reading the book of Proverbs, as I emphasized in the Preface. The book of Proverbs, in the Bible, is known for the wisdom it can bring to its wise readers. Here's what I learned from Dr. Charles Stanley on TBN (Trinity Broadcasting Network) as he preached on "Acquiring Wisdom." He used the first few chapters of Proverbs as a basis to his sermon, starting from Proverbs 2:1-7. His point was that if we want godly wisdom, we must seek it to acquire it. After diligently seeking, praying to God, and reading the Bible, wisdom can enter our hearts as we anticipate the results.[1]

I hope these thoughts have empowered you to fuel your efforts so you can understand how to become more wise.

ENCOURAGE GROUP INVOLVEMENT

The focused team player gets others involved equally in the same group effort. This strengthens the end results tremendously, simply because of the one or two involving more talent on the team. The project is scrutinized more closely with more persons evaluating the matter. Projects have more potential to be completed faster when all team members are involved and pull together. Accomplishing things quicker allows more time for additional work projects and evaluation in the follow-through process, where it often suffers. Team involvement is needed in all vocations and work environments.

Let's pretend you are the motivated leader and team player! What are some ideas that could be used to encourage others to get involved?

1. Remind other team members about what's at stake.
2. Keep an upbeat attitude no matter what is happening.
3. Develop more friendships outside the team.
4. Encourage others of the benefits for being a team player.
5. Use breaks and lunch periods as time to psyche up other team members.
6. Compliment others who receive monetary rewards.
7. Show appreciation with certificates of accomplishment.
8. Help to pull together all team members, **leaving no one off the team.**
9. Be very careful not to bully anyone.
10. Challenge team members with goals.
11. Join with those who are trying to be exemplary leaders in the group.
12. Point out the popularity of the social event or project to team members.
13. Associate the benefits of the event or project to community progress.
14. Appeal to others' common sense ideas.
15. Use upbeat wit and humor.
16. Brag on the prizes, if prizes are offered.
17. Center your compliments around helping someone or a group.
18. Use incentives and other connections honestly.
19. Make this "on the ball" philosophy a part of your job.
20. Consider connecting this effort with other successful efforts.
21. Brag on others' accomplishments no matter how small.
22. Some may not think they are able to do the task; show them how.
23. Remind team members what it will do for those who do well.
24. Talk to other leaders who are seasoned and experienced.
25. Pray to God who hears all our needs.
26. Point out how the project or event offers new and exciting information.
27. Tell co-workers thank you for their ideas.

ENTERTAINING GUESTS AT HOME

Maybe it starts by inviting a friend or guest to the local café. Eventually, I hope you can feel good about inviting guests to your home.

A host or hostess (person doing the inviting and entertaining) can try to make their guests feel comfortable. Prepare to do things they may find pleasing and interesting. Other times you may have to ask friends or acquaintances what their interests are in advance. If the timing is right, share with them what you had planned; ask them what they enjoy doing to have fun. Hopefully, both you and they can have some good times and laughs together.

Following are some possibilities to consider with your guest(s): watch a sports event together; celebrate a birthday or anniversary with a cake and ice cream; celebrate with snacks, or just a dessert, for an event at work, church or club, for instance. We've entertained friends, co-workers, and family to simply talk together about common interests or play games. It's always fun to serve fresh-baked pie or cookies with coffee or tea. Early in our marriage a stainless steel cookware salesperson helped us throw a dinner party. We were encouraged to invite several others we knew who would enjoy a sit-down dinner cooked by the salesperson and my wife. After dinner, the salesperson shared about their special cookware for approximately 30 minutes and paid us for the cost of the food. Just a precaution about this—make sure the guests know what kind of party it's going to be in advance. Otherwise, this might be a good way to lose friends if the guests are pressured to buy products.

GOODNESS GRACIOUS

The following paragraphs tell three stories of ways I think you could be gracious.

Story one: The boss and his spouse invite you and your family out to eat. Try to say yes even if it means changing some other plans. It's important to build a good relationship with the boss and his family. Support of family members can be very helpful in one's job.

By the way, in workplace circles, it is not unreasonable to say that spouses can make a difference many times in hiring practices, promotions, and longevity with the company. The boss encourages you to leave early because of the good week everyone had at work. He asks you whether you drove or need a ride home. If you decline, thank him by saying something like this, "Thank you very much for the offer, but that won't be necessary."

Story two: You see a hundred dollar bill outside the front door of your building at work and wonder if you should pick it up and stick it in your pocket. It's a good decision to not take what is not yours—no matter how small. You could get the next person coming or going involved so your respect is guarded when you pick it up. Report the incident by giving the bill to an office assistant; and also report the find to your lead person. It might be tempting to think this matter may never be talked about since no one saw it, but the consequences of theft are much more serious than the gain of $100.

Story three: You have been given a good promotion with a salary raise. Now, it's time to work even harder rather than resting on your laurels. The way to go up the ladder of success is the will to work and realize that getting more, may translate into giving more time. The real acid test is whether you can handle additional work and more efficient time management. Just realizing you must work even harder is the answer. I'm sure you'll figure out a way to step up to the plate and do well. Remember, you can't do it alone. Get others involved—share your appreciation

BEING COURTEOUS

Hopefully, you will find the following examples as courteous things to do.

First example: Let's say you are at a community event. Some people are standing in the background. Your boss is visiting with an employee from your place of work. You may want to avoid walking closer to join their conversation. Usually, the courteous thing to do is to go visit with them and be sociable. But in this case, they could be discussing some information about a private project at work. If their conversation changes and seems more light-hearted, then go visit with them. Most of the time, joining in conversations is appropriate.

Second example: If you're attending a special luncheon, take a moment to wait and look around, it looks full. Someone may invite you to sit with them. If not, you could ask someone whether it is OK to sit at the table with them. Thank them. Be prepared to show acceptable social table manners.

Third example: You're coming to a busy four-way stop in town with four stationary stop signs—four drivers from opposite corners arrive about the same time. Who goes first? Is it the fastest one to the accelerator? As you probably know, the rule of law says, when two cars approach the stop sign at the very same time, the car to the right has the right-of-way. If there is doubt in your mind who was first, the courteous response is to let the other driver go first. Give the person a "move ahead first" hand motion and smile. In our town we have a similar busy four-way stop. When I motion to the other driver to go ahead of me, we can usually see each other. Now the opposite is, if I bolted out with my V-8 in front of them, not even bothering to wave hello, they may think I was being rude. Eventually, if I drove like that by failing to be courteous, I could soon build up a not-so-good reputation for myself, not to say how many accidents I would have caused. This bad reputation could follow me and take years to overcome. And, when we are in a hurry, this kind of situation can happen..

If we are thinking of the other person's well-being, maybe it could be helpful to let other people go first when appropriate, to actually experience more satisfaction.

Fourth example: Let's say the company you work for designs, manufacturers, and sells helicopters. You have just joined the company. Your job is to stock shelves and assist people in the engineering area. The company has developed a voice command guidance system in the research and development department. It is scheduled to go on sale soon. The company is planning a preview of the new model for a large number of potential customers. They are serving a buffet dinner for all the people signed up to see the new voice command guidance system at the grand finale. Even though you are not salaried, you have been assigned to be one of the six employees working on a special team. Your team has been assigned to host several guests at the dinner. This would be your way of showing commitment to the company, and another way to learn new skills as an employee at the same time. The courteous thing to do is treat this as an opportunity.

MAKE IT RIGHT THE FIRST TIME

Many years ago, I was in business as a repairman, and then five years later as a general contractor, with two crews of employees. We worked at carefully planning our success by doing things best the first time, so we didn't have call-backs. We also had customers who knew we charged more than the competition, but we wanted them to be able to count on us for having a better finished product. Our company did not take needless shortcuts. The skilled employees who worked for me knew that fixing or constructing something with second-grade materials or using a quick fix was not the expectation for our customers. I shared with each new hire that if the code called out for four screws and gluing, they must go the second mile by using five screws and a better water proof adhesive or glue. My theory was to have it done just a little better, allowing for the unexpected. Why? If something let loose or an extra force were to be placed upon the situation, it could handle the extra stress.

Let me share something that happened recently. Our region received 10+ inches of snow and hovered around 32 degrees. The walks were scooped, leaving a thin layer of ice on the concrete from the sun melting the snow. Approximately 10 years ago, I can still remember putting up a banister along this same step and short walkway, and thinking to myself, "I really need to anchor the bottom of the banister well. If someone were to place an extreme amount of pressure on the top, I wouldn't want it to come loose, causing the railing to fail and the person to fall." Well, you're probably already guessing what happened. I went after the newspaper on the porch. The newspaper was not on the porch, but on the sidewalk. I took one step down, and a second step onto the ice and flipped. Luckily, I was holding onto the top of the rail with my left hand as I broke my fall, putting an extreme amount of shearing side-thrusting force on the railing. If the stud bolt base mountings on the bottom of the lateral railing had not been installed deeper than only adequate, I might have had serious head injuries from possibly hitting the top step. The strength of the railing might have failed without deeper stud bolts.

The same can happen at our job, as an employee. It's imperative that we do our work correctly the first time so it doesn't cause frustration or injury to the customers who put their trust in us. Customers expect us to go the second mile. If a customer loses trust in the one providing the service or the product, from experiencing something bad or even hearing about someone else's bad experience, it can have devastating outcomes from the loss of sales.

I'll end this chapter with a quote from the book, "Customers for Life," by Carl Sewell & Paul Brown who used the following quote from Leonard L. Berry, "The best system in the world for providing customer service is also the simplest: do what you say you are going to do, and do it right the first time."[2]

CHAPTER ELEVEN SUMMARY

Going the second mile means you are not satisfied, unless you've displayed your best work for the employer, the customer and yourself.

CHAPTER 12

CONSIDER THESE CLOSELY

JOY IN SEEING OTHERS BECOME SUCCESSFUL

Other people can be encouraged when you show happiness for their successes. Friendships are made by encouraging others to share about what is going on in their lives. It's very important to show interest in others' good fortune. Do you know anyone who becomes unhappy if their neighbor or acquaintance gets something they've always wanted? Joy in seeing others get ahead is primary to experiencing joy in our own lives.

If our heart is in the right frame of mind, we can be happy for others. We will show kindness and talk about the joys others are experiencing. I believe God likes to see people get along peacefully and show love in their hearts for one another.

DON'T WAIT, CALL BEFORE YOU'RE LATE

Reporting early to your job is important—this shows you are responsible and respectful. Start a habit of letting the boss know when you are running late. Make sure it's not a hit or miss situation! When company people have to wait for you because of being late to work, it causes embarrassment. Worse yet, it may cost them financial loss, loss of productiveness or affect someone's job credibility—maybe yours.

Years ago, I purchased a brand new Dodge Dakota pickup so I could expect more dependability versus relying on my older, existing pickup. The brand new pickup had 250 miles showing on the odometer. By purchasing a new vehicle, I would never have to be late because of the dependability of the new vehicle. But, on this morning the pickup's computer shut down. There I was, sitting on the side of Interstate 35, without a cell phone and not knowing how I was going to keep from being late. Embarrassment was inevitable. I was going to be late. To make matters worse, I was about to miss a television interview appointment. Even worse, I had doubts about my boss believing a story of how I was stranded along interstate without a cell phone with a brand new pickup. That kind of thing is not supposed to happen, but it did. Who would have ever thought by buying a new vehicle, one would have this kind of experience, but it happened. I hope it never happens to you. In retrospect, I should have had back-up plans in place.

THE TEST IS GETTING REST

We've all experienced staying out too late and then trying to be productive the next day. Sometimes we are out having fun. Some of us have experienced taking care of necessary responsibilities, or taking care of a child off and on all night, or dealing with an illness. Then, we may find ourselves too tired to be at our best during the working hours on the job. There are other times when we must avoid situations where the activity will deprive us from getting proper rest.

What are some ideas about staying awake when you have a lack of good sleep? If we are tired on the job, maybe there could be a few minutes during the lunch hour for us to rest our eyes and take some deep breaths. Changing the routine for a bit can offset sleepiness. Certain foods lend themselves to giving us more energy. Coffee or a cold drink may help keep an active mind. Mild isometric stretching exercises can counter sleepiness. A brisk walk may help wake you up. Lively music can help keep some people at their best, and there is other soothing music that puts me in a sleep mode. Try the following for getting better sleep. It works for me—and might work for you. As you close your eyes, program your mind by thinking something like this: "I'm going to forget that specific problem happened and get the sleep I need. OK, now I'm going to sleep." Or: "God, you know I need sleep. Forgive me and help me to forgive others, so that I can have peace of mind as I drift off to sleep." We can talk to the Lord God in prayer about our concerns.

CHANGE WITH THE TIMES

Try to have an open mind with a flexible mindset. Understand that things change often. Before forming a quick decision and getting upset, I hope you'll become more open to seeing things in other ways. Keep a perspective. Stephen Covey might call this a "paradigm shift." It isn't any surprise that Covey points this out in his book, *The 7 Habits of Highly Effective People*. He calls it the "Aha experience."[1]

Sometimes we can get caught up with bad habits of outdated paradigms. For instance, thinking "It worked the last ten years, so why not do it again the same way this year?" I'm not saying you can't do it again just like last year, but you may want to consider the variables. As an example, the coach sent a play around the right end and it worked well. Next time, the coach sent the same play around the left end. That is OK; he mixed it up slightly. I've seen employees who were hopelessly set in their ways to the point of putting their job on the line before making a change. They could only see it done a certain way. Employers like employees who are willing to try new, creative ideas, and be open-minded. Just because something works once and then again, doesn't mean it's going to continue working time after time.

I heard a story about an older man who went repeatedly to his favorite fishing hole to fish. Oh, it was very good year after year. He would catch all the fish he wanted in that same spot, no matter the circumstance. However, as the years went by, the stream began to change its course. Finally the hole in the stream dried up, but this man continued to fish the same spot because the spot was good. He had become accustomed to fishing the same hole, which had once been so good, that he didn't even notice the stream had changed course. He needed a "paradigm shift."

Are you changing with the course of the stream? I hope so, because the job world is like that. Keep up with the changing times to allow yourself to land the big one.

ADAPT TO CRITICISM

Is it hard for you to accept criticism? If you have difficulty accepting criticism, consider some of these simple guidelines. First and foremost, be very careful not to get angry when others are trying to help!

Drop your pride and

It's not fair!

1. look for the best in what's happening.
2. enjoy the fragrance or aroma around you.
3. consider a new direction.
4. seek God's help and ask for forgiveness.
5. listen with an open mind.
6. concentrate on the heavenly spirit of God.
7. encourage others to share as you listen.
8. reflect on how you're functioning.
9. let the decision grow on you before deciding.
10. talk it out quietly and constructively.
11. learn from your mistakes.

I was told years ago that if mistakes aren't being made, then you are probably not accomplishing much either! Learn from your mistakes. It's how you handle mistakes or criticism that counts. Pride can get in the way too often! Think about it this way: if we cannot accept criticism, how are things going to improve?

> **Next time someone wants to give you criticism, count it as a helpful opportunity.**

PERMISSION TO POST MATERIAL

As you know, bulletin boards offer information in many forms. Be careful about posting messages in writing, and then regretting what you said later. You can be sorry, but the damage has already been done if false information was made public about someone or something. The bottom line is, don't put things in writing unless you're absolutely sure of the timing, confidentiality, and accuracy of the information.

I've made up the following story about getting information approved before sending or posting it.

Let's say you've posted a For Sale ad for the company's pickup truck on a general website. You did not take the ad to the boss for proofreading. A stranger reads the ad. You did not receive an OK prior to posting it. In the meantime, the boss finds out about the ad. Your boss brings a current company rule to your attention. The rule states that an ad of this kind should not be posted publicly before allowing employees first chance at buying the item. Now a person outside the company had seen the ad and wants to buy the truck; you've almost made it a done deal. What comes next? You may have already disappointed the boss.

Double-checking the procedures for a project is important. Taking time to send important information back to the boss for confirmation will help to avoid mistakes. What you may think is small stuff, could have long-lasting effects on the company. There may be consequences in deciding who is or is not promoted simply based upon matters of confidentiality and the ability to make safe decisions. In this case, two incorrect decisions were made. First, the employee did not bother to check if posting an ad of this nature was part of company policy. Secondly, it's common courtesy to have the boss give the final OK before posting it. That's pretty much true about working as an employee in any job.

In summary, use media with discretion to make life easier for yourself and others. You could check out the appropriate process to use company time and equipment, including bulletin boards, e-mail, e-Bay, etc., for important matters.

PREPARE FOR BAD WEATHER

People are counting on you at work "come rain or shine!" As an example, let's say the news forecasts bad weather. It is the first of November and winter in Kansas has arrived. The weather forecast shows colder temperatures with rain, and maybe even snow. If you live in Kansas, you know we have a wide range of weather. What has been done to prepare for this change of weather, so you can stay healthy and get to work on time?

If you care about "carrying your own weight" as the saying goes, you must prepare for the changing weather unless you're living in Phoenix, Florida, southern California, or in an area where the climate is nearly always good. Even in those situations, a back-up plan should be ready for an unplanned, unpleasant emergency.

Following is a short check list for cold, inclement weather preparations:

- Water resistant shoes or insulated weatherized shoes
- Umbrella and preparing additional clothing for cold rainy weather
- Gloves, heavier coat, scarf or ear muffs, and something for covering the head
- Extra containers of water placed in the vehicle each day
- Check the car radiator for low temperatures
- All-weather tires and good battery for the car
- Wax the car for road salt conditions
- Clean the garage to put the car inside
- Car window scraper w/brush under seat
- Blanket and survival emergency kit in trunk that includes: flashlight, batteries, dried foods, blankets, first aid supplies, matches, rain coat, knife, pliers, compass, flares, Bible, notepad, pencil, Kleenex, paper towels, washcloth, and more
- Prepare to leave much earlier for poor road conditions
- Extra sweater, heavy coat, and blanket
- Arrange for vehicle parking space much closer to the residence
- Someone you can call if the car doesn't start
- Warmer clothing for outside conditions

- Carry emergency phone numbers
- Closed container for carrying the office agenda
- Leave a phone number or message at home outlining your travels
- Money for warm drink like hot coffee or hot chocolate
- Snow scoop and ice melt for the sidewalk
- Set the alarm earlier than normal
- Place to leave emergency notes at home for others
- Place rugs by doorways to shake off snow
- Additional weight in the back of the vehicle
- Telephone directory under the car seat or in the side door panel
- Back-up baby sitter and/or pet sitter
- Front drive vehicles handle better on ice and snow
- Vitamin C tablets may help prevent colds in the winter
- Wash hands with soap and water regularly to kill bacteria and germs
- Watch the five-day weather forecast
- Prepare to drink plenty of water

The following cold weather story is a likely telephone message from an employee named Bill, to Karen, a company receptionist, because he is late:

"Hello, Karen. This is Bill and I'm still at home. My car won't start because it's too cold. I'll try to get it started by 10:00 a.m." Karen knows what it means to come late and inconvenience others because of being late. Bill should have given his car more attention with the little extras before the cold weather. The car should have had a check-up to make sure it was serviced for winter, like: checking the battery life, battery terminals, anti-freeze level of protection, and fuel deicer in the gasoline tank. Would a frost plug help warm the engine block if the car is parked outdoors at night? Was there preparation to park the car out of the cold, direct winds?

Bill was late. Others had to fill in for Bill. He has not been convinced that his employer could lose hundreds of dollars from his lateness. When an employer hires, they want a person to come on time to the job no matter what. A valuable employee knows that a company can lose money just from lateness one time with one person, not to say what it would do if there are more absences in the course of the day. As employees we can prove ourselves to be more dependable and responsible in planning and preparedness.

Do you own an umbrella? Without using an umbrella, we can miss an opportunity to keep dry and presentable at work as we help customers. Whether there is rain in the forecast or not, have an umbrella or vinyl poncho handy just in case. In the work world where we stress teamwork and often work together, we want to be presentable.

Other bad weather preparations include drinking more water and orange juice. You could ask your doctor if taking vitamin C once a day would make a difference. Washing hands regularly and avoid touching our face may help us stay well. Try to avoid eating with your fingers. I have low-cut boots for my shoes when a winter snowstorm blows in to keep my feet warm. A sweater or coat could be taken and left at the place where you work in preparation for cold weather emergencies. I always wore a hat, hood and/or scarf to work on bad days just to keep from getting chilled and getting a bad cold. Employees going out into a more rugged job need to take layers of extra clothing just for the surprise of a weather change.

Very few people are comfortable being around someone who is coughing and has a bad cough. Is it appropriate to call in sick because of a bad cold? The answer for this question varies with different employers, but the common rule may be to not come to work with a fever.

Plan ahead and get prepared for the bad weather season in advance. Put together a back-up plan. As we know, it's worth it to work hard to be on time!

CONFIDENTIALITY

Keeping confidential information to ourselves may be challenging, but necessary. The best rules are: one, share things that are positive and helpful, and two, don't tell everything you know, especially without thinking; keep it confidential.

Think about it another way. Employers are looking for people who can handle a company secret or a special company formula without the information leaking to their competition. Often it is better not to share things that sound important with others, because it can be blown out of proportion with a completely different connotation. Some companies ask you to sign a confidentiality form saying you will not give out any confidential information about the company that has hired you.

There are expectations for a professional work atmosphere where employees can be trusted to respect the managers and other employees. Keeping information confidential is part of the workplace. The rule is to keep confidential information to ourselves.

YOUR SMART FRIEND

As you may already know, spell check is quick and simple on a computer. Today dictionaries come in many shapes and sizes. Many small electronic devices not only have a spell check on them but also a thesaurus. A thesaurus gives words to choose from which are similar to the word being used. Whatever the case, much of our communication depends on the way we perceive words being spelled, pronounced, and defined. Many schools offer classes if you find the English language hard to use. Some places charge a fee to teach English while others are free. It's easier to communicate, if you understand what words mean, and are able to spell correctly. In this section, spelling is emphasized. Writing will be given special attention in another part of this book.

E-mails, memos, letters, and notes can be error-free and effective if we take more time to proof-read and use spell-check. Business writing and using e-mail is efficient, as well as the "texting language." Abbreviated short hand communication like we have in texting, is fast and efficient. It may help with quicker response time to make a sale or finalize a business deal.

You might be surprised how helpful it is to have a dictionary at your finger tips. Consider buying one at a used bookstore or garage sale. I used a very small pocket dictionary for several years during high school and college to work at expanding my vocabulary.

One way to pronounce words better is to make a special effort to spell them right. Words must be visually comprehended correctly for good communication to happen. Recently, my wife suggested I might want to pronounce Afghanistan correctly, not "Afi-ghani-stan." I did not have a good visual of the spelling to pronounce the country of Afghanistan correctly. If the spelling of a word is not visually comprehended, words are much more difficult to pronounce.

Words can also have different meanings, if the emphasis is given at the beginning of the word, versus the end or visa versa, even though it is spelled correctly. This is the case with words like research, data, garage, and industry, which are mispronounced regularly. Just like correct spelling, groups of syllables can be studied from the dictionary to see which letter or part of the word gets the proper pronunciation.

You can buy games that help strengthen your spelling, such as Scrabble or Anagrams. Our family had a lot of fun playing the dictionary game. When playing the game, one player would find a difficult word in the dictionary, spell it, and then proceed to give its definition. Here is the funny part—the person giving the word could have also made up the word, spelled it wrong, or gave the incorrect definition. Quite often, it was hilarious when someone read a word they had made up, especially when it was a made-up, wild definition. You see, the other players had to decide whether you were telling the whole truth or not. We had some real laughs and learned a whole lot of new words and definitions from the dictionary. It is a fun way to strengthen your vocabulary. In fact, this game could be a clever way of entertaining some of your closest friends and perhaps their children for an evening of fun.

AVOID INDIFFERENCE

I watched a TV show called "Deal or No Deal." On this occasion, the guest on the show was trying to make a decision to choose the deal (money) offered them. The same person was able to ask three of her close friends, also invited to be at the show, whether to accept the deal of approximately $65,000 or not to accept it. Her friends advised her to accept the money. The crowd was motioning her to accept it. She chose to push the "no deal" button. And, as I understood her to say, "I do the opposite my friends tell me to do because I am an individual making my own decisions." To continue the story… she turned down another offer of $110,000 even though her three friends, and many in the audience, were yelling, "Take the deal, take the deal," but she said "no deal" and passed up a large sum of money. She ended up with $1,000.

What a tough decision to choose whether they were right or wrong. When friends mean well and are unanimous in their decision to help us, it may be a good idea to accept their decision, unless it is against your convictions. Having friends to support us in life is a great advantage! Friends should not be taken for granted!

HAVE A BACKUP PLAN

Early on in this Chapter under the topic, "Don't Wait, Call Before You're Late," where it talks about calling in if you know you're going to be late, I shared how a back-up plan was needed even though the pickup was new. It just goes to show how a good back-up plan is needed no matter how good the plan looks.

The following illustration shows how even a prairie dog digs a tunnel to a second hole to have a back-up plan in case they have to escape from a predator.

CHAPTER TWELVE SUMMARY

It's important to think about what we are going to do or say in advance. Planning our next move is good common sense, so we choose the best option. As an example, if we are going to be diving into water, it's wise to check the depth and whether there are sharp, shallow rocks directly under the surface. This could help us to avoid getting hurt. Another example is when we're communicating with people. We can choose not to dive right into the answer to a question or conversation before knowing some facts. There may be exceptions to this rule while driving a vehicle, if there are decisions that must be made quickly. But for the most part, we need time to think through the situation of an issue to help us zero in on the best decision.

CHAPTER 13

STRENGTHENING CHARACTER

Educating the mind without educating the heart is no education at all.

Aristotle[1]

IS A MENTOR LIKE A GPS?

What is a mentor? Do you have someone whom you admire and hope to become more like that person someday? Maybe this person has something you admire very much. This person may be someone who makes good choices. The mentor may or may not know he or she is your mentor. As we admire and learn from an effective, productive person or employee, we may be trying to imitate a part of their lifestyle, personality traits, or goals. When someone has been extremely successful at doing something, they might have someone looking up to them—even a brother or sister for example. So, if you do not yet have a mentor, consider doing yourself a favor—find a successful mentor for your life soon.

A mentor is something like a GPS for our life and workplace ambitions

Perhaps there was an excellent teacher or youth pastor in your life who stands out in your mind above all others. Think about how and why this may have made a big impact upon you. Now determine to learn from their accomplishments. Chances are these kinds of experiences with a mentor will have a positive effect upon making you a better person. This process may have a lasting impact, as well as strengthening and improving you as a person.

Here is your challenge. Think of someone in your life whom you have really admired and write their name(s) here as your mentor:

(1)_____

(2)_____

Perhaps the next step is to share with them how much you admire them. If you do, you may want to tell them some complimentary thoughts that have made you feel that way.

Here is another challenge you can consider. Can you become the person who someone else would want to claim as their mentor?

SHARPEN UP YOUR PRESENCE

Many authors have written about grooming and attire. The way you groom yourself and what you wear makes a big difference in the way people perceive you.

Mannerisms are equally important. If you feel good about how you present yourself, you probably show a positive self-esteem, which is a much needed attribute in the workplace.

When I was about twelve years old, we lived on a farm, and would go into town to pick up groceries and shop for whatever we needed. We hoped to find some of our friends at activities in the park or around the town square. People gathered along the park sidewalks or sat on benches to visit. We would watch kids and adults walk by, and notice what they were doing, eating or wearing. We were amazed sometimes and learned from that experience.

First: Grooming. Consider the way you care for and style your hair. Notice some people whom you admire. What are some of the latest trends for the workplace? You may want to consider a new hair style, such as easy care, inexpensive, and one that inspires you and your supervisor for a possible new job or promotion.

As suggested in the second topic of Chapter One, it is good to practice sitting and standing up as straight as possible for your body. The body functions better with good posture, whether we are able to stand or are in a wheelchair. When I practice good posture, my disposition feels better. When we work at having the best posture possible for us, we are telling the observer that we are self-confident.

There are other things of importance like fingernails, clean teeth, and avoiding too much jewelry. These grooming practices can make a positive impression. There is so much more to be said about proper grooming for the job. You will probably want to become more aware of other successful people on the job and how they present themselves.

Second: Attire. Have you picked out your outfit or clothes for your next meeting with an employer? Here's something that works well for me: I ask my wife or daughter, if I don't feel confident about what to wear. Clothing retailers are good at wanting to help you put together outfits that complement you. Clean, color-coordinated, stylish clothes that fit well are always appropriate. When planning for our wedding, I found a quality, inexpensive suit to wear for that special day. I felt great! What I'm emphasizing here is that it doesn't take a lot of money to look good for whatever the occasion. Even carpenters and construction workers need to be dressed like they are proud of their profession.

It is probably best to avoid wearing a plaid shirt with another color of plaid slacks! Most of the time, the rule is that you try to fit in and not stand out in the crowd. However, there are occasions when the rule is changed because an event or occasion calls for the unusual, such as a costume party. You want to have clothes that fit well to avoid looking like you slept in them. Maybe you could ask a brother, sister, or friend who might have some ideas about your clothing choices to wear at a job interview. As I said before, leaving a good impression and a professional presence is necessary to land the best job possible.

MORE THAN SKIN DEEP

Have you ever been walking along and someone asks, "What's wrong"? Our body language may tell others what is going on inside. If you have your faith values in order, you will be much more energized from the heart out. It matters! Oh sure, there are exceptions to the rule just like anything else we experience, but most likely, persons are worth much more to an employer, if the heart is radiating kindness outwardly from within. Persons on and off the job must move in positive directions! For every negative in the opposite direction, you probably lose two strokes in the right direction. If you allow little wrongs to inch their way into life's experiences, the heart and brain may become accustomed to making not so good decisions. So, it's your decision to work on the inner health (perhaps better known as your heart and soul) so you can grow strong and healthy inside and out, moving in a positive direction, projecting an energetic look of kindness and strength.

DEMONSTRATE INTEGRITY

What does Webster's Dictionary say about integrity? "**1 :** an unimpaired condition : soundness **3 :** the quality or state of being complete or undivided : completeness **syn** see honesty, unity."[2]

Do you have integrity with others and with yourself? In my opinion, to experience meaningful work as an employee, it must start with you. Next, it is helpful to have a team spirit with you and your boss. In addition, team spirit, support within your family and good friends can help so much as a source of strength at work.

Integrity and honesty played a big part in our country's heritage. I can't say enough about being an honest person. The story about Abraham Lincoln returning the two cents later, after being overpaid, is a good example of honesty in effect.

SENSE OF HUMOR

Zig Ziglar in his book *Top Performers* says, "A sense of humor is vital to good leadership," as one of the top performance principles.[3]

Remember the quote by Virginia Tooper of Pleasanton, California, known as the Laugh Professor back in Chapter three? In her noon luncheon seminar, she said "positive uses of humor on the job…improves your health, your outlook on life, and your ability to communicate."[4]

I think having a sense of humor and being able to laugh, even being able to laugh at yourself, strengthens character.

William Davis is quoted to have said, "The kind of humor I like is the thing that makes you laugh for five seconds and think for 10 minutes." This quote came from a presentation given by Al Schmidt about using humor to live well.[5]

It's fun to be around someone who has a sense of humor. My youngest brother and father-in-law were both good at telling jokes. When my brother was still living and before he died of cancer complications, I would see our local law enforcement officers occasionally come and go from his home, still laughing, as they had heard Gary tell them a joke.

FIRST IMPRESSIONS ARE LASTING

"Did you know that…you have about four minutes to be either received or rejected when you first meet someone?"[6]

In many of my experiences, if a first impression is made in seconds after initially meeting someone, it is quite often impossible to change those feelings later.

Gary Dessler, professor of business administration at Florida International University, in his article published in the Wichita Eagle-Beacon called "Job Talk," said that "bad first impressions are often all but impossible to overcome." It becomes a skill of knowing how to make someone like you at first glance. He points out several ways you can make yourself likeable in the short run by quoting three persons of authority on first impressions. Julius Fast, in his book "Body Language," and Thomas Sannito and Peter McGovern, versed in court room psychology, share several ways of producing liking in the short run:

1) Grooming is important. Studies indicate that most people, including adolescents and adults, are more attracted to people who are neat and well-groomed and who dress crisply.

2) Flash your eyebrows. Studies of people in many cultures indicate that an eyebrow flash (raising both eyebrows almost instinctively in rapid movement and keeping them for about a half-second) is almost always an unspoken signal of friendliness and approval.

3) Smile right. Everyone knows that there are smiles and there are smiles. The pained smile of a flight attendant who's been on duty for eight hours does little to say, "I like you." And the oblong, or "hostess," smile in which the lips are parted in a sort of ellipse around the teeth comes across as dishonest. On the other hand, a smile of easy friendliness in which the top teeth are exposed and the corners of the mouth are pulled up says, "Hello, pleased to meet you."

4) Lean forward. A person who doesn't like someone often leans back as if repelled. Liking is produced by leaning forward.

5) Nod your head. This is another effective way of producing liking, although it can be overdone. People like people who agree with them and who are attentive to what they're saying. Nodding (almost unconsciously) while the other person is talking thus helps to say, "I agree; I'm listening; I like you."

6) Open up. Generally speaking, a position in which your arms are crossed in front of your chest may project the impression that you're resisting the other person's ideas, as will clenched hands. Open, frequently outstretched arms and open palms project the opposite.

7) Look for similarities. Once you start talking, look for similarities in experiences, values, opinions, and interests. People tend to like people who are like them, so common experiences and interests are often a starting point for producing liking.

8) Importance is important. To produce liking, keep in mind Dale Carnegie's classic law of human conduct: "Always make the other person feel important."[7]

APPRECIATING YOUR JOB

Joy happens when your supervisor can give you compliments. It comes from having purpose, fulfillment, and satisfaction in a job that is challenging and exciting.

> **Joy takes place from a job which makes a contribution to humanity and God.**

Joy is felt when colleagues at work tell you they appreciate you and you return the compliment. Joy happens when your loved ones support you in the job. Joy in your heart can

136

help you work better. Joy can be experienced after working hard to achieve goals that you've set out to accomplish, and they come true.

"…The important thing for us is…stirring up goodness and peace and joy from the Holy Spirit." –Romans 14:17 [8]

A COMPASSIONATE PERSONALITY

How do you live your life with radiance and caring? Does your life show an attitude of radiance? I don't know how you feel about it, but living this kind of life is much easier said than done. This is something I have to work at all the time. Others whom we meet on a daily basis can appreciate people that radiate a caring personality. Do you work hard at putting on a pleasant face each morning? We all leave lasting impressions with many people as we go about our business. Others observe us often as we move around in our daily lives without us knowing it. Do you usually show happiness and compassion? Do you try to share compliments when appropriate? Your success of caring, helping others and being sensitive to their feelings becomes a very big part of your journey, as expressed in Chapter One!

If an apple or orange has a bad spot on the inside, a bruised area shows on the outside often times. We may be like the apple and orange in a way. If something is going wrong in our life, our faces and actions might show a lack of caring.

My wife and I were traveling on a trip quite a few years ago, and I recall a vivid memory in my mind. We stopped for lunch at a quaint outdoor open dining area. As we were enjoying our delicious lunch, I observed that some of the birds didn't seem to be as happy or healthy. Some had scuffed and dirty feathers, seemed extra hungry, or had been pecked on by other birds. Many of the birds were chirping, as if to say, "stay out of my way, you can't have that French fry, its mine." They were being selfish.

Even with people, there are noticeable signs and messages all around us, if we take the time to slow down and observe. I think the story above has a message to be learned in the way we treat one another. I've only used birds as a metaphor to point out the ways we care for people and things around us.

EXTRA PERSONAL CARE

Paying attention to good personal hygiene is a very sensitive topic, as noted previously. There is so much information on the Web and in the stores under personal hygiene. Even more information is available in magazines and books from the library and other sources. Following are some personal hygiene products that my wife and I use. Keep in mind, other product brands are probably equally good to those listed. These are products we use at our house.

- Mennen Skin Bracer after shave and Speed stick deodorant
- Electric triple head cordless Norelco shaver
- Bath & Body Works products, Dove bar soap, Redken hair conditioner
- Crest tartar protection whitening cool mint toothpaste

Give your employer the benefit of the doubt that you know how to take care of your hygiene, just like you'd care for the institution or company and customers.

USE UPLIFTING LANGUAGE

Our language and mannerisms have a lasting effect upon the people we meet. What kind of language is not uplifting? If derogatory and degrading remarks are aimed at pulling someone down, the language is probably unnecessary. Does it help to use swear words to emphasize certain feelings? Doesn't that kind of language simply get in the way of good communication?

Words from the Bible, in Matthew 5:22, say, "And if you curse your friend, you are in danger of the fires of hell."[9]

Developing a personal goal to stay away from words and language that carry a negative connotation is a positive way to communicate! It becomes a matter of making a decision to use uplifting words as you talk with people. There is a danger that young people pick up words like this, thinking it's cool to say them. I challenge you, as you speak with or about others, to take care while communicating, using uplifting respectful conversation.

ALLOW TIME FOR DEEP THOUGHTS

For many, meditation time is for quiet contemplation, spiritual insights, personal evaluation with one's self and friends, or a time to reflect upon God's plan for us. It may be a time to pray and allow the spirit of God to open new paths of insight for our life. It is a good time to get right with God and a time to receive vision for the next day.

There are many books on the market which can be a guide to having a meditation each day. Periods of meditation need not be long. It only needs to take a few minutes, or take as much time as needed. Some people take time away from the weekly routine by going to a cabin, the lake, or to the mountains. People choose places that are a restful change from the weekly work schedule. Others arrange special times with a spouse or friend(s) to reinvigorate their minds. It can happen as you drive; listen to a CD, contemplate challenges, hum, sing favorite songs, or whatever direction your meditation takes you. Quiet time in this way helps us to think deeply and consciously within. You may want to arrange for this meditation time in your life, if you are not yet doing so.

Meditation (a time to connect with God) can build you up! It will make you a better person!

MIRROR MIRROR ON THE WALL

The mirror speaks volumes. Take a self-inventory of yourself by starting in your own home. Look around. What is your life all about? Study what hidden things you can see physically in the mirror about yourself. Do you wear a smile? Does your face reflect good hygiene practices? Do you take good care of your hair or does it look like you just jumped out of bed?

Does your hair length reflect the expected style for an interview with a potential employer or promotion at work? Do you look sad or glad? Do you have clean white teeth? Do you look like you had enough sleep? Does your facial skin look alive or drab? Do your eyes portray an energized look?

Please analyze what you see! It may be helpful to have a close friend help you with feedback. Many times a friend or family member may have some good thoughts which could be very helpful! They may be reluctant to offer their thoughts **unless you make a special effort** to ask for their honest opinion.

In summary, would you impress a human resources person, who has been educated for conducting interviews, by his or her first impressions of you?

MUSIC—GREAT FOR OUR WELL-BEING

What type of music is your first choice? Consider listening to a variety of music. We can expand our appreciation and love of music. Some music may make us feel like moving and dancing to the songs, or make us feel relaxed. It may mean you will listen to and attend events that aren't always your first choice! That is why the music appreciation course in college is one of the required courses for many college degrees. In my college music appreciation class, I learned to appreciate a variety of music.

As an example, when I married my wife, going to a large concert or eating broccoli and other vegetables would not have been my first choice. But, with some encouragement, I learned to savor broccoli by tasting and mixing it with other foods. I eventually began to appreciate its taste and delicacy. So it is with music: after taking a music appreciation class in college and encouragement from my wife, I now enjoy going with her to musicals, choir performances, band concerts, and attending all kinds of musical and theatrical events. We often go with friends or family to enjoy a wide range of music. Good music gives us enjoyment. We also believe that soothing music is relaxing and beneficial.

Challenge and surround yourself with good listening music. Experts and studies tell us that music can have a positive effect upon us, just as one of my dairy farmer friends has learned that some music can calm the cows for higher milk production. So it may be with all of us…soothing music may inspire us to be more productive.

MORE THAN LISTENING

You've probably read or heard this before: "The best thing you can do is to become a good listener." Larry J. Bailey, the author of the book called *Working: Learning a Living*, points to "poor listening costs employers billions of dollars every year."[10]

As I heard on the news, when past President Bill Clinton would speak, the listener may receive a completely different message versus the person who both **watched and listened** to him speak. The reason given by the news reporter was that he uses a great deal of non-verbal communication techniques during his speeches. If you think about it, combining the non-verbal and verbal communication by a person or by the electronic media, is incredible. Read more about this in Chapter 14 under the topic, "A Picture is Worth a Thousand Words."

"The average mind can handle about 600-800 words per minute."[11] I wonder how much more that number would increase if we disciplined our mind to handle speaking and non-verbal communication comfortably at the same time? It would probably be mind-boggling to know the answer for that question!

The following statement was shared by Dr. June Alliman Yoder, a communications and preaching professor, in a seminar attended by my wife:

> **"According to communication research, oral communication is 7 percent vocabulary, and 93 percent other non-verbals, such as facial expression, eyes, posture, tone of voice...."** [12]

The spoken word can be retained best if you concentrate fully on the person speaking by both **watching and listening** as the mind processes what it **sees and hears**. Associate things you hear with thoughts of your own, using association for more understanding.

I realize that I'm repeating the following story, but it is so good. I knew an accomplished business friend and lecturer, Murray Bandy, who shared with me during our first visit together that he used a method of association so he would not forget another person's name. He said, "My name is Murray Bandy and my red hair looks like a rooster. Now you won't forget my name"—and I didn't.

Admittedly, persons have and use different sending and receiving systems for both **listening and watching**. Science tells us that we'll experience more retention if we use as many of our sensory mechanisms as possible at the same time, such as hearing, writing, saying it aloud, reading, smelling, touching, seeing a picture, and through association.

Watching and listening go hand-in-hand. This does not take into consideration if there are impairments. Then, overcompensation or special help probably needs to occur to offset the handicaps and/or complications the best you can.

Listen and watch for hidden messages! Do the non-verbal actions say the same as what you're hearing? Sometimes, the non-verbal actions do not play out with the same meaning as the words being spoken. When listening to someone, don't let the words spoken verbally mislead you. Is there double-talk going on? Again, watch to see if the verbal and non-verbal communication match with what you are hearing. If you're listening to a speech, invariably the person speaking may share the real heart of the matter toward the end of the talk. If you are truly listening and giving yourself the benefit of **hearing and seeing** everything possible, then you will receive the most from the message.

> **Paying attention to both verbal and non-verbal language from people or situations is paramount. Prepare to pick up on the non-verbal messages simultaneously while listening to conversation. This gives the full implications of the communication.**

PRACTICE MAKES PERFECT

Practice makes perfect even in a speech. It takes many pages of notes and study to narrow a speech down to several pages. Much practice precedes a speech before it is perfected and recognized as good. Just like a professional athlete, it takes many hours of practice before an athlete is ready for the main event. Life is that way. Before you get the reward, many hours of practice must precede the real thing. Sure, there is the exception to the rule, but we're not talking about exceptions. Do your homework before showing someone the real thing or getting too far into the project. Even auto racing drivers practice run after run before the real race. Use the five questions— what, when, where, why, and how, before you act on something and then put the final test to it.

Following are a few suggested practices to use before you put the finishing touches on perfecting something:

- First, have you done your homework w/findings, calculations, measurements, etc?
- Draw on the strength of others to review things with you.
- Check with the lead person so they feel good about the project.
- Be quietly respectful of everyone's suggestions.
- Respect laws, rules, safety, specifications sheets, licenses, codes, etc.
- If it's a speech, review the topic on giving a speech in this book.
- Even putting in a pipe line or working on an oil rig, go over procedures many times.
- Do things in sequential order, don't skip around.
- Avoid activity that might create conflict which could weaken the outcome.
- Take good notes and then review them many times.
- Use proper chains of command for the activity or project.
- Conduct business with the highest ethical standards, reporting misconduct.
- In many jobs, accepting gifts of value is not permitted; avoid being bribed.
- Try to remain focused.
- An automobile mechanic must have studied and reviewed the job over and over.
- Use error-free communication so you don't have set backs.
- Continue to proofread work so it is done correctly.
- Keep things clean and safe on a regular basis all through the duration of the project.
- Use a good problem-solving approach for more effectiveness.
- If you don't succeed the first time in the practice run, try, try again until you do.

"IN GOD WE TRUST"

I am grateful that "In God We Trust" is printed on the face of our currency. This is significant, with the potential of reminding you and me from where our strength comes.

What would it be like if we didn't have God to trust in? We have the opportunity to seek God's will at any time and know God will hear us. If you don't have this personal relationship of trusting God to hear you at any time, then you may want to consider changing your life. You may want to read Psalms 139.

Proverbs 2:3-5 says, "Yes, if you want better insight and discernment, and are searching for them as you would for lost money or hidden treasure, then wisdom will be given you, and knowledge of God himself; you will soon learn the importance of reverence for the Lord and of trusting Him."[13]

Also Proverbs 3:4-6 reads, "If you want favor with both God and man, and a reputation for good judgment and common sense, then trust the Lord completely; don't ever 'only' trust yourself. In everything you do, put God first, and he will direct you and crown your efforts with success."[14]

We can have the option to pray often to God, asking for wisdom and strength to meet our needs. Perhaps you already trust God to help you—great! After making that choice, we need to keep a perspective of God's power to help us.

God has the power to change things for us, but in his own time frame.

In conclusion, to be all that we can be in life, we need to have a personal relationship with God through Jesus Christ our Lord.

THE GIFT OF GRACE

Why would the suggestion to "nurture the gift of grace" be recommended as a tip for becoming successful? The dictionary in the back of my New American Standard Bible gives this definition for grace: "Unmerited favor coming from God."[15]

God has given us the books of the Bible to learn about His unmerited gift of grace. The gift is there to enjoy for those who want to learn about it. All we have to do is believe in God, and allow Jesus to come into our life as a witness to God and His followers. This is our responsibility, then, to accept and practice the gift. Grace is a gift to creatively present one's self as a servant to help all God's people.

Grace builds on the motto found engraved on our national penny currency, "In God We Trust." It changes who we are and the people around us because of Christ's love generating from within our hearts. Be patient and stay focused on nurturing this gift of grace. Cherish this gift by guarding against all unethical theories and practices of getting ahead. Develop leadership abilities by nurturing this gift of grace while interacting with people in a respectful, patient way.

The Zondervan Pictorial Bible Dictionary defines grace as …"(1) Properly speaking, that which affords joy, pleasure, delight, charm, sweetness, loveliness; (2) Good will, loving-kindness, mercy, etc;…"[16]

Another definition I especially like defines grace as: "The growth of grace is like the polishing of metals. There is first an opaque surface; by and by you see a spark darting out, then a strong light; till at length it sends back a perfect image of the sun that shines upon it."[17]

I especially like what my pastor, John C. Murray, said about grace: "God extends grace to us whether or not we seek after it. The question is, will we accept it?"[18]

So I see the challenge as, will you accept developing exceptional abilities as you nurture the gift of grace in life?

RE-ALIGNMENT

Perhaps you feel like life has cheated you. God loves you and wants you to have a life of joy. There is time to fix things now, no matter how messed up it looks. If it's a matter of regret, doing something you shouldn't have done, God wants to help. If you'll pray to Him, asking for forgiveness of your wrongs, He will forgive you. This promise is told in 1st John 1:9.

Too many times our motives may not be in alignment with God's plan for us. As an example, if our car gets out of alignment and wants to drag to the right or left, we constantly have to work on keeping it driving straight. The car needs fixed. A person doesn't want to let this problem go too long or it will start wearing the tires in the wrong places. Have you ever experienced this in your life? Sometimes we need a re-alignment, so it doesn't wear on us anymore.

Maybe it's the case of handling something we shouldn't have done; evil forces were there to prod us into thinking it was OK. If our desire is to please God rather than people, we will want to keep free from the grips of the opposite forces in the world! You can read the story of Adam and Eve in the fourth chapter of Genesis. The serpent tempted Eve to the point of causing her husband to let his guard down. Both became guilty of sin. Try to keep from putting yourself in a position of entrapment. We have the opportunity to build our character decisions upon God, who sent His son as a living example for us to follow. You could read the New Testament of the Bible to find more ways of strengthening your character.

Jeremy Kingsley wrote a book called *Getting Back Up When Life Knocks You Down*. It was copyrighted in 2011. I can recommend this small paperback book of 120 pages that sells for only $10 at this printing. Find more about this little book of encouragement and practical help under **Other Sources to Read**, page 188, in back of the book.

REPUTATION

I volunteered to pick up a friend of my grandson at the airport. After waiting in front of the airport terminal a few minutes, I decided to go inside to look for him. While walking past the baggage claim, I heard a man talking on his cell phone: "You can't do that because it will not be good for our family reputation!"

We go through life making a name for ourselves and our family. As time goes on, all the good or bad follows us into our day-to-day activities. As a person may choose to live a life of honor and following after Jesus, the opposite forces may also be there trying to spoil the good in building a reputable reputation. A person must always be on guard against rationalizing about something that is only attractive for the moment. We must train our minds to seek after righteousness!

> **The good or the bad, whichever it is, has a way of following us right into the workplace and all other life experiences.**

If it's striving to live our lives as good law-abiding citizens vs. going against our better judgment, it can make a huge difference in our ability to move up in the ranks of honest, successful employment.

As I said above, even family names carry a degree of reputation. We can try to help our families have a good reputation by being responsible and supportive.

CHAPTER THIRTEEN SUMMARY

Wow! One of my editors thought there could be entire books written about some topics you read in this chapter. Let's review part of the quote from Dr. June Alliman Yoder about, "oral communication 'being' 7 percent, and 93 percent other non-verbals…." I understand this to mean that what others see is much more powerful than what they hear. All the features and movements of our bodies, clothing, apparel, facial expressions, and especially the eyes, tell the listener much more without saying a verbal word. What kind of impression are you projecting?

If I'm the employer: (1) I'd need employees who look energized. (2) I'd want to hire someone for the long haul who shows they are listening and thinking. I'd be interested in having them show a respectful professional dignity as part of their personality. (3) I'd want them to have a good work ethic.

CHAPTER 14

FORGETTING THINGS TOO EASILY?

INVEST IN A PLANNER

Back in Chapter 6, page 56, I encouraged you to invest in a calendar book planner. Many office supply stores or bookstores sell daily, weekly, or monthly planner books. Most bookstores offer a wide selection in both, small or larger sizes. Your planner doesn't have to be expensive. A calendar book planner helps me to remember what happens on each day. Recording appointments and times in your planner, which you have with you regularly, will help you remember when to do what.

IMPROVE PLANNING TECHNIQUES

Sometimes I have missed important details and should have taken more time to record it. I'd just dive into the project without thinking about my first step. Recording steps and procedures of the event, participants, and their contributions develops good planning habits.

Observe and study other methods of planning on occasion from other productive people. Pick a mentor for yourself as discussed in Chapter 13, someone you think could offer you some good job-planning tips.

Observe other methods of planning and setting priorities. Arrange a time when you can compliment other people for something you've really learned to appreciate about them. You might want to ask if you can sit and talk with them about some pointers on being a better planner. Realize this should probably be someone you know and who would not give you a bad time about asking. You may feel more comfortable discussing this subject if you know the individual well.

Good planning comes from making a conscious effort. Designate a certain block of time each week so good planning becomes habit! Don't let other things take priority. Then ask yourself: what is the primary thing I am trying to accomplish in my planning? What are the next higher priorities?

And all-important, reward yourself for developing good plans!

THE MENTAL EDGE—MIND OVER MATTER

I addressed in Chapter 7 the matter of eating healthier and committing to an exercise program. I guess by now it's no secret where my priority lies in relation to staying in good physical condition. By the way, my mind stays focused better when my physical condition is at its best.

As you work into higher paying jobs, you may find yourself doing more sitting, much less walking, and less moving around physically. This is not always the case, but if it does happen to you, you need even more reason to have a regular exercise program. Increased heart rate from exercise is healthy. By staying in good physical condition, you could accomplish much more in the working day. I heard a quote from Dr. Oz recently: "You can't be wealthy without being healthy."

When I was young, my dad needed brain surgery. My two brothers, one sister, and I missed having him healthy. During a slow recovery due to paralysis, he realized what was at stake if he wanted to regain strength. After brain surgery, one half of his body was partially paralyzed. Dad took his doctor's suggestions very seriously. He appreciated all the support from our church, family, and friends. I credit part of his recovery to his very strong desire to become well again, even though the doctors told him that he had a window of five years to live. To make a long story short, he did experience a nearly full recovery. Dad was able to enjoy life again. After my mother's illness and death 12 years later, he was married to my stepmother and they had two children. We enjoy getting together as a family for dinners, playing games, and attending activities.

During my Dad's recovery period, he drank close to seven or eight glasses of water each day. By drinking this amount, he said, "My whole system works much better." I've heard this from others, that good exercise and drinking plenty of water helps a person stay healthier.

I guess my point is this—even though the odds were against my Dad's recovery in health, he had the will to improve. Dad did outlive some of his friends with the help of doctors, family, friends, and by God answering many prayers.

"A PICTURE IS WORTH A THOUSAND WORDS"

Sometimes we picture in our minds what we want to accomplish. In this age of "electronic information knowledge explosion," pictorial graphic information is key. The old saying, "A picture is worth a thousand words," applies to this matter. Often more productive people can keep abreast much faster from being very selective in both their **watching and listening.** As an example, the news channels often use several different methods of bringing you the news, all going on at the same time. They can show a central picture with three smaller highlighted pictures to the right or left, a constant scrolling line of live news alerts at the lower area of the screen, and a caption of the discussion in the center and below the main picture. This method of imagery gives us phenomenal coverage.

That's only part of what is being learned. There are hundreds of subliminal messages in the background being carried on at the same time for listeners like you and me. I've heard that some companies pay for these subliminal scripts which often surround the screen. Looking for non-verbal subliminal graphic messages in some form or another can help productive people. In doing this, they live up to the expectations of their colleagues on the job as they are able to **listen and watch** for more information faster.

"The average American is exposed to over 5,000 ad messages every day. However we only recognize about 287 ad messages a day." [1] So, what's my point? We must train our minds to find the right things in this electronic media blitz so our lives are enriched and our appetites are not poisoned!

One of my book editors flagged the subliminal stuff, asking "What do you mean by that?" As an example, some equipment manufacturers pay to have their piece of equipment in the background as an advertisement showing off one of its latest products. Or, a tractor manufacturer wants to keep the colors in the mind of its probable patrons. Maybe there was a gorgeous picture of the snow-capped Colorado Rocky Mountains in the background, simply and subtly to remind viewers about vacationing in the mountain states during the hot weather period.

Many more things can be learned such as the live expressions and tactics used to get a point across with changing hairstyles, word pronunciation, or background music to make a picture richer and more meaningful. Perhaps a company wants to do a soft sell to promote a certain clothing fashion, so this company arranges to have people appearing on the TV show wearing their most up-to-date clothing fashions for the coming season.

Seeing things first-hand is very important in this fast-paced age. Allow me to repeat a story shared earlier about watching a KC Chiefs football game on T.V. The next morning I wore my bright KC tie to work and found that it led to conversations with several colleagues The benefits from that social exchange of conversation paved the way to more serious talk on the job later. The exchange of conversation with friends may have never happened had I not worn the bright tie.

We can work at training our mind to focus totally on the screen. **Watch and listen** for all kinds of hidden subliminal messages which our brain may receive without us consciously realizing it. This may be another way for you to keep up with the latest news and trends every day, which may affect your job sooner, rather than later. And, probably even more important, the other side of the issue amounts to limiting our use of the aggressive behavior media consumption that we subject ourselves to in the course of the day, not to say how much time is lost?

If you have one or more children, isn't it even more important that parent(s) and teacher(s) monitor their interests for helping them select the right kinds of electronic media blitz placed upon them? The potential is that we all could train and discipline our minds to block out the bad and accept the good. Or, little subtle hints can divert our minds, and limit our ability to go after that raise or promotion we'd like to have so much.

SAYING LESS CAN BE MORE

Listen more and talk less. It's been said that you want to come out of an interview feeling you didn't say everything you wanted to say. Why? Employers want persons who get to the point and do not waste their time. Prioritize and only give what you're asked to give until you know the person much better. Telling someone too much may also indicate you have trouble handling confidential information. In some situations, telling others more information than what is necessary is not a good trait! Share only what's necessary.

Selling a house or property is the same for real estate salespeople. Their professional schooling has trained them to **watch and listen** and allow the buyer to look and make their own quiet decisions..

When you visit with people, what's one example to start conversation? Say something they would enjoy hearing and be brief! The other person is not ready for a lecture. One day at the donut shop, I caught myself talking about something I had done the previous day. One of the two men hearing the conversation pulled his chair over to listen to another group close to us. I was probably boring him. I forgot the rule of needing to share less about me and more about things that would interest him.

I once met a person who we'll refer to as Bill. He told a story about attending a Realtor Association meeting. As an architect, he shared how the local building inspectors were not upholding the local building codes. He mentioned that he had talked about some of the inspectors, sharing the things they were doing incorrectly. He was apparently trying to decide what he would do about the situation. Bill realized he disappointed others in the group with his remarks. He was sure he had given some, who were in attendance, an incorrect impression. The association meeting was meant to be an evening of discussing exciting things the association was experiencing. He was probably right in everything he shared, but had not shared with the appropriate conversation. Usually persons who speak less and are positive in their approach are listened to more often. In all situations, it is wise to think through the situation and what should be shared.

Summing up these thoughts, we could be more careful by sharing stories and information that people will be interested in hearing. That's good advice for me, too. Smile and enjoy the stories from others. Share some, but don't share everything you know. Give more than equal time to others. Look them in the eye. Give the other person a sign of affirmation (maybe with a slow nod) that you heard what he or she said. People feel good about having someone genuinely interested in them who doesn't try to monopolize the conversation.

THE UNFORGETABLE CHARACTER

What you see is not always what you get. I'll refer to a used automobile as an example. A car could look really good on the outside. But, my philosophy is to become interested in a purchase, only if I know how the vehicle has been cared for by the previous owners. What does the vehicle look like under the shiny paint? When an owner does not change the oil regularly, the engine may not last as long. It would probably be difficult for some people to tell if the automobile engine was abused just by looking at the engine. For that reason, I will not buy a used car if the history is not well-known. I want a car to have been serviced with good care. To get more miles of dependability from a car, care has to have been on the owner's priority list.

And, possibly like the car illustration above, when a company hires employees, they probably want to know the history of the person being interviewed. They want to know what's underneath the skin and who the person hangs out with. Most often, they want to know about a potential employee's goals and strengths. They want to know the person as an open book. Supervisors want potential employees to have had a rich experience so they can look forward to keeping their employees for years to come, advancing with the company.

Prepare ahead and continue to be a person of integrity and good character. Allow your interviewer or employer to know you. Share examples or thoughts about your character. "By your actions they will know you." Show them why you can be at the top of the new-hire list or deserving of that raise!

MORE TIPS FOR REMEMBERING

Let's review some ideas about preparing for a test, interview, job evaluation, a special event or committee meeting, etc., so you can remember and not overlook important matters.

- First, give yourself reasons for doing the study—prepare rationale for yourself.
- Get plenty of rest, exercise, and eat right so you can be at your best.
- Decide what you can say during an interview that prepares you for the job.
- Be genuine and truthful—your face may show these traits.
- Take good legible notes for your referral later.
- Give yourself a visual of the details you're trying to remember.
- Prioritize the high points with bold print or highlighter—use what works for you.
- Abbreviate as much as possible, using parts of words in shorthand style.
- Mark all handouts and spec sheets with a date and reference.
- Use a laptop or handheld computer device when appropriate to record important information fast.
- Decide how you memorize best.
- For studying, set some goals or limitations before you start studying, such as, finding a place with good light, quiet atmosphere, soft chair, cold water, and anything else that will motivate thinking ability.
- Study or prepare for an interview for one hour.
- Pull together one page of notes for this project.
- Use current spelled notes and text.
- Reward myself with pizza and a soda after two hours of good study.
- Take a deserved break after 30 minutes.
- Avoid letting another person coax you out of finishing the task.
- Use the 5 Ws—what, where, when, why, who and how—to use all your five sensory mechanisms more routinely.
- Could choose not to confuse or boggle the mind with reading unhealthy, unwanted, information!
- Concentrate to hear everything clearly (turn up the volume if needed).
- Touching or feeling.
- Find a place to read something out loud.

- Visualizing the spelling.
- Repetition (doing it over and over).
- Associating it with something that is easy to remember.
- Repeating what you heard word for word softly to yourself.

Here is another technique to use association for remembering. Think to yourself, I want to remember this because_____, and you'll be surprised what this will do for your recall.

Another method which may work for you: make yourself a deal, such as this example. "If I remember to talk with Mary Jones who offered to give me a better job next year, I'll be able to afford a better car." Now you have raised the bar for remembering something very important by giving yourself a challenge to remember.

Continue to work on aspects that you think will work best of you. Find information using Google or using your favorite Web site, giving additional pointers on recall, good study planning habits, tips on remembering or memorization so you will not forget things so easily. By the way, if I've repeated something, forgive me for senior moments and forgetting thoughts I've written about earlier.

CHAPTER FOURTEEN SUMMARY

If I concentrate on **watching and listening** intently to someone while they are talking, I find that I can remember what they said much easier at a later time. It is also good if we make a note to remind ourselves, as well as hear and see it for the second time, so we don't forget something so easily.

CHAPTER 15

WANTED: QUALIFIED WORKERS

MARKETING YOUR STRENGTHS

Successful businesses spend big money to market their company and product. It's much like needing to market your own strengths. Many people have different strengths. Do you market your strengths?

In my opinion, marketing yourself is all about developing a positive, appropriate first impression with people regularly. It's about leading a life worthy of praise with purpose in your step, making a contribution to the lives of others. Try to have the acceptable behavior people would expect of you. Show that you can surround yourself with people and activities to energize your strengths. It's about motivating yourself to be all you can be. Show that you are genuine and inspired to be an excellent employee, or would be if you were hired. This is your decision to choose between being average or the best you can be. Which will you choose?

Maybe It Would Be Good If You Placed A Note In A Convenient Place To Read When Waking Each Morning, To Remind You Of All Your Strengths And Potential.

CUSTOMER APPRECIATION

Repeat business might depend on how your customers are greeted. Work hard at being pleasant with customers; as you may have been told, customers are right most of the time.

Occasionally, we are faced with challenges. But does that give us the right to be indifferent or difficult to be around? What do we really gain by causing problems for others? Let's spend our time looking for the pleasant side of life. We can choose to move past any negative attitude with patience and encouragement for others. Being positive and receptive to helpful criticism at the work setting can be contagious.

By now, you know which personality most employers prefer for their new hires on a long-term basis to take care of their customers. As the saying goes, "Birds of a feather stick together." Do you run around with friends who are pleasant? It's obvious who will help the organization thrive—the person with a kind heart, who lifts people up when they're down. My grandmother gave me a plaque that says; "Bloom where you are planted." This may be one of the top prerequisites for leading a fulfilling life in the workplace "where customers are the king."

Summing it up, the chances of getting a good job or moving up the ladder in your present job are better if you practice ways to have a pleasant personality with customers.

PRODUCTIVITY

Strive to create an atmosphere of satisfaction and productiveness to produce better end results. Helping to create an atmosphere of this quality will be beneficial for you, co-workers, and the company. Ask yourself:

"What will help me do a better job?"

Try giving yourself job deadlines and time limitations to do certain tasks. Just like a track runner, efficiency improves as you challenge yourself. I'm challenging you to develop an aura of self esteem, but not to the extent that we become stressed out! Energized workers should be creating pleasant vibes in an atmosphere of satisfaction and productiveness. Just one of many possible examples: red colors are inviting and energizing for my wife. So, she decorated her office with shades of red décor in wall hangings and accessories.

Did you realize light colors of brown and gray tones, sometimes called neutral tones, are restful? The colors are subdued and help me feel less tense. As an example, natural lighting helps me concentrate, leading to more satisfaction and productiveness.

Music has the potential to create a productive atmosphere as you read about in Chapter 13, "Music—Great for Our Well Being." As the story was told of my friend playing soft music while the cows were being milked, this music helped the cows to reach a higher milk production. Perhaps pleasant music has potential to improve you.

The order of your interior décor, furniture arrangements, desk arrangement, files, and cleanliness of your work area all play a part in your daily potential. Organization of the work area is also key to satisfaction and productiveness, not only for you, but the people with whom you associate daily.

Supervisors have opportunities to try harder at creating a fun atmosphere while still accomplishing a lot on the job. So can you. However, let me caution you, it can be overdone. Josh Billings has said, "There's not much fun in medicine, but there's a lot of medicine in fun."[1]

Just for a moment, think about the following—someday you may be a lead person and have a similar challenge. How will you motivate people to produce better workplace results?

QUALITY OVER QUANTITY

Stephen Denby in the VICA Professional: VP article "Foundations of Quality" says, "Quality products and service drive the world economy..." Denby also says, "we must teach new employees about their responsibilities..."

Following is Denby's basic quality theory process in seven parts:

(1) "The Customer is King...Customers' needs must be met."
(2) "Empowerment...An employee is in the best position to know customer needs."
(3) "Quality is Measurable"...Customers should be satisfied every time.

(4) "Employee-Set Standards…Employees are happiest when they are involved in setting standards and defining how their company can meet them best."

(5) "Continuous improvement…'Next generation employees' should have the attitude that any product or service can be improved."

6) "Do It Right the First Time…Nothing causes customers greater consternation than finding a malfunction in a new purchase…"

(7) "Systems Fail, Not Employees…Employers know that usually the employee wants to do a good job. The employee who understands this is most helpful in finding solutions."[2]

As an employee, you may be considered as having the ability to make the difference in the quality of your employer's product or service. Treat this as both a challenge and opportunity to improve product quality.

Just like the nation needs quality products and services, our nation needs quality employees trained with three types of skills: "(a) occupational skills, (b) employability skills, and (c) basic academic skills."[3] (a) Occupational skills are the skills you'd pick up while training for the specifics of a manual job. (b) Employability skills are the kind I've been stressing in my book: interpersonal skills such as telling the truth, giving a good image, having a good attitude, sending the right non-verbal communications, etc. In my opinion, one without the other will not get you very far, except giving much frustration. (c) Finally, you need good basic academic skill training such as math, English, and science.

All three skills can usually be acquired within two years after receiving a high school degree or equivalent. This can be your decision to prioritize your time to receive more training for your current or desired job.

CALCULATING RISK TAKER

Have you ever observed a person who takes all kinds of risks? This person may be in a hurry, and might be unorganized. The same person may not want to prioritize the day in advance, but want to rush into it.

On the other hand, the calculating risk taker looks at several ways of doing something in advance, weighs (calculates) the advantages and disadvantages of the outcomes. He or she has learned that taking time to study and research the situation cuts down on poor risks. More time is left for productivity, fun and relaxation.

PSYCHED UP

If you have a process to become motivated, you're right on. And if not, then consider starting the process of psyching up yourself. Find solutions and reward yourself for successful outcomes. No one else may take the time to reward you. This builds self-esteem for yourself.

Like many others, I must work on psyching myself up. I'm sharing my golfing story for the second time because it is so relevant as a lesson in life. Thoughts go back to a time when I was golfing with friends and doing very poorly. As I allowed myself to feel badly about my luck, I struck the ball even worse. I allowed myself to feel like I couldn't do anything right.

Do you know the feeling? In fact, the situation got so bad that I felt like giving up the sport. Then, I realized my problem—me and my attitude, the way I was handling the matter! I felt like doing what the golfer did following us on the fairway. He threw his good golf club at the green flag stick. However, that didn't seem to help him much, from what I could tell. Although, I chuckled at myself and the situation, which may have helped me! This leads me to three points.

1) It does some good if you can laugh at yourself. Laughing relaxes muscles and gives you better circulation, making it possible to be more efficient. It's been said that laughter is good for us and our health. When taking a deep breath or relaxing, you can think more logically than when under pressure.

2) Take responsibility by making the best of each day. Live your life as if this is your last day. Step back repeatedly during the day's agenda—then reflect and assess matters. How could I have done better? What is it going to take? Shall I do it myself, or who can help me? When is the best time to start? Where could I find the answers? Why should it change? You might be saying, I already handle matters using many of these questions. Great—but remember, inevitably the time you are really having problems is the least likely time you'll put these problem-solving principles into practice.

3) A challenge to consider—it seems to me that some people go through life thinking they can do it alone. We can learn to trust and utilize other people, including God, to help us now.

SMILING IS CONTAGIOUS

The real truth is, it takes less energy to smile compared to the energy loss that comes with a frown or causing problems for others. An employee's smile says something about his or her personality. Employers are looking to hire and train persons who have a contagious smile. Smiles win people over while a frown could make a discussion more difficult. I wonder if smiling might be the least expensive and most effective management tool. With a smile illuminating your face, you make it easier for people to associate with you. As you consciously work on practicing a smile, it becomes easier and easier, until the smile becomes effortless. A smile can make you feel better.

A real smile tells others that you appreciate their company. "Something of a person's character may be discovered by observing how he/she smiles. Some people never smile; they only grin" –Bovee.[4]

Back on page 22, I showed a sketch of a person with a big smile. Smiles can be contagious. Observe people with smiles on their face. Doesn't it feel good to meet people with contagious smiles?

NON-SMOKER

The following stories may or may not apply to you. Please consider the effects that can develop from secondhand smoke.

My brother is now allergic to secondhand smoke. Smoke from cigarettes and cigars make him feel ill. The problem began when he worked with smokers in the department where he shared office space. He now says, "My employee productiveness for the company could have been better had I not developed an asthmatic problem. My health would be better today, if I had not experienced secondhand smoking on the job."

I know someone who experienced a similar problem. Still today she must be very careful to not go into places where people are smoking or have smoked. Secondhand smoke can have a negative effect upon some people.

I challenge you to check out this information from Google about what smoking can do to you. If you are a smoker and want to quit smoking, I would encourage you to seek help. Several people have shared with me how they kicked the habit, and are happy about their decision.

SOCIAL ETIQUETTE

Many of the topics up to now have touched on the expectations of social etiquette. Whether we are in an interview, visiting casually with co-workers or giving a speech, as described below, our conversation is so important. Mannerisms have a huge impact on relationships with others. Employers are looking for these attributes. Most employers do not care if you are rich or poor. They are looking for someone who will put in an honest days work and willing to work well with and for their customers.

If your employer invited you to come to their home or meet at a restaurant for a 6:00 p.m. dinner, how would you respond? Hopefully, you will accept the offer and enjoy the opportunity to visit together.

Putting on your best social behavior is as important as wearing neat clothes. A genuine friendly smile tops the list. This is a time to consider saying thank you for taking your coat, serving coffee or a meal, having been given a compliment, and finally, for their invitation as you leave. I'm sure your employer wants you to practice using the expected social graces. Our attitude can help prepare us to be polite and respectful. The same things would apply if you're going for an interview.

Speak in a kind, pleasant manner when you visit with others. Speak distinctly, and not too fast, to help others hear what you're saying. Maybe there will be others invited to dinner. Wait your turn; look at the people to whom you are addressing your conversation, so you can hold their interest.

Avoid dominating the conversation. Refer to the section on listening again. Respectful listening can signal you understand the more important values of conversation. Try to give others equal time in conversation.

When visiting, and this is my opinion, try not to get too close (less than 14 inches) to someone. Otherwise, they may be uncomfortable. And if you stand or sit too far (more than four feet) from the people in the group, they may feel there is a reason you're trying to distance yourself from the conversation.

The social expectations placed upon you go hand-in-hand with being hired for a good job and advancement. Sometimes, several little hints from the other person can show you how to change the way you are being perceived.

TEAM UNITY

I have a story to share with you about the importance of team work, as found in the PTA Monthly News, called "Something to Think About." It goes like this: "This is a story about four People named: Everybody, Somebody, Anybody, and Nobody. There was an important job to be done and Everybody was sure that Somebody would do it. Anybody could have done it, but Nobody did it. Somebody got angry about that, because it was Everybody's job. Everybody thought Anybody could do it, but Nobody realized that Everybody wouldn't do it. It ended up that Everybody blamed Somebody when Nobody did what Anybody could have." [5]

This story points out these workers' lack of a work ethic; this can happen if no one steps up to do their part in the group. The final decision or outcome will probably be no better than the strength of the weakest person in the group. My theory is: we all owe it to ourselves to help bring the weakest member of the group, the team, or even the family up to speed, so the final outcome will reflect the best. Now, we're talking about work ethics, which becomes crucial for the degree of success as a team in an organization.

When team efforts in sports are truly a team effort, the team is exciting to watch. Strong teams draw spectators to the event. Business can be the same. People appreciate going to a business where the employees seem to be working as a team. A company teamwork concept draws people into the business as opposed to running them away. This common sense effort enables the team to have much more opportunity to do great things. Both the strong and the weakest members will benefit from the unselfish team concept. So continue trying to use all your God-given talents and allowing others the same when you get together. Remember—everyone has something to contribute. Wonderful results come from all working together with harmony and love for one another, giving encouragement and complimenting others at every opportunity.

Private and public organizations spend thousands of dollars teaching employees to be good team players. If you aren't getting along with someone or some group, then think hard about why that is happening. Perhaps you're afraid or do not know how to resolve it. Get help from someone. A good team player will work out differences one way or another, rather than letting the challenge become a bigger problem. You could ask to meet with your supervisor; let your cooperative attitude show that you want some direction from him or her on how you can help to resolve the situation. If that doesn't work, get a third person involved who will help work out the differences. If that doesn't work, go to a professional for advice, a counselor, good friend, administrator, or pastor. Try to avoid procrastinating about something so important! Team players usually want to work together. Team players have the strength to rally their teammates and not grab the glorification only for themselves.

The strongest teams, just like a strong workplace encourage all people to work together, allowing each and every one to be a valuable part of the whole process.

MODESTY IS THE POLICY

Modesty is a humbling topic for me to talk about, especially because I do not want to push my thoughts or suggestions onto you. But remember, I want you to have a better working relationship to be more successful on the job, while at the same time, carrying with you a spirit of modesty and humility. Hang in there with me, please.

A modest, humble person does not always dominate conversations or think too highly of his or herself. There is no need to try to force your agenda onto others. Allow others to have their own opinions, also. Think about how your own actions look as you work with others to avoid being arrogant or conceited. You may want to avoid giving others the impression you have it too good, or that you always know all the answers.

Yes, your life can be rewarding, while holding onto a spirit of hope, humility, humbleness, and sufficient self-confidence.

HANDS OFF

Many companies have a harassment policy. If they do, read it in detail. As an example, touching another person while on the job is not generally acceptable in our society today. In business meetings and occasions, a handshake is a professional way to greet or say goodbye to another person. Touching may cause some wrong impressions and needless problems with loss of time. For example, you are trying to get someone's attention, so you speak louder and may reach for the person. Generally, there is no need to touch someone to get your point across.

POSITIVE APPROACH

I especially liked the following paragraph found in a mailing sent to me about having a positive influence, published by Mennonite Mutual Aid.

"Optimistic thinking may have benefits beyond just making you more pleasant to be around. According to the Mayo Clinic, some studies show positive people have greater resistance to colds, reduced risk of cardiovascular disease, and a longer life span, perhaps because they deal better with stress. If you're not naturally optimistic, you can become more so with practice, replacing negative thoughts with positive ideas, being open to the humor of situations, and surrounding yourself with positive people." [6]

Positive employees say yes in a number of ways, as I've already discussed back in Chapter 3, "Choosing Encouraging Words." Think about setting a goal to say yes in special ways as much of the time as you can. Positive feedback is appreciated very much. It builds up both parties. For the person hearing this, it's immeasurable. Affirmation of this kind is not difficult, if you think about it. Let it become a spontaneous habit for you. For the person giving positive remarks in the workplace, this may help to develop a productive attitude with other employees and the entire department may benefit. Employees choosing to use positive reinforcement are very valuable in the workplace.

> **Positive communication ranks high on the list to become eligible for receiving pay raises!**

STRENGTH COMES FROM PATIENCE

Patience is a virtue—we can choose to use it. If you practice patience with the small challenges that come along on a daily basis, the bigger problems will not seem so large. As an example, if your neighbor needs your help, take the time, go help them and you will probably be happy you did so. Be patient if they have requests. Learn and show a genuine interest in them. There may come a time when they take time to tell you about leaving your car lights on at the end of the day. Maybe they wouldn't have done this if you had not taken time to learn to know them. Now, because of the neighborly friendship you have developed, you didn't have to come out and find a dead car battery.

Your patience is valuable as you live your faith in the neighborhood or at work. Be patient with people in all situations. They may have an unusual deadline or trying to recover from an illness. They may be rushing to the hospital with a loved one in the back seat. Only God knows. Finding strength within us can help us make the best of the situation. Many times in my life, there was a problem to solve one day, and the next day the questions or challenges were resolved.

We live in a fast-paced world with employers who sometimes want us to work fast and to be a superman or superwoman. That doesn't mean we can't be cautious, think and plan projects well, stop briefly to "smell the roses," think before we talk, wait for the right moment, and sense God's leading while being patient with others.

I conclude this topic by quoting a saying by Bp. Horne in *The New Dictionary of Thoughts*. "Patience strengthens the spirit, sweetens the temper, stifles anger, extinguishes envy, subdues pride, bridles the tongue, restrains the hand, and tramples upon temptations."[7]

Be patient with the people and companies you work for or want to be your employer, after all it works both ways. They want good workers and you want good pay.

If you think about it in that way, it's a good decision to be patient.

CHAPTER FIFTHTEEN SUMMARY

To summarize the chapter, let's examine three words from my computer thesaurus in the title of this chapter, "Wanted: Qualified Workers." The words suggest someone is recruiting a competent employee for their workforce who is fit, has practiced skills, capable, experienced, and eligible now.

CHAPTER 16

RISING TO THE OCCASION

"Those who aim at nothing usually hit it. To aim at something we must know what it is." [1] *– Millard J. Erickson*

WHEN THE GOING GETS TOUGH, THE TOUGH GET GOING

Dale Carnegie knew what it meant to fight the odds. As a young person, and as a junior in college, "he was struggling against many odds. His family was poor…. Study had to be done between his farm chores. He withdrew from many school activities because be didn't have the time or the clothes." [2]

Dale Carnegie did not give up. He "knew he could do anything he wanted to do…." [3] Dale Carnegie fought the odds and knew what it meant to tough it out.

He went on to publish several books. One of them which stands out in my mind is entitled *How to Win Friends and Influence People.* "More than two decades after it's publication, it 'was' still selling over 250,000 copies a year and 'had' topped the 5,000,000 figure." [4]

Another paper back book published later by Carnegie was entitled, *How to Stop Worrying and Start Living.*[5] Even though both paper back books were written over fifty years ago, they both have stood the test of time, being incredible books yet today.

Successful people like Dale Carnegie rose to the occasion when they had set their sights on something valuable and dear to their hearts. Contrary to the attitude of the pessimist, the person who trains their mind and senses may achieve more. This becomes a matter of wanting to excel past the expected!

Have you ever heard the statement, "Your attitude is showing?" Webster defines attitude as "1: the arrangement of the parts of the body or figure : POSTURE" The definition also makes reference to "more at aptitude" which deals with the capacity to learn.[6]

I've often thought to myself—"I don't want to let my attitude get in the way of being able to do better." Also, if a person does not choose to do more than the bare minimum, maybe nothing more than the minimum will happen. This is not what I call toughing it out. If we're going to tough it out, we must try to set our sights on reaching our fullest potential.

Following are seven pointers about making tough decisions, suggested by Dr. Barbara Varenhorst, a psychologist, and Daralee Schulman, a career and stress management consultant.[7]

■ "Be aware of how you can't control the final outcome of a decision," only the process.

- "Identify your wants and needs" in the beginning.
- Rank your needs even if some are contradictory while asking yourself, "Which would I choose?"
- "Gather all the information" you need to make a decision such as "alternatives, consequences, advantages, and disadvantages," and please don't let your emotions get involved.
- "Determine how much of a risk you're willing to take." Choose the strategy that is the safest. Which one has the highest odds of success with the best outcome?
- "Eliminate any option" which might be hard to live with later.
- "Picture how you would deal with negative consequences."

Train your mind to get tough, making aggressive decisions for an outcome you'll be proud of "after the dust clears!"

LEADERSHIP

There are all kinds of books, classes, seminars, and audiovisuals suggesting ways to be a leader. Basically, a big part of this self-help book is about becoming a leader. Everyone is different in the way and number of people they feel comfortable in leading.

As an example, a person may find it hard to sell a certain brand of cars, when in fact, they are personally sold on another brand. Here's my point—it is important to feel good about the designated products which the team is to sell. It would be very hard if you do not prefer your product group. So it is with people. You must first convince yourself to feel good about the company or assigned group! It would be a big challenge to fix a situation if you didn't like the product or people in the group representing the company for whom you work. You must work hard on having good feelings about being in the right place. I hope you can consider buying into the following statement: Do the very best you can within your group, regardless of the situation!

These individuals stand out in my mind when leadership is mentioned. Zig Ziglar quotes Andrew Carnegie in his book, who once said, "No man can become rich without himself enriching others." Andrew Carnegie developed motivated followers.[8]

Here is another quote from the book *Launching a Leadership Revolution*, by Chris Brady and Orrin Woodward: "Sooner or later, we are all called upon to lead. Whether at your job or in your home, in your community or in your church, one day you will need to step up and take control."[9]

Think about why someone would want to follow you as a leader.

WORKING THE EXTRA HOUR

The following may be hard to hear, but staying after the normal hours is expected when the demand is necessary. In my opinion, the difference between a person earning a minimum hourly wage, versus having a better paying job, may be as simple as offering to stay after the normal quitting time to finish helping a customer or doing a project.

Can you be excited about coming earlier, staying over or coming after hours to help the boss with special projects when the demand is necessary? A willing attitude of interest for making things work well within the company or establishment happens with your help! You must work hard with a frame of mind that exhibits going the extra mile. After the boss sees the potentially good attitude in you as an hourly employee, exciting things may develop to improve your position with the company. As an example, management may be thinking, let's find out if Susan or Sam want to come help us do sales for the company display this weekend at the car show. If either turn down their supervisor about doing volunteer work after hours, even though he/she had good excuses, the opportunities may go away. Refusals may be announcing that you are an 8:00 a.m. to 5:00 p.m. person and your personal interests take precedence. Instead, it is advisable to find within yourself to say, "if my boss wants me to help with special projects after hours, I will consider it."

Overtime may be or may not be paid. Either way, advancement depends on you. The "can do" attitude may directly contribute to wage increases.

SCANNING SAVES TIME

Publications can easily be scanned for interesting reading or trends in the field of your expertise. Find a time daily—say five, ten, or 30 minutes to scan information and reports that have implications for your field of interest. If possible, try to protect that reading time. You may want to scan the captions and titles of articles first. Look for interesting headlines in magazines or the newspaper. The Wall Street Journal, USA Today, and trade subscriptions are all good reading sources. After scanning, come back and read more interesting reading material more in-depth.

When I was a young businessman, I realized how important it was to plan, but didn't take enough time to practice scanning reading material.

Saving and filing interesting articles for referral at a later time is helpful. It's worthwhile to set up a useful filing or retrieval system. Be sure to date and label the file to find easily. Review Chapter 4, Topic six, "Keeping Copies of Important Information."

PROBLEM SOLVING STRATEGIES

Have you done a big job lately which called for more depth of understanding? Do you consciously or unconsciously use a problem-solving strategy? Maybe you use a unique decision-making pattern similar to the full blown problem-solving strategy like the following.

When doing my graduate studies, I was required to do an extensive research project called a thesis. After many days of trying to figure out what would be of interest to me and still be of benefit to others, I settled on researching problem solving strategies.

I value my year of studying at Ball State University and preparing my thesis called, *Problem Solving Strategies*.

Following is a simplified version for solving small or large day-to-day problems.

Stage 1— Identify the problem (something which makes things uncomfortable).

Stage 2—Review the situation (thinking more about the troubling matter).

Stage 3—Arrive at possible solutions (looking for tentative ideas to fix the problem).

Stage 4—Collect support data (builds support evidences).

Stage 5—Reach a decision (reviews support data to draw conclusions).

Stage 6—Apply the decision (follows through by solving the problem thoroughly with a fix).

Regarding data collection stage 4 above (collecting information): usually, one would think first about getting data from books, magazines, or the Internet. If you're going to build support to solve the problem, spend some time taking notes of your thoughts and how or where you should go for similar support material; then do it. At this stage, you should not be trying to decide which data is best. The business of paying attention to detail while collecting data cannot be over-emphasized.

More about collecting data: visit the library or bookstore. Research the Web for finding more information. It is amazing how the computer can find information simply by typing in the question on the Google line. If it is about researching the marketplace for industrial product information, it is hard to beat the Thomas Register, which contains many volumes of valuable information. If it is about researching the construction industry, try the Architectural Digest, which also contains many volumes of information.

Some people may choose to stop after stage 5 above and do not see it through to the end in stage 6. I discussed this in Chapter 4 of my book, in the section called, "Following Through." The problem solving process can be used for nearly all decisions, large or small in life. I catch myself making decisions too fast sometimes when I'm playing cards. If the card has already been laid, the saying is, "A card laid is a card played," meaning you can't pick it up and play another card after you've already laid down the first card.

Be cautious about rushing your decisions!

LIVING A SIMPLER LIFESTYLE

Can anyone be successful and live a simple lifestyle? The Amish people seem to enjoy living a simpler lifestyle, focusing on less material conveniences, working together and sharing their religious beliefs as a community. Perhaps we can learn from their simpler lifestyle. They seem to have mastered a simpler way to live on less and experience self-sufficiency, all the time living a worthwhile, dedicated life. If you want to learn more about the Amish, you can purchase the small paperback book, **Amish Values for Your Family** by Suzanne Woods Fisher.

> Have you ever heard the statement, "The more you make, the more you spend?" What choices can we make to take us down a path of living within our means or budget? Budgeting goals can help you or your family. Encourage others who live with you to help with the process. Personally, I think one way to gradually improve living a simpler lifestyle would be writing down realistic goals discussed in Chapter 7, topic 5, entitled PLANNING PERSONAL GOALS. You may want to decide what you can comfortably live without. Consider buying things you need, not always what you want!

If you're serious about this aspect of living a simpler lifestyle, there are books to buy on this subject for only a few dollars. A small investment for a book and a little time reading the material will pay dividends over and over again. Try to stretch your dollars so you can enjoy more of the things you need. Like I have stressed, "need," rather than things you'd like to have. Can you eat good, nutritious food for less? Can you be less wasteful with foods by developing a good system for leftovers? Can you decide to be happy with a smaller variety of entertainment? Slow down and savor each moment. My wife reminds me often, "we can slow down and enjoy, the finer things in life, our faith, family, friends, and reaching out to others with the love of God."

It's a mental decision to live a simpler lifestyle! Some very productive people aren't noticed as much because they are living in this way. They may own a comfortable, landscaped, new looking home and car. They may own acres of land and have other wealth but it never shows. That could be another reason they live within their budget and a simple lifestyle. They may have learned that giving to the church and people in need means spending less on themselves. This simpler lifestyle has the potential to add years of happiness.

> **Pastor John C. Murray says, "Those who intentionally plan their generosity are uniting the values of careful planning and management with the values of compassion and care for others—that is success even if a project fails."[10]**

THANKING OTHERS

The habit of thanking people for their accomplishments by word of mouth, with letters, notes, phone calls, or an e-mail after finishing an event or project, is paramount to your success! This can include thanking God daily for his constant watch over us.

Begin now, if you haven't already, to thank and recognize people who have contributed to the success of something they've done in the community or workplace. Share with them how special it was to have them participate. Share with them how their involvement played a big part in the success of the project. Make the note or message short. It's the intentions that are the most significant, not the length of the communication. If you forgot to thank them immediately, follow up with a passing remark next time you see them. Even though you may feel you are not good with words, remember, it's the thought behind the thank you note that counts. It is kosher (the acceptable thing to do) to recognize people for their extra effort whether it was for pay or volunteering. I hope "thanking others" becomes a big part of your life.

BECOMING SPIRITUALLY EXCITED

Webster defines spirituality as "sensitivity or attachment to religious values."[11]

This topic is my personal testimony and interpretation for becoming spiritually excited. Again, according to my interpretation of the definition, a spiritually active person is someone who is both sensitive and excited about promoting values of religious living in their daily life. I invite you to deepen your spirituality in your own tradition.

Here is a thought you might want to ponder. It comes from Millard Erickson's book *Does*

It Matter How I Live? Erickson's title to Chapter 1 is, "If the Gospel Is So Simple, Why Is Godly Living So Hard?"[12]

Choices to be made are around us every day. Christian living does not have to be hard.

Are you choosing to let your life shine with a joy that promotes values of Christian living? Let's take a look at the Beatitudes, found in Matthew 5:3-10. When Jesus walked on the earth, he found himself surrounded by crowds of people. Jesus possessed that magnetism talked about in Chapter 1. Crowds of people wanted to hear from Him on how they could become more spiritually like Him. We find Him speaking to them, and I quote from the book of Matthew: "Humble people are very fortunate...for the Kingdom of Heaven is given to them. Those who mourn are fortunate! for they shall be comforted. The meek and lowly are fortunate! for the whole wide world belongs to them. Happy are those who long to be just and good, for they shall be completely satisfied. Happy are the kind and merciful, for they shall be shown mercy. Happy are those whose hearts are pure, for they shall see God. Happy are those who strive for peace—they shall be called the sons of God. Happy are those who are persecuted because they are good, for the Kingdom of Heaven is theirs."[13]

My challenge is arranging daily work around God's instruction for myself, rising to each occasion when struggles come along. Included in this challenge is to live a more fulfilling life of happiness, becoming more spiritually motivated by following Jesus's teachings daily.

MOTIVATED

Kevin Wilder specifically prepared this topic on motivation for Chapter 16.

"First, a working definition of motivation is about either moving toward something for a reason or away from something for a reason; moving away from the chocolate chip cookie to fit into a new dress or suit or moving toward the cookie because it would taste good.

Second, Abraham Maslow had a theory that people move up to reach higher needs after lower needs are met. If we don't have food and shelter, then we are not as concerned about friends and the meaning of life.

Third, we know that people respond more positively to clear, specific, measurable goals as opposed to broad and undefined goals. An example of this is a student who thinks, "I will create a two-sided note card with key terms and concepts over each chapter of the book and will read each chapter by Thursday," rather than the vague goal of, "I will get an A" or "I am planning to do better."

*All that being said, **let's apply these three ideas to unemployment.***

It is best to frame your goal for employment in the positive such as: "I want to get up every day and contribute to my family and my community." Versus, "I don't want to starve." More energy is generated from using the positive approach.

Second, taking a job to meet basic needs will be fulfilling for awhile, but it is important to also think about higher needs like friendships, family time, and quality of life issues as well.

Third, state your goal in looking for a job. Specifically, plan to submit two resumés a day or make four phone calls or check three websites for employment each day."[14]

Whether you have a job or not, get motivated on a new level to find happiness in employment, looking for quality of life on and off the job.

CHAPTER SIXTEEN SUMMARY

Rise to the occasion. Continue to give up on old practices that you do not really want to keep, allowing more time for the quality of life that God would want you to enjoy. Try to move up to your new expectations that bring true happiness and fulfillment.

Chapter 17

MORE IMPORTANT TIPS

FAVORS HAVE LIMITS

Listen for subtle comments shared by the boss, friends, and colleagues. Gain a deeper understanding by listening to their likes and dislikes. Take an active interest in group discussions. Become friends with co-workers at work by only sharing kind things about them. Do not go against your better judgment when a time comes that you need a special request or favor. If it doesn't feel like the timing is right, then drop it and work out another time to discuss the request.

Sometimes, asking for a favor before we think more about it is not the best decision. Give it much thought before actually asking them for the request. If it's something big, I'd recommend trying this method. Before you ask for the favor, quite often the pros and cons can be sized up on each side of lined paper. On one side, write the pluses, and on the other side, write the negative aspects of the issue. The answer to your request for a favor may become clear as each of the pluses and negatives are evaluated. Your intuition, or inner common sense, will kick in, giving you a sense of the situation. Then, focus on asking for a special request or favor only if you think the answer would probably be a yes.

Asking for too many favors is a good way to put a strain on the relationship whether it's your boss, co-worker, family member, neighbor, or whoever. So think it over once, twice and three times before you ask them for something that might not be appropriate timing.

CLUTTER-FREE MENTALITY

This paragraph is to encourage me, too! We can start at home by keeping our hat and coat hanging in the right places. It's just too easy to drop both a hat and coat on the closest chair as we come home or arrive at the office. I'm still working on this one. More than your hat and coat, everything could have a specific place to be stored and returned again—"a place for everything and everything in its place." Our daily routine can happen easier if we know where to locate our car keys, bills, purse, or important papers immediately. This can be an excellent habit to enhance productivity at home or work. Employers appreciate employees who practice good housekeeping.

A clutter-free mentality energizes me and it may do the same for you.

UP FRONT SEATING BONUS

If you choose to sit up front at meetings, seminars, performances and events, you may get more from the speaker. You may miss the non-verbal part of the speaker's message when you sit too far from the front. In Chapter 13, the topic entitled "More Than Listening," Dr. Yoder pointed out that "93% of all our communication is non-verbal."[1]

Upon this premise, what's being heard may be taken differently based upon how far you are from the person(s) featured at the event. The attendee in close proximity of the entertainment or speaker might be able to pick up on more by watching facial expressions from the person(s) as well as responses from people up front in the audience. Maybe I should define my "up front" point of view. If you're able to see the eyes of the presenter or group giving their performance, you're up front. Facial expressions and other slight movements, tell much about what the speaker or entertainer(s) are truly trying to get across. Obviously, you can hear what they're saying if the audio speaker system works well, however, you may be still missing out on the heart of the event. That's why people sometimes pay more for up front seating. Here's another thought to think about when being seated up front. There will be other successful people up front and value the opportunity of socializing with one another before the event, at the breaks, and visiting afterward as another important bonus for coming to the meeting or event.

In conclusion, if you arrive early, you can find the right place for yourself and those accompanying you.

RESPECTING OTHERS' PERSONAL SPACE

Have you ever experienced a person who was too close to you as you were talking together or made you uncomfortable because they were in your space?

What is an appropriate distance to be from someone's face while they are speaking with us? I'm referring to our culture. What is acceptable in America may be different in another country. But in America, I've read we shouldn't be closer than approximately two feet to someone when talking together. If you're closer, the person may feel uncomfortable. Using appropriate social skills like this is so important, especially in the workplace.

Respecting others' personal space applies to waiting in line, parking spaces, stadium seating, bosses office, and seating in an airplane. When parking our vehicles, we should avoid parking too close to another vehicle so the doors do not dink the neighboring car. Also, I try not to take up more than one space. It is a matter of showing respect to other people for their personal space.

FRIENDS FOR THE RIGHT REASONS

What are some of the ways we can receive help from family, friends, and acquaintances about job opportunities? If a friend, for instance, knows you are searching for a job, they can help by calling you if he or she hears of an opportunity. Connections and networking can be an asset to us in the job search. Developing friendships within our community, church, and workplace might give us a lead for a much needed job. Most good jobs are found by word of mouth through referrals from friends and acquaintances. I continue to advocate that we try to make friends with others, except those who might be wanting to show us they do not want our friendship. We can still be kind to others.

Try not to take advantage of friendships by over using their kindness. Sharing can be a give and take situation with friends. Friends can take turns helping each other. Sometimes, one or the other might need more help because of an unexpected accident, illness or death in the family. A wonderful goal to reach would be—to treat others as they deserve to be treated and we would like to be treated.

Trustworthy family and friends are priceless. True friends probably know how to handle confidential job search information. Finding the best in everyone is key to finding friends for the right reasons.

SUBTLE REMARKS

Listen for information, such as gentle hints, shared between the lines. Try practicing the use of helpful advice through honesty, humor, and puns. Building each other up is team-building, and bringing each other down is the opposite. It is human nature to like something that brings our spirits up instead of down. So, we may want to share what needs to be told in an up-beat indirect way, such as a story, or in the form of a question.

At times we might do better watching and listening for obvious remarks as a story is told, and not miss something, maybe an opportunity of a lifetime.

CONDUCTING MEETINGS EFFECTIVELY

In a publication called Communication Briefings, Carol L. Barnum shares the following in an article called "Here's How To Manage Your Meetings Effectively."

■ Plan the meeting well. If the meeting is not planned well with objectives to meet, don't have it. Think about the key players involved and the positions they may take. Develop your plan around winning them to your position. Seven members in the committee is recommended.

■ Notify each committee member in advance with the agenda to be discussed. Give the date, time, and place. It should be far enough in advance to help them prepare to be active participants. List the items in order of priority with the highest priority at the top of the list. The agenda should include these points: Date, start time and end time, directions to the meeting, brief descriptions and who will be addressing the topics, time allowed for each person on the agenda, and attached preparatory reading.

■ Assign someone to facilitate (someone to take notes and make sure the group stays on target). Consider the seating arrangement. Find multimedia visuals to reinforce your strong points you want to make and to convince them of your leadership. "A study, sponsored by 3M, showed that when visuals were used, the audience remembered up to 10% more of the information." She found that "visuals also bring faster decisions." "Visuals reduce meeting time." She points out that "a university study has shown that when computer-generated overhead transparencies or slides were used, the presenter was perceived as being up to 43% more persuasive. In addition, the presenter is seen as more professional, more credible, and more interesting."

- "Problem-solving groups aim for a consensus." A circular arrangement encourages discussion and invites each one to participate.
- "Decision-making groups seek specific actions." Putting persons in rows with the chairperson standing in front gives assertiveness to the chair's position, steering the group to a quicker consensus. Try not to pit one side against the other. Prearrange the seating order, where the chair places agenda for each at the table with their names on the materials in advance.
- Eye contact is very important. Eye contact can determine who is encouraged to give more or less input to the discussion. Barnum says that in leaderless groups, if you want to claim the leadership role, arrive early enough to position yourself where you are most likely to receive and give the most eye contact, such as on the side where two persons are sitting and where three are sitting on the other side. Position people who are at odds with one another side-by-side so they have reduced eye contact.

In summary she says, the best way to ruin a meeting is to "arrive late, open on a comic level, come unprepared, allow for telephone (or other) interruptions, resent questions, monopolize the meeting, lose control," and do not follow prepared agenda.[2]

SPEAKING WITH EFFECTIVENESS

As we speak with others, we want to remember that the other individual has important information to share with us, also. We can share our thoughts, and then be aware to give time for them to share and/or listen. What impression does he or she think of us after we have had a discussion? We can only hope they have enjoyed conversing with us. Could it be that we show more strength and awareness when we minimize our speaking and concentrate on listening strengths?

Have you heard someone say after their interview, "I really feel good about everything that happened. I was able to get all my questions answered." That is not always a good omen. I've been told some questions need to be unanswered in an interview, otherwise it may be a sign you're too forward or talking too much. Leave your listener with some questions. It's much like giving a book report.

Sometimes in a debate, maybe the way to close is "agree to disagree."

I'm not an authority on debate, but when two are debating an issue and neither wants to give in to the other's opinion, they could agree to disagree. Contrary to opinion where there is an argument or big difference of opinion, the one to get in the last word has probably won the fight, but maybe lost the battle. The more mature employee will show restraint, patience, and calmness. They have learned that an organized, self-assured person will normally prevail.

Here's a thought on speaking tips—if you are giving a speech and know where, when, who the speech is going to be addressed to, and what the subject is about, why not invite a person or two who could appreciate the topic of the speech? Then, if they come to hear the speech, you could publicly thank them for coming.

Carol Driscoll, in an article from Communications Briefings, says that good speakers "make it a point to entertain as well as inform." She goes on to give six other good pieces of advice. Speakers are:

(1) "thoroughly prepared and comfortable with their material." They outline their main points on multimedia and have checked it out to see if it works in advance.

(2) Speakers get the audience involved "by soliciting answers and information." Use creative ways to have them stand or a show of hands.

(3) Speakers "enhance the presentation with other things like newspaper clippings, cartoons, music, appropriate quotes or relevant experiences."

(4) Speakers "use self-deprecating humor to get a point across. This allows the audience to identify with the speaker's foibles."

(5) Speakers may want to try meeting people at the door prior to the speech. Move around while giving the speech, "a technique that makes you seem accessible."

(6) Speakers avoid boring an audience with material that is known.[3]

I really like the following speech tip. It comes from *How to Speak So People Will Listen*" by Ronald L. Willingham. "To develop genuine enthusiasm for speaking, you'll need a *goal*, or an *objective*. Make up your mind what you want to do."[4]

Use limited hand, arm(s) and body movements to reinforce points in your speech.

"Look at your listeners...Pick out four or five people in different parts of the room and speak to them, shifting your eyes from one to another."[5]

Bring the audience along with a joke and a story line. This can often be a good way to start a speech, but takes much practice to get the punch line across effectively.

Include wit and humor in your speech as pointed out in Chapter 13 under the topic of **Sense of Humor** by William Davis who said, "The kind of humor I like is the thing that makes you laugh for five seconds and think for 10 minutes."[6]

To quote Ronald L. Willingham again from his book, *How to Speak so People Will Listen*: "If you want to learn to speak, you must be conversational."[7]

STREET WISE

What I mean to pass on to you here is, don't be naïve to the exchange that goes on between some people or groups as you travel about on foot, by bus, train, car, or plane. I'm cautioning you to be mindful of time that could be taken away from the productiveness in your job. We see and hear of weird, devastating things on TV sometimes. Are there ways we can be more aware and prepared for this type of situation? Why not take precautions against being in the wrong places at the wrong time by practicing some serious preventive measures? This means more than just minding our own business. I personally try to stay away from places where it could get roudy.

If you have a premonition against something, listen to the small inner voice within. It might be a passing thought telling you to stay away from places where crimes could take place. One example—if you have that feeling coming or going to work, go home before the streets become empty of people carrying on their daily routines.

Blend in socially with the times and places where you go rather than looking like a stranger or a tourist in the area. Go places with others rather than by yourself. As an example, if you go to a large city and are constantly gazing up at the tall buildings, you may be noticed. You would look like an outsider. Plan your trips in advance. Pick the safest routes. Go about your life in a straightforward, quiet, dignified manner. It's good to let close family or friends know where you're going or staying when traveling.

Don't flash around your purchases or prized possessions. If you go into the store and purchase some things, bring them back and lock them in your car, then go back in to finish your shopping, you may have just given the thief an advantage to know you've gone back in the store to shop for awhile again. Lock your belongings up just prior to leaving the parking lot or area. Park your vehicle in a well-lighted parking area in the flow of things. Keep the windows up and car doors locked.

Walk down the street with confidence, in the openness of the area, away from cars and closed corners or blind alleyways. Don't leave valuables or personal items unattended for any stranger to grab easily. Try to fit in with the people who live and work in that community. Carry a very limited amount of cash so if someone did rob you, you wouldn't be out of very much. Keep your wallet in your zipped part of the purse or buttoned in your pocket when out and about. Try not to have direct eye contact with strangers who pass you by. You can tell others hello when appropriate, but limit your conversation with strangers. Watch out and steer away from suspicious looking characters. Eat in quiet established eating places that have a good following and others that frequent the place daily.

Keep records of important documents with identification numbers of each, so if stolen, you could cancel credit cards, etc., in minutes. Carry a cell phone or other devices that signal you need help. Carry it so you could go straight to it in a moment. There is much more that could be said about being street wise, but we should always be mindful at all times of our power available in knowing and praying for God's protection that is there for us at any time.

POWER OF FORGIVENESS

Jeremy Kingsley in his book entitled *Getting Back Up When Life Knocks You Down*, writes a whole chapter about "finding freedom in forgiveness." [8]

—If they have hurt you—

People, including you and me, have setbacks from time to time. This can cause grief or bitterness and then "We must find ways to break down and mend the walls of hurt," as shared with me by my pastor's father, John F. Murray.[9]

It may not be a matter of changing the person or group(s) decision who hurt you. **You**… may have to take steps to mend the walls of hurt that you are experiencing.

As Billy Graham states in the preface of his book, *The Journey*, "Whatever has happened in your life so far—both good and bad—cannot be altered, and all the decisions and events that have made you what you are today are indelibly inscribed in the story of your life…. No matter what your life has been like so far, God wants to put your feet on a new path…a better path…His path."[10]

The book of Matthew gives us a big part of what we might know to point our lives in a positive direction of action. I find it especially uplifting to read the words from the book of Matthew 1-28, especially the print in red, spoken by Jesus, in my red-lettered edition of the Living Bible. It gives me new hope and a freshness of mind. It allows me to focus on the real important issues facing me now, and not only on the past.

Jesus was sent to earth as a baby, to live his life and teach as a model for our lives. Jesus tells us how to live our lives with others by breaking down the walls of hurt, anger, grudges, resentment, hurt, hostility, bitterness, grief, heartache, and unhappiness through the power of forgiveness.

—If you have hurt them—

How do you start the process of asking for forgiveness? You simply ask Jesus or the Lord God to help you. If it involves another person or group, go with sincerity and tell them that something has been bothering you. Tell them something along this line of thought: "I am sorry that it happened the way it did, and I hope you can forgive me for _____ . I was wrong." Thank them for allowing you to visit together. Tell them you feel much better having had the chance to visit together. Find other good things (do your homework before you go) to add to the conversation. Keep it short and end on a friendly note. Maybe it's the case where they have died, and now what? How do you ask someone to forgive you if they've died? Jesus tells us in Matthew how you are a special person. He loves you. Simply get on your knees and ask Jesus to forgive you for all you have done wrong. You are special to him. If you're sincere, and by the way, Jesus knows all things, He will hear your call for help—and now all you have to do is have faith as you carry on with a new life—allowing Jesus to help you each minute, each hour, each day, and each year for the rest of your life.

Accepting a value system of this magnitude will help free your mind for being all that you want to be. Forgiveness breaks down walls of unhappiness which would otherwise have impeded growth of the kind Christ desires of all of us.

RAISING THE BAR

Have you ever been to a track meet where the high jumper or the person pole vaulting was expected to jump even higher to stay in the competition?

Are you equally aware that therein lies this paradox? According to Dr. Ruby K. Payne in her book, *A Framework for Understanding Poverty*, "an individual brings with him/her the hidden rules of the class in which he/she was raised. Even though the income of the individual may rise significantly, many of the patterns of thought, social interaction, cognitive strategies, etc. remain with the individual."[11]

If this does not pertain to you, skip to the next topic. If this does pertain to you, let's talk more about changing those uncomfortable feelings about moving up, especially in the job world. What this change may mean is that you can choose to develop an ambition like never before. Develop a burning desire of "I can" as discussed in Chapter 6. As I understand implications to Dr. Payne's quote, some may want to think of new and different ways to improve their current life style immediately by applying many of the tips in this book. Consider how and when you're going to start practicing the patterns of expectations (hidden rules) of the income level you would like to have, while earning more money. Think about your history, present situation, and where you are going in the near future. If you do have that burning desire to change, and now you've read about many of the attributes employers are wanting in an employee—go for it. As time goes on and you're being paid more, the hidden rules and expectations generally increase as the yearly income increases.

Even if you are handicapped or disabled, or close to living in poverty, it is difficult. Remember, I've been there as a kid growing up. I want all my readers to experience something better and enjoy a better style of living. Raising the bar of expectation will take a determined aggressiveness! Hopefully, I've inspired you to apply suggestions which can work, if given time. Perhaps it would be a good time to visit with a trusted friend about these matters. It could be an opportunity of prayerfully and earnestly talking with God to feel the glimmer of hope you so desire.

ENJOY PICTURE PHOTOS

Do you carry a picture of someone very special to you? Or have photos like this at home or work? Or hanging on the walls? Could this be good for your health? Consider this, it can be a way to enjoy precious memories and the finer things in life. If you're already doing this, great. If you're not practicing this, you may want to think about enjoying life more completely. Fill your life with photos and mementos which can add much happiness to your life.

They make my life worth living!

MORE ABOUT ENTREPRENEURSHIP

I wrote a couple of paragraphs about entrepreneurship back in Chapter 9, as you may recall, and a few more tips in other places. I'm sharing more about this subject since the time and money in owning your own business is so critical in the planning stages, much more than normally expected. For that reason and more, owning your own business while still under employment may hamper your effectiveness in your primary employment job. So I recommend you think clearly before venturing into something new too quickly. Find articles in books and the local library to read. Visit your local small business administration (SBA) office.

Starting your own business may be a way to generate more income. I say this reluctantly, because even though you may earn more, starting your own business has big start up costs and huge risks. There is a very high failure rate of people who started their own business, then lost it or became bankrupt. So here is my advice. (1) Talk to others about your plans. Get feedback about the pros and cons. (2) An entrepreneur is a person with special gifts. I would recommend you have an outgoing, pleasant personality. Read all about the kind of personality people have who have been successful. 3) Most people need thousands of dollars to start a business. Do you have that kind of money? (4) In Chapter 8, I explain the need for a business plan to include a trip to the bank sooner or later. The business plan is paramount. (5) Do you know a skill or vocation very well? (6) Have you been encouraged by someone to consider going into business for yourself? (7) How well do you know the product or customer need for this venture? (8) Are you willing to take several educational classes to bring yourself up to speed on the aspects of starting a business? (9) Are you willing to spend 60 hours a week running your own business versus 38-42 hours a week drawing wages from an employer? (10) Will you start the business on a part-time basis without jeopardizing your full-time job? If you can answer all ten of these questions and necessities with affirmation, then maybe you can consider starting a small business.

All I ask of you is to think long and hard about starting your own business, because you are ultimately responsible for everything that happens.

COMING FROM ABROAD

When we were in Branson, Missouri recently, we attended a dinner and performance by Yakov Smirnoff, who came to America from Russia, when he was younger. Yakov told a story during the show we attended, that he had to learn not only English when he arrived here, but a whole new language of expressions, word meanings, and accents to communicate with others.

He learned that many restaurants and businesses have baby changing tables in their rest rooms. Yakov laughed as he told the story, because the first time he saw the sign, he thought this meant that, if you wanted to, you could exchange your baby with another person's baby. He commented about some of our interesting expressions, words, and phrases which often have double meanings in our country. In addition, there are long lists of American slang and collections of common words with opposite meanings to learn.

If you're serious about moving up in your job, you can benefit from arranging more time to socialize with others and learning the jargon people use both on and off the job.

FREEDOM TO MAKE GOOD CHOICES

I'm fortunate my great grandfather chose to come to America. Where he was born, they were not given the chance to make some of their own choices. The country's leaders required its people to follow their lead.

My great grandfather traveled to America as a young man to start a new life where he would have the freedom to worship, make choices on how much he wanted to earn, and was free to choose his own lifestyle.

After arriving in America by ship, he found work with farmers, digging miles of clay tile trenches by hand so their fields would drain and produce better crops. I'm glad he chose to look for a life of purpose, a life that was not dead ended and open to leading a strong Christian lifestyle. I'm sure he was not only thinking about his own life, but the generations following him, including my family. Sometimes we cannot experience the rewards of hard work in our own lives, but only to have future generations reap the rewards.

What path would you have chosen and just how hard are you willing to work for the freedoms our forefathers have laid out for us? There are and always will be difficult decisions for all of us as we strive to make things better in the sight of God.

CHAPTER SEVENTEEN SUMMARY

Whatever your background may be, and if you are trying to break into a new lifestyle, put away the past and practice raising the bar for a new standard of living. You may choose to reach for new opportunities where you set your sites on family harmony, hope, honor, humility, hire, health, healing and happiness that can occupy each day of your life.

CHAPTER 18

LOOKING TO THE FUTURE

LIFE UNDER THE MAGNIFYING GLASS

What would you like to see if you were examined under a magnifying glass? If someone were to examine me that closely, I hope they would see everything at its best.

I believe God sees us as though He were looking through a very high-powered, clean, lighted magnifying glass. I also believe the almighty, all-knowing Lord God not only sees but hears everything we do, as I understand from reading Psalms 139. Why shouldn't we take advantage of a good thing, and consider allowing God to see us very plainly, loving, pleasant and showing kindness to everyone we see and meet daily. My pastor, John C. Murray, sums it up this way: "No matter what God sees, God loves you and God's grace wants to help you continue to grow and change."[1]

WITH A CIRCLE OF BELIEVERS

Being active in a worship group is good for maintaining a well-rounded lifestyle. I believe it's good to worship with other people of similar faiths. It is a time when you can praise God and sense His Spirit's leading in your life as well as in others.

My wife and I are grateful for our pastors and others who lead us in worship, praying, sharing, singing, and having fellowship. I have learned that for me, there's no going it alone. I need a time in my life to go meet God in worship.

What avenue do you use, or will you use to strengthen your Christian life? If you are not going to church, but are active in a worship group, great. God is willing to meet you where you are. Whether you're an active member at church (which I recommend) or not, I hope you're allowing God to work in your life and not taking Him for granted. Our God loves and cares about you and everyone.

I've encouraged the value of meeting God through actively joining friends in worship. Consider letting God lead you minute by minute, hour by hour, day by day, every day. Here are a few suggestions for giving God a part of your daily life and worship experiences:

- Offering problems up to God in prayer for Him to help guide your thoughts
- Arranging special times of rest away from the busy workload to meditate
- Building strong, mutual, respectful relationships in the workplace and at home
- Striving to be joyful through Jesus Christ and with the support of friends
- Strengthening business decision-making by referring to the word of life, the Bible
- Allowing God to raise you to new heights of service for others in need

- Studying the Bible both by yourself and with a circle of believers, learning how it applies to you in real life experiences as you work and deal with others.

Without experiencing what friends in faith are all about, we can miss a large segment of discovering the joys in life. Both church and worship groups have played an important part in my life. I've learned the expectations that are placed upon me as a child of God. Perhaps it could be looked upon as a maintenance program—a way to take care of what I've been given and sometimes taken for granted. I must be responsible and contribute more than just to my own life. My life is about ways I can contribute to others; my family, community, job, country, friends, church, and those I meet daily at home or from other parts of the world. We are God's caretakers of everything around us, including other people or animals, and the environment. What is your position as you pass through this earthly life and what can be gained? I suggest you owe it to yourself, and if you have family, to your children and your children's children, to explore these options.

BREAKING BREAD

Brokenness can be fixed. Forgiveness is part of the equation. Jesus broke bread with his disciples, announcing they were ordinary folks preparing to spread the word of God's saving grace for everyone who would accept his presence in their lives.

You may want to consider breaking bread with your loved ones and others as an expression of your faith.

The Bible tells us that one of the two men, who were hung on a cross to die alongside Jesus, recognized Jesus as God's son who could forgive him of his sins and allow his spirit to leave his body upon death, going to heaven to be with Jesus forever. The choice was made, he accepted the challenge. He would be able to leave this world to spend eternity in heaven, leaving all his troubles behind.

Many people have turned to Jesus early, rather than later, to live a more complete life. If you have not yet done this, please consider making that choice. God's love and guidance can help all of us.

TO NEW BEGINNINGS

The following story has been made up to depict a segment of our society.

A year ago, I needed lumber to build some Bluebird Houses. One of my friends knew I was looking for used cedar fence boards. He told me that Jack had a pile of used, rough dog-eared cedar fence boards that would make good bird houses. Well, I got excited about the offer and picked up the phone. Jack offered me a chance to come get the pile of old Western Red Cedar fence boards as soon as possible. So, I went to look at the boards. When I found the boards piled alongside weeds in a field, I chuckled and imagined hearing one board telling another board, "Do you see that old guy who wants to make beautiful bird houses out of us? Who's he kidding! We're not good enough for that! We're too rough around the edges. We do not look good." I had to think about this scenario. My first impression was, the boards did not fill the bill for my needs right then. Some were dirty because they were stacked close to the soil in the field. They would need a lot of TLC. They probably were there for two years or more. Some had bad markings and scratches. Others had been slammed together making nail marks on the face side. Many of the fence boards had gouges from being mishandled. Others had been split off from the main part. Many boards simply showed a lack of care.

I was thinking to myself, "I can cut out the bad and surface one side of the board with my 6" jointer. After some cleaning, people will like the way they look. They've already stood the time of becoming weathered, and now I can change them into new, beautiful bird houses. About that time, I started pulling the best boards from the pile.

Again the boards are complaining. "Oh, that hurts, it's giving me a headache and burns along my side. You're making me so uncomfortable. I don't want to be hammered, sawed, sanded and nailed just to help a family of birds. In fact, I don't like birds that are blue. I'm already feeling blue enough from being kicked around. "That is for the birds." I'd rather be burned for firewood than go through so much.

I began to cut and build the Bluebird houses into works of art so my retailers would want them from me in the spring. They would sell for $24.95 a piece. One day when I was loading them for delivery, I again heard a voice saying, "Why back then, no one wanted me, I was not so happy with the way I looked. No one would seriously talk to me about what I could do for them. In fact, sometimes they would talk bad about me, even though I tried to feel good about myself. Many times they would act as though I didn't even exist. And back then, I had a poor place to stay, but look at me now. I'm changed into something useful and wanted. I'm happy. It's working and I'm exciting. The changes have been worth all the discomforts in the process of being made new. I have caring neighbors now who sing pretty and treat me as "King in my own house."

Isn't this metaphor much like the story I'm telling about in my book? If you haven't had your special job opportunity yet, or haven't been doing well, you have a chance to be real useful in society, successful, and living a happy structured life, full of meaning and productiveness. Allow people to help you make changes. Do the best you can, while rising to the occasion. I encourage you to feel charged with that challenge.

A DECISION FOR ETERNITY

Joel Osteen ends his book *Starting Your Best Life Now* by challenging his readers to develop an enthusiasm, "doing everything with your whole heart," not just being mediocre. He says, "Do it with passion and some fire. Not only will you feel better, but that fire will spread, and soon other people will want what you have."[2]

Please consider allowing Jesus to fire you up in your daily associations with people now, preparing for the job or the interview, in your workplace, and in your home life. I encourage you to be excited about your proactive stand!

Remember, little things become big things many times over in life. Try bringing to each occasion a smile of happiness, remembering all the blessings God gives you.

Looking back in your life, how many times have you prayed asking God to help you through a difficult situation? God wants to help us fulfill our dreams! He wants us to be part of the family of God. Without including him in our actions daily, life can become confusing, empty, and meaningless. Make him a special part of each day as a close friend and confidant. Please consider asking God to help you regularly, and then thanking him in your prayers. If you are a person who has never allowed Jesus our Lord and God into your life, or have not been born again, then consider it now! Be more than you ever dreamed possible. A whole new lifestyle is set in motion when you're born again. Suddenly you are not so interested in self, but in the welfare of others as you go about your daily work.

You'll want to turn away from the sinful things of the past and commit yourself to the Lord's work. Life within your work setting will take on a whole new meaning! Maybe your question is…how do I accept Jesus into my life? Simply pray and tell the Lord you want a different life, a life filled with love and meaning for life with Him and "with all God's people." Ask God to fill you with his power to become someone special. Perhaps you're thinking, "I'm not worthy of the Lord. I've lived in sin too long. I've done too many things wrong." The Bible tells us all we have to do now is believe. Believe that God can forgive you of all your wrongs. Back in Chapter 8, I quoted Gracia Burnham who said, "That is exactly the kind of situation that God specializes in…making good come out of hopelessness." We can read in the latter part of the New Testament of the Bible from First John 1:9, that if you'll only confess these wrongs to Christ who died for you on the cross, he'll forgive you. Believe in him and he will hear you. Now, what's next? After accepting Jesus, each day, learning more and more about his love for you. Find others who have accepted Jesus as their Savior. Focus on putting into practice many of the suggestions shared from others and from the prior chapters you just read.

realize this growth period in your life is on-going

Go about your work showing gratitude for all that Jesus is and can do for you. Live your life as an example of your love for him. The lyrics in the song, "Get all excited, go tell everybody that Jesus Christ is Lord," composed by Bill and Gloria Gaither, describe the kind of love which has no end. Your life should be a reflection of God's love!

My mother once told me, and I can still picture her telling me this at the breakfast table one morning just like so many other suggestions, "Roger, the way you treat others is like the way you treat God." As I recall that day, I realize what a profound statement she gave me to live my life. She went on to Heaven with the Lord after an illness took her life when she was 44 years old.

In closing here, my prayer goes out to you. I hope you are appreciating many of the words of encouragement while finding the real meaning in life. Don't do it for me, do it for yourself! Allow the spirit of God to bless you over and over and over again!

A FRESH START

If you have accepted a new faith or want to deepen your faith in Him, need answers to hundreds of questions and some straightforward answers, remember we can't do it alone.

Ask one or two friends to help you to live a new life of commitment and responsibility. Seek out a prayer group or worship group to study God's word. Pray to God every day, asking Him to give you wisdom and strength to meet life's challenging struggles and difficult experiences.

TIME CAPSULE

Have you heard of high school graduating classes that chose to have each one in the graduating class predict their own future? Then many years later at a class reunion they would open and read each one's time capsule as a novelty to have a few laughs. What would you like to read about yourself 20 years later? It is my belief you could actually come near to planning for this prediction to come true if you were to have strong convictions toward reaching your personal ambitions and end goals.

Please consider allowing Jesus to help you in your daily associations with people, preparing for the interview, in your working job, and in your home life. Remember, little things become big things many times throughout life. Bring to each occasion a smile of happiness for all the good things that are happening around you. Time is precious.

Looking back in time, when was the last time you prayed, asking God to help or guide you with something?

> **"God also wants to help us shape
> our goals so they are meaningful."**[3]

Life can become confusing, empty and meaningless without having God to guide you through the path of life here on earth. Please consider including God in your life daily and making Him a close friend and confidant.

DREAMS CAN COME TRUE

I invite you to imagine for a moment—what would you be doing if you had any wish from a crystal ball? Dreams can come true without magic if you will dream to be all you can be. What is your dream?

As a young boy growing up in Iowa, I watched the farmers prepare the fields for planting corn. Farmers would add fertilizer or manure to give the planted corn a head start. My dad was careful to buy the very best seed corn he could find. After the soil was prepared and the moisture was just right, farmers would plant the little kernels of seed corn. After several days, small sprouts of corn started popping through the soil. Think about this for a moment—a wonderful thing happens when one kernel of corn develops into a whole ear, two little kernels can produce hundreds. During the growth period, my dad would care for the field of corn by cultivating past the little plants of corn as a way to brace them, aerating the ground and hoeing out the unwanted weeds. Dad would listen to the rain forecast each morning. He shared with me that it was important to keep the fields cared for and clean from weeds. This would produce a better crop of corn, growing tall and strong, producing large, full ears of corn, for which he could be grateful.

The story of the seed corn growing into something of which to be proud could be much like the story for our lives. Dreams can come true if only we'll plant our best, water and care for our life with nutrients. We can work to keep the bad weeds out of our lives. We can cultivate our life by reading and watching for things that make our life grow strong and prosperous, always reaching for our "field of dreams." Much like my dad would care for his corn, so we can take care of our life as we grow in understanding.

WISHING YOU THE BEST

I leave with you this special message. One wish would be, that I'd be able to sit down and visit about how some things stand out in your mind from reading this self-help book. Of course I can't visit with everyone who has read my book, but I can pray the spirit of God could be with you each day and become an active part of your life. I encourage you to invite the spirit of God within to lead you. "Listen to your body," as some people might say…

> **Listen to the quiet inner sense of God's Holy Spirit in you which comes with believing He is there at all times.**

Think about what needs to happen first, second, third, and so on. I'd encourage you to commit to your decisions of finding new and refreshing ways of dealing with life, first with God and self, next with family, and also your employer.

In the final part of my writing, I'm wishing you the best in moving up to God's speed in doing for others what you would want them to do for you, things that give you joy and an inner peace. May God bless you and keep you; and may God show his love upon you and your family always.

THE NEW YOU WITH COMMITMENT

I've been encouraging you to begin a new way of living! Living daily with a radiance of self confidence can be your choice. There can be immediate inspiration available for you to do your work with a higher degree of expectation.

> **"We can make our plans, but the final outcome is in God's hands. We can always 'prove' that we are right, but is the Lord convinced? Commit your work to the Lord, then it will succeed."**
> **Proverbs 16:1-3**

CHAPTER EIGHTEEN SUMMARY

So I leave with you to consider: commit each day to be the most you can be, avoid ending the day angry at someone, and continue to seek out good choices which will make positive improvements. Allow others to contribute to your decisions at home and at work for the good of all—young and old, rich or poor. All of us could benefit from finding and practicing job and life opportunities each day to make the world a better place in which to live. And, always remember—

You are not alone!

NOTES & RESOURCES

Preface

1. Charles Ray Van Nice. *Tact And The Teacher*. Lawrence, KS: Plainview Publications, 1929. Pg. 8.
2. *The Living Bible*. Wheaton, IL: Tyndale House Publishers, Inc. Reference Edition, 1971. Proverbs 1:1-2.

Introduction

1. Chris Isidore, "Skilled Worker Shortage Hurts U.S." (New York: CNNMoney.com, Jan. 5, 2007), Pg. 1 of 3.
2. "Survey: Fewer skilled workers." (The Wichita Eagle, National Assoc. of Manufacturers, Towers Perrin Co., Published by Knight-Ridder Tribune News Nov. 23, 1991), 2A.
3. Ibid., Wichita Eagle.
4. Zig Ziglar with Krish Dhanam, Bryan Flanagan, and Jim Savage. *Top Performance*. Grand Rapids, MI: Fleming H. Revell, Division of Baker Publishing Group, 2003. Pg. 11.

Chapter 1

1. *The Living Bible*. Wheaton, IL: Tyndale House Publishers, Inc. Reference Edition, 1971. Proverbs 6:20.
2. Ibid., Proverbs 1:8.
3. Ibid., Jonah, chapters 1 & 2.
4. Ibid., Galatians 5:22.
5. David Bowman and Ronald Kweskin. *How Do I Find the Right Job? Ask the Experts*. New York: John Wiley & Sons, Inc., 1990. Pg. 67.
6. *The Living Bible*, Romans 1:28-32.
7. Ibid., T*he Living Bible*, Matthew 7:12.
8. Marlene Caroselli. *Interpersonal Skills: The Professional Development Series*. Rochester, NY: Southwestern-Thomson Learning, 2003. Preface vii.
9. *The Living Bible,* Matthew 18:19.

Chapter 3

1. Thomas M. Camden. *The Job Hunter's Final Exam*. Chicago, IL: Surrey Books, 1990.

Chapter 4

1. Larry Axline (Managing Director of Management Action Planning, Boulder, CO).
2. Laura Brill. *Business Writing Quick and Easy*. New York, NY: American Management Association: Second Ed., 1981. Back cover flap.
3. Sharon B. Molzen, "Homemaker's Chats," (Newton, KS: The Newton Kansan, Oct. 15, 1985), Pg. 2.
4. "A Phone Tip," printed in Communication Briefings, April 1994. Source: Customer Service Newsletter, Silver Spring, MD, cited in Team Management Briefings, Portland, OR.
5. Matt Weaver, "Texting and Social Media."

Chapter 5

1. Virginia Tooper, "Positive Uses of Humor on the Job," (Newton, KS: PrairieView Inc., Growth Associates Seminar Flyer), Feb. 20, 1986.
2. Elwood N. Chapman. *Your Attitude is Showing: A Primer on Human Relations*. Palo Alto, CA: Science Research Associates, 3rd Ed. 1977. Pg.14.
3. Henry Ford, "50 Most Inspirational Quotes," in Conrade Insurance Group Pamphlet, Newton, KS, #22.

4. "How to Deal With Verbal Bullying," www.ehow.com/hour, Nov. 16, 2009, Pg. 1 of 3.

5. "How to Stop Bullies," Nov. 16, 2009, Pg. 2 and 3 of 6. Http://realparenting4realkids.com/2009/04/06/hour-to-stop-bullies/,

6. Mark Twain, "50 Most Inspirational Quotes," in Conrade Insurance Group Pamphlet, Newton, KS, #44.

7. *Compton's Sout-Sy Encyclopaedia by Britannica*. Vol. 22, 2008. Pgs. 670-671.

8. Author known as c1989, DLS, "101 Ways To Cope With Stress," list from Hutchinson Community College Campus Bookstore, Hutchison, KS.

9. John C. Murray quote, pastor of Hesston Mennonite Church, Hesston, KS.

Chapter 7

1. Lisa Bartel, stepsister to Roger Eichelberger.

2. Norman Cousins, "Lettin' Go and Holdin' On: Finding the Humor and Courage to Live Well," quips from Al Schmidt presentation (Wichita, KS: "Bits of Wits," printed by Affiliated Psychiatric Services, 1995).

3. Zig Ziglar with Krish Dhanam, Bryan Flanagan, and Jim Savage. *Top Performance*. Grand Rapids, MI: Fleming H. Revell, Division of Baker Publishing Group, 2003. Pg. 75.

4. *The Living Bible*. Wheaton, IL: Tyndale House Publishers, Inc., Reference Edition, 1971. Matthew 6: 6-15.

5. William Damon, "Get A Life" (Newton Kansan USA Weekend Edition, June 12-14, 2009). Pg. 12. usaweekend.com.

6. Ibid., Damon.

7. Tony Dungy and Nathan Whitaker. *Uncommon: Finding Your Path to Significance*. Carol Stream, IL: Tyndale House Publishers, 2009. Pg. 63.

Chapter 8

1. "Personal Credit Score Notice to the Home Loan Applicant," Chester, PA: TransUnion, 19022.

2. Strathdee, Penner, Warkentin, Jantzi, Friesen, and Ollenburger. "Dealing With Overwhelming Debt," pamphlet. Faith and Life Resources, a division of Mennonite Publishing Network, Scottdale, PA, and Waterloo, ON 2009. Pg. 4.

3. Joe Dominguez and Vicki Robin. *Your Money or Your Life*. New York, NY: Viking Penguin, a division of Penguin Books USA Inc. 1992. Pg. 212.

4. Garner, Arnone, Pape, Barker, Nissenbaum, Rouse, and Voss. *Ernst & Young's Retirement Planning Guide—Take Care of Your Finances Now... And They'll Take Care of You Later*. New York, NY: John Wiley & Sons 1997. Pg. 43.

5. Casey J. Jacob, "Agape Offering Classes about Job, Meal Skills," Agape Resource Center, (Newton, KS: Article in the Newton Kansan, Weekend edition, No. 201), August 28 and 29, 2010.

6. Author unknown, "Vocational (Trade) Schools Worth It?," http://answers.yahoo.com/questions/index?qid=20080622191259AAffncZ, Pg. 1 of 1.

7. "Computer & Industrial Computer Drafting Technology," Flyer from Hutchinson Community College, May 2014. Hutchinson, KS, Machine Drafting – Associate in Applied Science.

8. Mennonite Housing, Wichita, KS 2010.

9. Gary Hill, Harvey County Habitat for Humanity Office, 2010.

10. Ronni Eisenberg and Kate Kelly. *Organize Yourself!* MacMillan Publishing Company, 1986. Pgs. 73-79.

11. Ivan D. Friesen, "Assuring Hope," (Scottsdale, PA: Zondervan Bible Publishers, Winter Adult Bible Study), 2010-2011 series.

12. Joel Osteen. *Starting Your Best Life Now*, New York, NY: Hachette Book Group USA, Joel Osteen Publishing & Faith Words, 2007. Pg. 13.

13. Gracia Burnham and Dean Merrill. *To Fly Again, Surviving the Tailspin of Life*. Wheaton, IL: Tyndale House Publishers, Inc., 2005.
14. Bryson Smith. "Ephesians 2:1-22, Lesson 3." Ephesians Study Guide, Faith Walk Bible Studies.
15. Jerry Weaver, Retirement Income Planner, Hesston, KS. www.jerryweaver.retirerx.com.
16. Luke S. Weaver. *Successful Living: A Study of Bible-based Economic and Lifestyle Principles*. Morgantown, PA: Masthof Press, 2010. Pg. 112.
17. Elaine Harms, Harms Insurance Services, North Newton, KS.

Chapter 9

1. "Total Quality Management," Britannica Concise Encyclopedia. Definition from Answers.com. http://www.answers.com.(2010). Pg. 1.
2. "Total Quality Management," (TQM): Accounting Dictionary. Definition from Answers.com. http://www.answers.com. (2010). Pg. 1.
3. *Webster's Improved Dictionary and Everyday Encyclopedia*. Nashville, TN: The Southwestern Company, 1956.

Chapter 10

1. Richard E. Riley, U.S. Secretary of Education, "Hope for future lies in education" (The Wichita Eagle, Jan 13, 1994), 9A.
2. Kendall Heier. *TeamUp Careers*. Career and Life Coach, Wichita, KS.

Chapter 11

1. Dr. Charles Stanley, "Acquiring Wisdom," TBN, Trinity Family Network, Channel 151. Sunday, 2/24/2013.
2. Carl Sewell and Paul B. Brown. *Customers for Life*. New York, NY: Pocket Books. Pg. 33.

Chapter 12

1. Stephen R. Covey. *The 7 Habits of Highly Effective People*. New York, NY: Simon and Schuster, First Fireside Edition, 1990. Pgs. 28-32.

Chapter 13

1. Tony Dungy and Nathan Whitaker. *Uncommon: Finding Your Path to Significance*. Carol Stream, IL: Tyndale House Publishers, 2009. Author of Quote: Aristotle, Pg. 3.
2. *Webster's Seventh New Collegiate Dictionary*. G. & C. Merriam Co. 1967.
3. Zig Ziglar with Krish Dhanam, Bryan Flanagan, and Jim Savage. *Top Performance*. Grand Rapids, MI: Fleming H. Revell, Division of Baker Publishing Group, 2003. Pg. 50.
4. Virginia Tooper, "Positive Uses of Humor on the Job." (Newton, KS: Growth Associates, Prairie View Inc. Flyer.) Feb. 20, 1986.
5. William Davis, "Lettin' Go and Holdin' On: Finding the Humor and Courage to Live Well," quips from Al Schmidt presentation (Wichita, KS: "Bits of Wits," printed by Affiliated Psychiatric Services, 1995).
6. Ibid., Ziglar, Pg. 110.
7. Gary Dessler, "Making Good First Impression a Learned Skill," (Wichita, KS: Wichita Eagle- Beacon Job Talk, Dec. 28, 1987), 5D.
8. *The Living Bible*. Wheaton, IL: Tyndale House Publishers, Inc., Reference Edition, 1971. Romans 14:17.
9. Ibid., Matthew 5:22.
10. Larry J. Bailey. *Working: Learning a Living*. South-Western Educational Publishing, 2nd ed., 1997. Pg. 198.
11. Ibid., Bailey
12. Dr. June Alliman, professor at Goshen College, Goshen, IN.

13. Ibid., *The Living Bible,* Proverbs 2:3-5.

14. Ibid., Proverbs 3: 4-6.

15. "Grace," New American Standard Bible. Nashville, Camden, New York: Thomas Nelson, 1977. Pg. 26.

16. Merrill C. Tenney. *Zondervan Pictorial Bible Dictionary.* Grand Rapids, MI: Zondervan Publishing House, 1967. Pg. 322.

17. Tryon Edwards. *The New Dictionary of Thoughts: A Cyclopedia of Quotations.* NY: Standard Book Company, 1954. Author of quote: Payson, Pg. 230.

18. John C. Murray quote, pastor of Hesston Mennonite Church, Hesston, KS.

Chapter 14

1. Peter Eash-Scott, "Electronic Media Sunday School Discussion," (Created for Seekers Sunday School Class, Hesston, KS: Assessing Our Electronic Media Consumption & It's Many Upsides and Downsides, Jan 12, 2014) Pg. 2 #3.

Chapter 15

1. Josh Billings and Al Schmidt presentation, "Lettin' Go and Holdin' On: Finding the Humor and Courage to Live Well" (Wichita, KS: "Bits of Wisdom," printed by Affiliated Psychiatric Services, 1995).

2. Stephen Denby, "Foundations of Quality." (Leesburg, VA: VICA Professional: VP, Volume 26, No.1 Sept. 1991.) Pgs. 10-11.

3. Larry J. Bailey. *Working: Learning a Living.* South-Western Educational Publishing, 2nd ed., 1997. Pg. 196.

4. Tryon Edwards. *The New Dictionary of Thoughts: A Cyclopedia of Quotations.* NY: Standard Book Company, 1954. Author of quote: Bovee, Pg. 601.

5. "Something to Think About," (Wichita, KS: Anderson Elementary PTA Monthly News, February, 1996).

6. "Toolkit" (Published by MMA, Volume 36, Number 5, Sept-Oct 2009).

7. Ibid., Tryon Edwards, Author of Quote: Bp. Horne, Pg. 453.

Chapter 16

1. Millard J. Erickson. *Does It Matter How I Live?* Grand Rapids, MI: Baker Books, 1994. Pg. 14.

2. Dale Carnegie. *How to Win Friends and Influence People.* New York, NY: Simon and Schuster for Pocket Books Inc., 1936. About the Author.

3. Ibid.

4. Ibid.

5. Dale Carnegie. *How to Stop Worrying and Start Living.* New York, NY: Simon and Schuster for Pocket Books Inc., 1948.

6. *Webster's Seventh New Collegiate Dictionary.* Springfield, MA: G. & C. Merriam Co., 1967.

7. Janet Bailey, "How to Make Tough Decisions," Communication Briefings, Alexandria, VA, Volume XIV, No. II ISSN 0730-7799, Pg. 8. Suggestions by Dr. Varenhorst and Daralee Schulman.

8. Zig Ziglar with Krish Dhanam, Bryan Flanagan, and Jim Savage. *Top Performance.* Grand Rapids, MI: Fleming H. Revell, Division of Baker Publishing Group, 2003. Pg. 51. Ziglar quotes Andrew Carnegie.

9. Chris Brady and Orrin Woodward. *Launching a Leadership Revolution.* New York, NY: Hachette Book Group, 2005. Front Leaf Cover.

10. John C. Murray, pastor of Hesston Mennonite Church, Hesston KS.

11. Ibid., Webster's Collegiate Dictionary.

12. Ibid., Erickson, Pg. 11.

13. *The Living Bible*. Wheaton, IL: Tyndale House Publishers, Inc., Reference Edition, 1971. Matthew 5:3-10.
14. Kevin Wilder, psychologist at Hesston College, Hesston, KS. Article on motivation prepared specifically for the writing of this book.

Chapter 17

1. Dr. June Alliman Yoder, Goshen College, Goshen, IN.
2. Carol M. Barnum, "Here's How To Manage Your Meetings Effectively" (Blackwood NJ: Communication Briefings-Encoders, Inc, April 1994) Volume 13, Number 6, 8a, and 8b.
3. Carol Driscoll, "How the Best Speakers Do It" (NJ: Communication Briefings, Volume XIV, No. II ISSN 0730-7799) from the Toastmaster, Mission Viejo, CA, Pg. 2.
4. Ronald L. Willingham. *How To Speak So People Will Listen*. Waco, TX: Word Books, 1968. Pg. 20.
5. Harold R. Wallace and L. Ann Masters. *Personality Development for Work*. South-Western Educational Publishing, 7th ed., 1996. Pg. 150.
6. William Davis, "Bits of Wits" quips from Al Schmidt presentation "Lettin' Go and Holdin' On: Finding the Humor and Courage to Live Well," from Affiliated Psychiatric Services, Wichita, KS, 1995.
7. Ibid., Willingham, Pg. 13.
8. Jeremy Kingsley. *Getting Back Up When Life Knocks You Down*. Bloomington, MN: Bethany House Publishers, 2011. Pg. 79.
9. John F. Murray, Hesston, KS.
10. Billy Graham. *The Journey*. Nashville, TN: W Publishing Group, Division of Thomas Nelson, Inc., 2006. Preface, Pg. vii-viii.
11. Dr. Ruby K. Payne. *A Framework for Understanding Poverty*. Highlands, TX: Aha! Process, Inc., 2001. Pg. 11.

Chapter 18

1. John C. Murray quote, pastor of Hesston Mennonite Church, Hesston, KS.
2. Joel Osteen. *Starting Your Best Life Now*. New York, NY: Joel Osteen Publishing and Faith Words, Hachette Book Group USA, 2007. Pgs. 124-125.
3. Ibid., John C. Murray.

OTHER SOURCES TO READ

Beers Ron, and Amy E. Mason. The NLT Bible Promise Book. Tyndale House Publishers, Inc. Carol Stream, IL 2007. (A very small alphabetized biblical resource pocket book with 94 different subjects of advice such as "Change" on page 6, "Comfort" on page 7, and "Consequences" on page 8.)

Burham, Gracia with Dean Merrill. To Fly Again: Surviving the Tailspin of Life. Tyndale House Publishers, Inc., Wheaton, IL 2005. (The whole book reflects the quote by Max Lucado on the front of her book: "A training manual for anyone seeking to fly above discouraging circumstances.")

Dungy, Tony, and Nathan Whitaker. Uncommon: Finding Your Path to Significance. Tyndale House Publishers, Inc. Carol Stream, IL 2009. (The author kept me interested page after page as I was repeatedly taken back to how Tony made the best of things.)

Eisenberg, Ronni, and Kate Kelly. Organize Yourself. MacMillan Publishing Company. 1986. (The book is packed with good ideas for getting more organized.)

Harper, Stephen C. The McGraw-Hill Guide to Starting Your Own Business. McGraw-Hill. New York, NY, 2nd Edition, 2003. Page xv. (Early in the preface the author says, "Few of these books are tailored to people who have limited experience and education in business…this guide is written for the first-timer.")

Kingsley, Jeremy. Getting Back Up When Life Knocks You Down. Bethany House Publishers, (a division of Baker Publishing Group, Grand Rapids, MI) 11400 Hampshire Ave. South, Bloomington, MN 2011. (Beau Eckert, pastor of Calvary Church in Lancaster, PA, says that the book is "Practical. Genuine. Relevant. Authentic.")

Lucado, Max. God Will Use This for Good. Thomas Nelson. Nashville, TN 2013. (Emphasis is on surviving the mess of life.)

Osteen, Joel. Starting Your Best Life Now. Published by Faith Words, Hachette Book Group USA, NY, NY 2007. (A very small colorful book with inspiring quotes and advice from Joel Osteen to get the most out of each day. If you need a jump start in your life now, this tops the list.)

Our Daily Bread, by RBC Ministries. (A very small but wonderful little daily personal and family devotional pamphlet booklet for three months, one page per day, of inspiring pages of good reading.)

WORD INDEX

A

Accomplishments, 2, 48, 58, 62, 110, 111, 139, 121, 133, 163
Activities, Extracurricular, 110, 115
Activities, Leisure, 46, 66
Adaptability, 37, 45, 59, 126
Adult, Unemployed Young, 80
Advancement, 62, 69, 78, 118, 155, 161
Aggressive, 62
Agreeable, 103
Ahead, Getting, 142
Ambition, 48, 107
Appearance, 50, 98, 107, 111, 118, 133-134
Application, Employment, 15-17
Appreciation, 122, 138
Aptitude, 159
Arrival, Early, 18, 52, 125, 166-167
Assets, 70, 84-85, 100
Associations With People, 1-14, 89
Attendance 51-52, 129, 148
Attire, 133-134
Attire, Grooming and, 135
Attitude, 3, 6, 10, 42-44, 53-54, 57, 103, 106, 111, 121, 127, 137, 151, 153-157, 159, 161

B

Backup Plan, 125, 132
Bartering, 95-96
Believe, 179
Believers, Circle of, 176-177, 179
Bible, 48, 74, 120, 177, 179
Body Conditioning, 113-114
Body Language, 52-55, 134, 136
Book, Calendar, 56-58, 62, 67
Born Again, 120, 179
Boss, 52, 55-58, 67,112, 116, 118, 127-128, 135
Breaks, Coffee, 6
Budgeting, 72, 76-84, 87-88, 95, 162-163
Bullying, 47-48, 108
Business, Personal, 27, 65, 66, 80, 81
Business Plan, 81-82
Buying, 96-99

C

Can vs. I Can't, 57
Cards, Business, 5
Cards, Credit, 92, 171
Caring, 6, 32, 37, 137, 176
Cash, 95-99
Cleanliness, 29
Challenges, New, 43, 50, 177-178, 133-144
Change, 4, 5, 59-60, 92, 107, 120, 126-127, 131, 133-144, 148
Change of Command, 57-59
Character, Building, 75, 92-93, 112, 133-144, 148-149, 154
Children, 80, 173, 177
Church, 112-113, 176

Circle, Confidence, 8-9, 64, 71, 77, 85, 176
Classes, 23, 34, 47, 69, 85-86, 108, 116-118, 130, 160, 174, 180
Cleanliness, 29, 106
Cleanliness, Job, 29, 59, 106
Clientele, 105
Clothing, 111
Clutter, 28, 30, 43, 49, 95, 111, 162, 166
Colleagues, 31-32, 50, 136, 146, 166
College, Enroll in, 116
Command, Chain of, 57
Commitment, 23, 172
Committee, 115
Communication, 10, 21, 23, 34, 40, 53, 55, 58, 59, 104, 107, 111, 130-131, 138-141, 144, 147-148, 155, 157, 163, 166, 168
Communication, Non-Verbal, 53, 55, 139, 140
Community, Involvement in, 6, 115
Company Policy, 102, 104
Compassion, 137, 163
Competition, 7, 71, 75, 99, 115, 123, 130, 172
Complimentary, 10
Computer Ethics, 28
Computer Software, 118, 130
Concentration, 48
Condition, Physical, 113, 145-146
Confidence Circle, 9
Confidentiality, 24, 39, 56, 120, 127-128, 130
Conflict Resolution, 42, 48-50
Considerate, 28
Contacts, Business, 5
Contacts, Personal, 89
Convention, Attending, 116
Conversation, 24-25, 56,147-148
Copies, Keeping, 30, 161
Courses, Taking College, 117
Courteous, 2, 23, 25, 40, 60, 88, 104, 122-123, 156-157
Credit Card, 82
Credit Score, 83
Critical Thinking, 37-40, 48-50, 91-92, 107-108, 135-136, 161-162
Criticism, Accept, 44, 126-127
Crossword Puzzle, 13
Curb Appeal, 71-72
Customers, 60-61, 105, 124, 151-152

D

Dealership, 107
Debts, 69, 83-85
Decisions, 1, 28, 34, 37, 46, 49, 63, 66, 77-78, 84, 93-95, 97, 99, 102, 109, 114, 128, 131-132, 135, 143, 148, 159-160, 162, 168-169, 171, 175, 181-182
Demeanor, Quiet, 108
Description, Job, 35-37, 40, 60, 61
Desk Area, 29

Details, Important, 19, 20, 38, 61, 68, 81, 125-132, 145, 149, 151-158
Dictionary, 19, 105, 108, 130-131, 135, 142, 158
Diet, 110, 113
Differences of Opinion, 44
Disclaimer, xii, xv
Distractions, 30, 91
Dollar, Stretching, 72, 81-101, 160, 162
Dreams, 1, 66, 69, 70, 80, 85, 90, 101, 116, 179-181
Dress, 3, 53, 111
Drinking, 28, 36, 72-73, 129, 146

E

E-Mail, 27, 31-32, 34, 40, 64, 68, 128, 130, 163
Eating Healthy, 72-74
Education, 16, 85, 86, 89, 100, 116-117, 119, 133, 146-147
Efficiency, 10, 39, 56-57, 70, 105, 152
Emotional Issues, 42-50
Employee Emotions, 42-50
Employment Applications, 15-17
Empowerment, 20, 120, 152
Encouragement, 10, 20-22, 103, 125, 163, 179
Energy, 20-22, 46
Entrepreneurship, 104, 173
Envy, 7, 10, 158
Eternity, 178-179
Ethics, Computer, 28
Ethics, Work, 27-28, 62, 103, 116, 156
Etiquette, Social, 155
Evaluation, Job, 51-53, 56, 69, 149
Evaluation, Self, 176
Everything Told, 24, 130
Evil, 6, 143
Exercise, 65, 113, 145, 146
Exhibition Display, 107
Expectations, Social, 155
Expression, 174
Extracurricular Activity, 46, 110

F

Facebook, 41
Failures, Learning from, 44-45
Fair, Job, 118-119
Faith, 35, 50, 83, 90, 93, 120, 134, 158, 163, 172, 177, 179
Family, 2, 5, 6, 8-11, 13, 16, 29, 34-35, 41, 44, 47, 49, 51, 60, 61, 64, 69, 71, 74-76, 83-84, 87, 88, 94, 97, 107, 111, 112, 114, 122, 131, 135, 139, 143-144,146, 156, 159, 162-164, 166-168, 171, 173-175, 177-179, 181
Favors, 58, 104, 166-167
Feelings, 24, 29, 38, 44, 50, 77-78, 135, 137, 138, 160, 172
Feet, 72, 130, 155, 167, 171
Filing, 94-95
Financial Planning, 47, 81-101
Flexibility, 2, 34, 45
Follow Through, 18 32, 61-62, 88, 105, 120-123
Forgetfulness, 145-150

Forgiveness, 42, 45, 49, 64, 76-77, 120, 127, 143, 171-172, 177
Fortune, Good, 88, 125
Foul-ups, Avoid, 31
Friendships, 5-8, 10, 32, 42, 46, 75-76, 78, 85, 108, 111, 114, 121, 125, 131, 164, 167, 176-177, 179
Free Time, 66
Freedom, 171, 174-175
Fruits of the Spirit, 5

G

Gifts, 10, 104-105, 142, 173
Giving, 5-6, 85
Goals, Personal, 20, 48, 66-71, 88, 107, 109, 116-117, 162-163, 172
God, 42, 46, 50, 62, 74, 90, 91-93, 126-127, 136, 141-143, 163-165, 171, 175-182
God, In God We Trust, 141-142
God Leading, 158
God, Spirit of, 127, 138, 179-181
Going, Tough Get, 159
Golden Rule, 10, 181
Gossip, 10, 41
Grace, Gift of, 142-143, 176-177
Graciousness, 122
Groceries, Stretching, 72
Grooming, 134, 136
Guarantees, 90
Guests, Entertaining, 121

H

Habits, 145, 150
Handshake, 19, 52
Happiness, 6, 35, 49, 52, 67, 70, 74, 111, 125, 137, 163-165, 173, 175, 178, 180
Harassment, 157
Healing, 49, 64, 75, 175
Healthier, Eating, 145, 72-74
Healthy, 72, 78
Hidden Rules, 172-173
Hired, 11, 15-17, 21, 46, 62, 66, 102-103, 106, 144, 155
Hobbies, 111, 115
Holy Spirit, 6, 137, 181
Home, Off Work at, 43, 64-80, 121
Honesty, 108, 135, 168
Honor, 47, 107, 143, 175
Hope, 4, 10, 24, 34, 46, 48, 57, 67, 71, 82-83, 87-88, 90, 93, 100, 107, 109, 112, 117, 120-121, 125-126, 133, 157, 160, 163, 169, 172, 173, 175-176, 179
Humility, 137, 156-157, 175
Humor, 47, 49-50, 65, 121, 135, 157, 168, 170
Hurt, 51, 132, 171-172
Hygiene, Good, 59, 134, 137-138

I

Image, Person's, 54
Immigrant, 174
Impression, First, 15, 18, 25, 39, 55, 135-136, 151, 177
Indifference, Avoid, 131
Information, Handling, 24

Insurance, 8, 35, 53, 69, 77, 82, 85, 94-95, 98, 99-101
Integrity, 2, 46, 135, 149
Interviewing, 18-26, 52, 90-91, 106, 110, 112, 119, 139, 147, 155, 169, 180,
Inventory, 32, 46, 61, 63, 82, 84-85, 94-95, 98-99
Investments, 20, 85-88, 90-91, 94-95, 145
Involvement, Community, 6
Isometric Exercise, 113
Issues, Emotional, 42-48

J

Jesus, 5, 11, 19, 48, 50, 62, 70-71, 74, 90, 92, 120, 142-143, 164, 172, 176-180
Job, 27-41, 43, 51-52, 57, 66, 78, 104, 121, 136, 152, 168, 172-173, 178
Job Description, 35, 60-61
Job Evaluation, 51-63
Job Fair, 118-119
Job Openings, 71
Job, Second, 51, 104
Jonah, 4
Joy, 75, 114, 121, 125, 136-137, 142-143, 177, 181

K

Knowledge, Added, 61-62

L

Landscape, 72, 106
Language, Non-Verbal Body, 3, 25, 52, 79, 134-136, 138-140
Language, Uplifting, 108, 138
Lateness, 27, 51-52, 125, 129
Laughter, 7, 43, 65, 135, 154
Leadership, 114, 121, 135, 142, 160, 168, 169
Leisure Activity, 66
Liabilities, 84-85
Life, 5, 48, 65-66, 80, 90, 143, 151, 171-173, 177-181
Life, Balanced, 112
Life, Prayer, 50, 74
Lifestyle, 162-163, 173-175, 179
Listening, 4, 5, 19-21, 32, 38, 44, 52, 79-80, 111, 136, 139-140, 144, 146, 147, 150, 155, 166, 168, 169
Lists, Mailing, 31, 118
Loans, 83, 86, 92, 196
Love, 5, 71, 80, 91, 125, 139, 142, 156, 163, 173, 176-179, 181
Loyalty, 102-103

M

Mail, 31
Management, 52, 102-109
Management, Time, 18, 37-38, 40-41, 122
Manners, 11, 13-14, 123
Manual, Company Policy, 102
Marriage, 78
Market, Job, 117-118
Marketing Self, 131, 133-141, 151
Material, Posting, 127
Media, Social, 40-41, 79
Meditation, 19, 35, 66, 75, 112, 138
Meeting, Conducting, 168

Memory, 33, 49, 113, 137
Mental Balance, 59, 75, 113, 145
Mentor, 133, 145
Mind Over Matter, 145, 159-160
Minding Our Business, 56
Mistakes, 2, 31, 35, 42, 44-45, 58, 90, 127
Modesty, 156, 157
Money, 1, 2, 10, 20, 30, 35-36, 53, 55, 68-70, 74, 76, 80, 83-85, 87-89, 93, 97, 99-101, 106, 117, 129, 131, 134, 142, 151, 157, 173-174
Moonlighting, 104
Motivation, 42-50, 61, 153, 164
Moving-Up, 107-109, 144, 152, 165, 172, 174, 181
Multi-tasking, 40
Music, 139, 152

N

Neighborly, 6-7, 47, 158
Networking, 6-7, 85, 167
Net Worth, 84, 196
Newspaper, Reading the, 67, 71
New Testament, 35, 48, 120
Non-Verbal Language, 19, 53, 111, 139
Note Taking, 38, 149-150

O

Observing, 125
Off Work, At Home, 64-80
Opinion, Differences of, 44, 60, 64
Opportunity, 1, 18, 21, 23, 45-46, 58, 62-64, 81, 85, 88-92, 107, 110-111, 114-115, 123, 127, 129, 141, 143, 153, 155-156, 167-168, 173, 175, 178
Optimistic Thinking, 157
Organization, Professional, 145
Organized, 27-41, 87-88
Organizer, 56-57, 87
Others, Encourage, 91, 111, 120-121, 127, 162
Overtime, 58, 76, 102, 104, 159-161

P

Paradigms, 126
Parenthood, 80, 173
Passion, 178
Patience, 157-158
Paycheck, 99-100, 105, 117, 119
Pecking Order, 57-58, 102
People Associations, 1-14
Perfect, Practice Makes, 140-141
Personal Business and Your Job, The entire book addresses this matter.
Personal Contacts, 1-14, 89-90
Personality, 5, 20, 66, 86, 103, 108, 111-112, 133, 137, 144, 151-152, 154, 173-174
Personnel Staff, 11
Physical, 65, 113
Phone, 9, 39
Plan, Personal Business, 81-82, 66-71
Plan, Business, 81, 173-174, 196
Plan, Savings, 77, 93
Planner, Day, 56-57, 66-71, 145

Planning, Financial, 35, 81-101, 104
Planning Habits, 66, 140, 181
Plans, Back up, 132
Player, Team, 120-121, 156
Pleasant, 137, 176
Point, To The, 10, 20, 24, 34, 41, 104, 126, 143, 147
Policy, Company, 29, 52, 102-104, 128
Position Yourself, 1, 57, 103, 151
Positive Approach, 20-22, 157
Posture, 3, 25, 53, 134, 140, 159
Potential, Job, 78,103
Power, 109, 172, 179
Practice, 140-141
Prayer, 19, 50, 58, 74, 78, 176, 178, 180
Preparedness, Weather, 128-130
Pride, 44, 51, 89, 127, 158
Priorities, Setting, 145
Proactive, 30, 46, 62, 73, 178, 180
Problem Solving, 57-59, 156, 161-162
Productiveness, 21 59, 62, 125, 139, 152-153, 155,
    170, 178
Professional, More, 17, 38, 107-108, 110, 115-116,
    130, 134, 168
Profit, 17, 63
Promotion, 43, 45
Proofreading, 29, 127
Protocol, 38
Psych Yourself Up, 142, 153
Purchasing, 96-99

Q

Quality, 73, 87, 96, 97, 105, 108, 111, 123-124, 134-
    135, 152-153, 164-165
Quantity, 73, 87, 96-97, 105, 108, 111, 123-124, 134-
    135, 140, 152-153, 164-165
Questioning, 55

R

Re-alignment, 143
Recall, 33, 137, 150, 173, 179
Records, Filing, 30, 38
Relationships, 1-14
Relaxation, 139
Remarks, Subtle, 168
Remembering, 19, 33, 42, 56-57, 89, 139, 145-150,
    178
Reports, 143-144
Reputation, 89, 97, 123, 142-144
Requests, 158
Research, 33, 71, 98, 106, 123, 131, 140, 153, 161, 162
Resolution, Conflict, 49
Respect, 1, 3, 4, 9, 11-13, 27-29, 37-39, 44, 47, 51, 54,
    58-59, 66, 78, 89, 105-106, 114, 122, 130,
    141, 167
Responsibility, 27, 30, 34, 45, 47, 56, 61, 142, 152, 154,
    180
Resume, Preparing, 15, 109-119, 194
Retailer, 8, 91, 98
Risk Taker, 153
Rule, Golden, 10

S

Safety, 170-171
Sales, 105, 107
Savings, 20, 68-70, 72, 77, 82, 86, 92-94, 101
Schooling, 116, 148
Seating Location, 166-167
Security Job, 41, 71, 115, 118
Seeing, 3, 10, 39, 75, 91, 125-126, 140, 147
Self-esteem, 64, 94, 101, 134, 153
Self Control, 5
Self, Giving of, (sharing) 10
Self Evaluation, 138, 140, 143
Seminars, 61, 68, 108, 116-117, 160, 166
Sense, Common, 3, 54, 36-37, 55, 79, 89, 121, 132,
    142, 156, 166
Shake, Hand, 19
Shopping, 91, 96-99
Sickness, 51-52, 130
Sleep Patterns, 75-78, 125-126
Smarter, Working, 28, 34-35, 38
Smiling, 22, 25, 43, 79, 103, 136, 154-155
Smoking, 154-155
Socializing, 114, 155, 167
Social Media, 40-41, 79
Software, Computer, 118
Solution Oriented, 46, 103
Solving Problem, 48-50, 161-162, 168
Space, Respect Personal, 155
Speaking, 20-22, 108, 131, 140, 166, 169-170
Speech, 140-141
Spirit, 5-6, 80, 137-138, 177, 179, 181
Spirit, Fruits of the, 5
Spiritually, Active, 112, 157, 163-164
Sports, 75
Spouse, 32, 47, 66, 76, 78, 122, 138
Street Wise, 170-171
Strengths, 19, 26, 46-47, 96, 110, 119, 148, 151, 169
Stress, 48-50
Study Habits, 145-146, 149-150
Subliminal Messages, 79, 146-147
Success, 1, 10, 11, 25, 29, 35, 57, 66-67, 83, 85, 91, 94,
    101, 111, 122-123, 125, 137, 142, 156, 160,
    163
Suggestions, 55

T

T.V., 79
Table Manners, 11-14
Talk, 10, 19, 108
Tardiness, 51
Taxes, Income, 95, 99
Teamwork, 7, 28, 32, 78, 103, 120, 129, 156
Telephone, 16, 23, 26, 29, 37, 39, 67, 95, 119, 129, 169
Teen Off Work, 80
Texting, 40-41, 79, 130-131
Thanking Others, 32, 104-105, 163
Thesaurus, 130, 158
Thinking, Critical, 37-38, 48, 91-92, 108, 135-136,
    161-162

Time, Company, 27-28, 128
Time, Free, 18-19, 66
Time Management, 37-38, 79, 120-124, 161, 180
Together, Working, 57, 92, 156, 162
Top, Desk, 29-30
Tough Get Going, 145, 159-160
TQM, 105
Trends, 117, 134, 147, 161
Trust, In God We, 141-142
Trust Worthiness, 108

U

Unemployed, 80
Unprofessional, 56

V

Vacationing, 69, 75, 147
Vehicle, Clean, 106
Values, 46, 163, 172
Visits, Clientele, 105
Volunteering, 6, 115, 163

W

Walls, Breaking Down, 171-172 Watching, 11, 19, 45,
   56, 71, 79, 81, 106, 117, 140, 146-147, 150,
   167-168, 181
Wealth, 92, 163
Weather, Prepare for Bad, 128-130
Welcoming, 121
Willingness, 23-24
Wisdom, 35, 120, 142, 146-147, 180
Wise, Street, 170-171
Working Smarter, 23-24, 34-35, 102, 108, 110-119
Worker Qualifications, 23-24, 27, 34, 62, 108, 151-158
Work Shop, 116
Worship, 174, 176
Worth, Financial Net, 2, 70, 82, 84-85, 94
Writing Skills, 34, 38

Y

Yourself, Marketing, 1-14, 151
Yourself, Motivate, 42, 48
Yourself, Organize, 88

RESUMÉ

DATE: _____

TELEPHONE: _____

NAME: _____

ADDRESS: _____

OCCUPATIONAL GOALS:

_____

_____

```
┌ ─ ─ ─ ─ ─ ─ ─ ─ ┐
╷                 ╷
   Space for
╷   Photo–        ╷
   Optional
╷                 ╷
└ ─ ─ ─ ─ ─ ─ ─ ─ ┘
```

Space for Photo– Optional

EDUCATION:

Diploma: _____

Degree: _____

Degree: _____

Skills: _____

CERTIFICATES OF ACHIEVEMENT AND AWARDS:

_____

_____

_____

PRESENT TO PAST WORK HISTORY:

Company: _____ Address: _____

Dates employed: _____ Job Title or responsibility: _____

Company: _____ Address: _____

Dates employed: _____ Job Title or responsibility: _____

Company: _____ Address: _____

Dates employed: _____ Job Title or responsibility: _____

Company: _____ Address: _____

Dates employed: _____ Job Title or responsibility: _____

OTHER INTERESTS, EXPERIENCES, AND LEISURE ACTIVITIES:

_____

_____

_____

_____

_____

_____

REFERENCES:

(name, position, organization, current address, current telephone number to be reached)

1. _____

2. _____

(See continued attachment(s) on page two if necessary)

194

MONTHLY BUDGET SHEET

EXPENSES:

Contributions..............................$_____	Groceries................................$ _____	Gifts ....$ _____
Giving & Tithing ...._____	Education...................................._____	Drugs.._____
Subscriptions… ...._____	Cleaners.................... _____	Clothing......................................._____
Baby Sitting..................................._____	Dental ...._____	Hobby Expenses........................._____
Counseling...................................._____	Rent....................................... _____	Auto Fuel ...._____
Children & Toys ...._____	Legal Advice .... _____	Vacation & Trips........................._____
Entertainment/Movies ...._____	Eating Out .... _____	Hair/Beauty Care ...._____
Computer etc.................................._____	Investment(s) .... _____	Car Payment(s)..........................._____
Cable Television............................._____	Dues....................................... _____	Driver's License ...._____
Parking Fees ...._____	Office Supplies .... _____	Paid into Savings......................._____
Taxi or Tolls ...._____	Tools & Equipment......................_____	Home Imprvmnts........................._____
Cleaning & Supplies........................_____	Vehicle Repair .... _____	Subcontracts..............................._____
Photography.................................._____	Penalties or Fines........................._____	Broker Fees etc..........................._____
Furniture Purchasing......................._____	Snacks and Breaks........................._____	Tips & Bonuses..........................._____
Carpet Cleaning.............................._____	Landscape ...._____	Pets and Same ...._____
Home Repair ...._____	Permits ...._____	Health & Beauty........................._____
Other.._____	Other ...._____	Other ...._____
Other.._____	Other ...._____	Other ...._____

INSURANCES:

Home Owner Ins...........................$ _____	Land Line Phone ....$ _____	Personal Property ....$ _____
Auto Ins. ...._____	Electric......................................._____	Property......................................_____
Life Ins. ...._____	Water ...._____	Auto Plates............................._____
Renter's Ins....................................._____	Internet......................................._____	Mobile Home..........................._____
Health Insurances............................_____	Assessments................................._____	Income Taxes..........................._____
Liability.._____	Trash ...._____	Tax on Interest........................._____
Boat.._____	Cell Phone ...._____	Tax on Investment ...._____
Motor Club ...._____	Gas Service ...._____	Other ...._____
Other.._____	Other ...._____	

1. **Clear Income** after employer deductions taken out ....$ _____
2. **Expenses** – All money to be paid out ....$ _____

3. **Subtract #2. Expenses** — from money **Income #1** ....$ _____

FINANCIAL BALANCE SHEET
(Figuring Net Worth)

COLUMN ONE
ASSETS– $ WORTH – Dollar Values

Cash ....$_____
Automobile..._____
2nd Auto ...._____
Checking Acct.._____
Savings Acct.._____
Coin Collection..._____
Education Fund ...._____
Personal Property..._____
Real Estate.._____
Mobile Home ...._____
Home ...._____
Stocks.._____
Bonds..._____
Life Ins. Cash Value..._____
Payments from Others .... _____
Pension Plan.._____
Company Business..._____
Hobby Value ...._____
Other.._____
Other ...._____

COLUMN TWO
LIABILITIES–BORROWED-DEBTS OWED

Loan to Bank..$_____
2nd Loan to Bank ...._____
3rd Loan to Bank ...._____
Primary Credit Card ...._____
2nd Credit Card ...._____
3rd Credit Card ...._____
Bills Unpaid ...._____
Car Loan.._____
2nd Car Loan ...._____
Education Loan(s) ...._____
Unpaid Home Loan Amt. ...._____
Unpaid Mobile Home Amt. ...._____
Personal Loan to Someone ...._____
Personal Property Loan.................................._____
Unpaid Medical..._____
Other.._____
Other.._____
Other.._____

COLUMN ONE
TOTAL ASSETS ....$ _____

COLUMN TWO
TOTAL LIABILITIES............................. $ _____

NET WORTH:

1st TOTAL ASSETS IN COLUMN ONE UNDER VALUES ....$ _____

2nd TOTAL YOUR DEBTS OWED IN COLUMN TWO .... $ _____

SUBTRACT COLUMN 2 FROM COLUMN 1 <u>YOUR NET WORTH</u> ....$_____

ANSWER SHEET
Body Language

1 Untied shoe

2 Arms showing disgust

3 No smile

4 Unshaven look

5 Unmanaged hair

6 Clothes that do not fit well

7 Frowning

8 Mean stare

9 Is cap necessary

10 Looks stressed

11 Wearing pants too low

12 Worn-out shoe

13 Soiled clothing

14 Questionable shirt

15 Tired blood shot eye

16 Rings around eyes

17 Too much skin showing

18 Improve posture

Crossword Puzzle

ACROSS

1 stuff

5 it

7 time

9 slow

11 napkin

12 can

13 of

15 waiter

16 sis

17 plate

20 celery

22 stash

23 as

26 jams

27 food

30 ice

32 no

34 host

35 notes

37 taste

39 trash

40 sort

DOWN

2 toon

3 fork

4 utensils

6 thanks

8 excuses

9 show

10 waitress

14 fake

18 at

19 tab

20 cajun

21 lamb

24 hostess

25 jokes

28 dinner

29 mouth

31 eat

33 odor

36 ear

PERSONAL INVENTORY

This is a random list of personal things you may own. Assess dollar values for each category entry. Add spaces for missing listings which you own, then add up each category, and then total all the entries to find a personal inventory total.

KITCHEN

Stove....................$____	Table......................____	Freezer ....____	Cabinets...................____	Compactor..................____
All Dishes ....____	Microwave ....____	Coffee Maker ....____	Towel Rack ....____	Toaster.....................____
Pans ....____	Mixer........................____	Hutch ....____	Skillet(s) ....____	Crock Pot..................____
Knives ....____	Can Opener ....____	Misc. Tools ....____	Corning Ware.............____	All Containers ....____
Cups.............................____	All Glassware ....____	Draining Tray ....____	Hot Pads ....____	Picnic Basket..............____
Plates ....____	Wastebasket ....____	Cutting Board ....____	Waffle Maker ....____	Place Mats.................____
Dicer............................____	Measure Cup ....____	Potato Peeler ....____	Blender ....____	Slicer ....____
Trays............................____	Mixing Bowls ....____	Refrig Contents............____	Freezer Contents............____	Bakg Cntainers ....____
Stool(s) ....____	Refrigerator...............____	Food...........................____	Knife Set ....____	Serving Cart ....____
Silverware ....____	_____ ......____	_____ ......____	_____ ......____	_____ ......____

DINING AREA

Table..................$ ____	All Chairs..................____	Silverware....................____	China ....____	All Small Glassware.....____
Flowers ....____	Centerpiece................____	Tablecloth ....____	Glasses ....____	Cups ....____

OFFICE

Computer ....$____	Paper Shredder............____	Small Bookcase(s) ......____	Printer........................____	Camera Equip ....____
Books ....____	Software ....____	File Cabinet ....____	Wastebasket ....____	Pen & Pencils.............____
Desk ....____	File Folders................____	Bookends....................____	Office Supplies............____	Printer Cart. ....____
Stapler.........................____	Calculator ....____	Speakers.....................____	Briefcase ....____	Keyboard ....____
Mouse ....____	Mouse Pad.................____	Planner ....____	Magazine Rack ....____	Special Cords ....____
Checks ....____	Chair Mat ....____	Surge Protector...........____	Office Chair(s) ....____	Lamp ....____
Stamps........................____	Ream Paper ....____	Paper Punch(s) ....____	Paper Labels...............____	Scissors ....____
Floppy(s)......................____	Storage Disks ....____	Adding Machine ....____	Date Organizer............____	Card Holder ....____
Desk ....____	Flash Drive Storage ....____	Phone Card.................____	Wood Bookcase(s).......____	_____ ......____
_____ ......____	_____ ......____	_____ ......____	_____ ......____	_____ ......____
				_____ ......____

CLOSET(S)

Jewelry...................$____	Shoe Racks................____	Women's Clothing ....____	Men's Clothing..............____	Men's Shoes...............____
Paper...........................____	Car Seat(s)................____	Child's Shoes ....____	Women's Shoes............____	Child's Clothing ....____
Belts ....____	Coats........................____	Men's Overcoat............____	Scarf(s)......................____	Vacuum ....____
Boots...........................____	Rain Coats ....____	Stuffed Animals...........____	Gloves.......................____	Pet Toys....................____
Hats.............................____	Caps.........................____	Games ....____	Cleaner Bags..............____	Key Rack ....____
_____ ......____	_____ ......____	_____ ......____	_____ ......____	_____ ......____
_____ ......____	_____ ......____	_____ ......____	_____ ......____	_____ ......____

HALLWAY(S)

Hall Seat.................$____	Umbrella(s)................____	Hall Tree ....____	Animal Mounting ....____	Silk Tree.....................____
Hall Rack ....____	Cane(s) ....____	Silk Flowers ....____	Pedestal Stand.............____	Coat Rack ....____
Table............................____	Throw Rugs................____	Security Camera...........____	Shelving......................____	_____
_____ ......____	_____ ......____	_____ ......____	_____ ......____	_____ ......____
_____ ......____	_____ ......____	_____ ......____	_____ ......____	_____ ......____

BEDROOM(S)

Bed(s) ....$___	Shoe Rack.............___	Cedar Chest ....___	Jewelry Hanger...........___	Nightstand.............___
Table(s) ....___	Shades ....___	Armoire.............___	Clothes Hanger(s) ....___	Purse(s).............___
Shirts.............___	Men's Socks ....___	Men's Underwear ....___	Ladies' Hose ....___	Lingerie ....___
Sweater(s).............___	Thermal Wear ....___	Vibrator.............___	Comforter(s).............___	Heat Blanket ....___
Bedding.............___	Dresser(s).............___	Pillows ....___	Alarm Clock ....___	Heating Pad.............___
Mattress(s) ....___	Box Springs ....___	Shoe Inserts ....___	Baby Things.............___	Ceiling Fan ....___
Chairs.............___	Chest of Dwrs ....___	Clocks ....___	Jewelry ....___	Mirror(s).............___
Lamps ....___	Light Fixtures ....___	.............___	.............___	.............___
.............___	.............___	.............___	.............___	.............___

LIVING ROOM

Couch..............$___	Love Seat ....___	Lazy Boy ....___	End Tables ....___	Organ..............___
Stereo.............___	Sound System ....___	Coffee Table ....___	Pillow(s) ....___	Ottoman ....___
Lamps ....___	Painting(s) ....___	Centerpiece.............___	Decorations ....___	Magazines ....___
Blinds ....___	Drapery ....___	Magazine Rack ....___	Floor Lamp ....___	.............___
.............___	.............___	.............___	.............___	.............___

BATHROOM(S)

Towel(s) ....$___	Wash Cloths ....___	Bath Hardware.............___	Shower Curtain.............___	Hand Mirror.............___
Lotion(s) ....___	Hair Dryer ....___	Shaver(s) ....___	Flashlight ....___	Dental ....___
Scales.............___	Medicine Cab ....___	Bath Supplies ....___	Hair Clipper.............___	Shower Mat.............___
Rug(s) ....___	Medicines ....___	Tweezer(s) ....___	Hair Care Supp. ....___	Teeth Supplies.............___
Soaps ....___	Brush(es) ....___	Tester(s) ....___	Carry Case(s).............___	Eyecare Item(s).............___
Combs.............___	Makeup ....___	Clock(s) ....___	Portable Light ....___	Night Light.............___
Contacts ....___	Hearing Aid ....___	Clothes Hamper.............___	Dentures ....___	Toiletries ....___
Overnight Case.............___	.............___	.............___	.............___	.............___
.............___	.............___	.............___	.............___	.............___

UTILITY ROOM

Washer..............$___	Clothes Dryer ....___	Shelf(s) ....___	Clothes Racks.............___	Flashlight(s) ....___
Stool(s) ....___	Buckets ....___	Mop(s) ....___	Broom(s) ....___	.............___
Apron ....___	Exercise Bike.............___	Washer Soap ....___	.............___	.............___
.............___	.............___	.............___	.............___	.............___
.............___	.............___	.............___	.............___	.............___

STORAGE AREAS

Linens ....$___	Blankets ....___	Shelving.............___	Game Mounts.............___	Canned Goods.............___
Toys.............___	Albums ....___	Paints.............___	Cleaning Supp ....___	Water Hoses.............___
Lumber.............___	Plywood ....___	Bird Seed ....___	Clay Pig. Thrower ....___	Welder ....___
Edger.............___	Barbecue.............___	Bicycle(s).............___	Outside Games ....___	Lawn Mower ....___
.............___	.............___	.............___	.............___	.............___
.............___	.............___	.............___	.............___	.............___

GARAGE

Oil..............$ ___	Lubricants.............___	Garden Tools ....___	Shop Equip..............___	Electric Tools.............___
Jack(s) ....___	Ladder(s) ....___	Hardware.............___	Tool Bench.............___	Vise(s).............___
Ropes.............___	Bicycle(s).............___	Motorcycle.............___	Rototiller ....___	Gun(s), shells.............___

Fillers............___	Chain Saw............___	Car Ramp ....___	Hde Tray Box(s)........___	Log Chains ....___
Mule ....___	2-Wheel Cart............___	Garden Tractor............___	Golf Cart ....___	Bench Grinder ....___
Battery Charger............___	Supplies ....___	Shop Vacuum ....___	Bar Clamps ....___	Fire Extinguisher ....___
Patio Lighting............___	_____......___	_____......___	_____......___	_____......___

BASEMENT

Table(s) ....$___	Toy Room ....___	Soft Water Conditioner............___	Lifting Weights ....___	Toy Box............___
Safe............___	P.T. Equipment ....___	Furn. Room ....___	Entertainment ....___	Elect Heater ....___
Lighting............___	Lubricants............___	Garden Tools ....___	Shop Equip. ....___	Electric Tools ....___
Food ....___	Containers............___	Sports Cab. ....___	Kit & Dining ....___	Alarm Systm(s)............___
_____......___	_____......___	_____......___	_____......___	_____......___
_____......___	_____......___	_____......___	_____......___	_____......___

MISCELLANEOUS

Clocks ....$___	Lamps ....___	Baby Bed ....___	Mirror(s)............___	Picture(s) ....___
Games............___	DVD Player ....___	Wdw Treatmnt ....___	Electrical Hde.............___	Hand Tools ....___
Barbecue ....___	Flower Pots ....___	Athletic Equip. ....___	Lawn Mower ....___	Lawn Tools ....___
Rugs............___	Radio(s)............___	Umbrella(s) ....___	Fertilizer(s)............___	Trophies............___
VCRs ....___	Floor Fan ....___	Memorabilia* ....___	Cell Phone(s) ....___	Telephones ....___
Safe ....___	Plaques ....___	Antique(s)* ....___	Speakers ....___	Area Rug(s)............___
Piano ....___	Card Table ....___	Wdw Blinds ....___	Dehumidifier ....___	Humidifier ....___
DVDs ....___	Decorations ....___	Birdhouse(s)............___	Plant Stand(s)............___	Broom(s)............___
Bulbs ....___	Magnifying Glass ....___	Area Rug(s)............___	Christmas Items ....___	Heating Stove ....___
Bench ....___	Space Heater............___	Piano Bench ....___	Music Instrumnt ....___	Bird Feeder(s)............___
Liquids ....___	Picnic Table............___	Cabinet(s)............___	BBQ Tools ....___	Fireplace tools ....___
Wallet ....___	Cushion(s)............___	Generator............___	Lawn Edger............___	Tree Trimmer ....___
Swing Set............___	Candles ....___	Pet Supplies ....___	Lawn Chairs ....___	Video Screen ....___
Pet(s)............___	Tape Measure(s) ....___	Toy Chest............___	Hearing Aid ....___	Watches............___
TV(s) ....___	B. B. Goal ....___	Trailer............___	First Aid Kit ....___	Med. Supplies ....___
Boat............___	Fert. Seeder............___	Pond Heater............___	Medical Equip. ....___	Swim Trunks ....___
Jet Ski ....___	Doll(s)............___	2-Wheel Dolly ....___	Bracelet(s)............___	Water Skis ....___
Trellis ....___	Binoculars ....___	Water Vests ....___	Ice Cooler(s)............___	Hunting Vest............___
Bats ....___	Swing Set............___	Sump Pump ....___	Puzzles............___	Skateboard ....___
Cage(s)............___	Ice Skates ....___	Pressure Gauge ....___	Tennis Rackets............___	Ball Glove(s)............___
Jug(s)............___	Sunglasses ....___	Pet Bed ....___	Heat Lamp ....___	Tripod ....___
Toys............___	Livestock............___	Garbage Can ....___	B.B. Goal ....___	Garbage Cans ....___
Camera ....___	Elec. Cords ....___	Ice Cream Freezer............___	Large Water Container.............___	Roller Shades ....___
Hammock............___	Roller Skates............___	Dog House ....___	Hockey Sticks ....___	Paintings ....___
Cane(s)............___	Car Pillows ....___	Fire Extinguisher. ....___	Fire Lighter ....___	Stroller............___
Plants ....___	Cedar Chest ....___	Tool Box(es) ....___	Christmas Décor............___	Heat Lamp ....___
Mirror ....___	Video Camera ....___	Video Camera ....___	Clothes Hamper............___	Folding Chairs ....___
Gun(s)............___	Patio Furniture ....___	Deck Furniture ....___	Deck Lighting ....___	Playhouse............___
Skates ....___	PingPong Table............___	Porch Swing ....___	Sack Swing ....___	Work Bench............___
Heating Pad............___	Pool Table ....___	Barbecue Equipment ....___	Hammock ....___	Extension Cords ....___
Framed Pictures............___	Fishing Equip ....___	Golf Clubs and Bag............___	Golf Cart ....___	Wheelchair ....___
Skis ....___	Tennis Equip ....___	Exercise Equipment............___	Medical Equip. ....___	Hobby ....___
Collectibles............___	High Chair ....___	Gas Can(s)............___	Business Sales Inv............___	Bow & Arrow Set ....___

Total All Categories .... $_____

"...more than just a single reader self-help book."

FOR FOCUS GROUP MEETINGS

The following is only a brief outline of just another way to use the book while taking advantage of its broad spectrum of topics. This focus group outline is not the only way to pull together individuals as a group who may be searching for more opportunities to enrich their lives.

1. This new self-help teaching tool can be used effectively for small focus groups. Leaders are encouraged to review the entire book to get a perspective of its content before group arrangements have been made.

2. Send out invitations to prospective clients and participants. Give them an overview of what to expect in the focus group. After a couple of days, make a quick phone call. Ask them whether they are interested in pursuing the invitation to become part of a life changing discussion group.

3. If they are, arrange to get them a copy of the book or run off a topic in the book to be studied at the first meeting. After assigning a particular topic to be studied at the first sitting, give a time, date, and directions where the first meeting will be held.

4. Prepare how you are going to handle each small group. At the first meeting, share why you are meeting together and the objectives you expect to accomplish. How long will the group stay together? Reinforce the issue that all participants will have a chance to be involved in group discussion and shared reading at their own discretion and comfort level.

5. During the focus group meetings:

   1) Participants will be encouraged to raise questions for discussion.
   2) Special guests will be invited for specific subjects.
   3) There will be other media used to reinforce certain parts of interest.
   4) Show & tell times can be set aside for given time periods.
   5) Meetings will start and end on time, lasting no longer than one hour unless it is announced differently in advance of the meeting.
   6) Prayer time will become a valuable part of each session.
   7) All persons regardless of their gender are welcome to take part.

CPSIA information can be obtained
at www.ICGtesting.com
Printed in the USA
FSOW02n1122010716
22267FS

9 781683 013334